PUTTING IT ALL TOGETHER

A Consumer's Guide to Home Furnishings

PUTTING IT ALL TOGETHER

A Consumer's Guide to Home Furnishings

Peggie Varney Collins
Shirley Wright Collins

Illustrations by Philip F. Farrell, Jr.

Charles Scribner's Sons   NEW YORK

Copyright © 1977 Peggie Varney Collins and Shirley Wright Collins

Library of Congress Cataloging in Publication Data

Collins, Peggie Varney.
    Putting it all together.

    Includes bibliographies and index.
    1. House furnishings.   2. Consumer education.
I. Collins, Shirley Wright, joint author.
II. Title.
TX311.C57   645   77-1885
ISBN 0-684-14883-8
ISBN 0-684-14884-6 pbk.

1 3 5 7 9 11 13 15 17 19 Q/C 20 18 16 14 12 10 8 6 4 2
1 3 5 7 9 11 13 15 17 19 Q/P 20 18 16 14 12 10 8 6 4 2

Printed in the United States of America

CONTENTS

ACKNOWLEDGMENTS

P UT T I N G this book together has been an adventure that has been fun, hectic, and above all rewarding. We could not have done it at all, however, without the support of our friends and associates in the industry. The people working daily in home furnishings and allied fields have generously contributed their vast practical knowledge gained from many years in their specializations, and we gratefully share this with you.

Although it would be impossible to list them all, some of those who have been especially helpful are: Glen Albright of Albright and Zimmerman, furniture manufacturers; Thomas Cushman, head of the laboratory of the State of California Bureau of Home Furnishings; David Finner, wallpaper and paint contractor in the San Fernando Valley, Calif.; Ran Hedger, sales representative for Kentile Floor Company; George Montgomery of Montgomery Draperies in Canoga Park, Calif.; Shirley Nash Mossman, professor of interior design, Chaffey College, Alta Loma, Calif.; David Naccarato of David Julian Designs, upholstered furniture manufacturers; Ernest Owens, designer and manufacturer, Design Guild, lamps and accessories, Los Angeles, Calif.; Shelley Sidlow, carpet sales for Paul Singer Floors, Los Angeles, Calif.; Eva Taubman Steinberg, collector and former art gallery owner, Fullerton, Calif.; Howard Voien, sales representative, Albright and Zimmerman; and Alan Wilson, Woodland Hills designer and fabric consultant.

Special thanks go to Howard C. Winslow and the staff of the California Bureau of Home Furnishings, who were most diligent and cooperative in providing information and who opened our minds to the problems we needed to face, shared some of their solutions, and reminded us that there are no pat answers.

Our gratitude also goes to William Jarrett, who encouraged us to continue with our project; to Barbara Plumb, who saw its potential; to Elisabeth Crawford, who saw us through the most difficult time of "putting it all together"; to Hank Baum, whose class and later support opened up the world of art to us; to friends and associates who were especially helpful and supportive: Bob Lopez, Florence Simon Rosenbloom, Sylvia Rindge Adamson Neville, J. Robert Finley, and very especially Arlene Marconi Hoffman.

We've always wondered why many authors mention their typists in terms of undying devotion. It is now crystal clear to us, and we express awe and gratitude to Virginia (Ginger) Frerichs and the yoga that kept her going when we were down to the final draft.

It is, however, to our families that we dedicate this book. We think this is the least we can do when about the only kinds of home furnishings any of them have been exposed to recently are wall-to-wall books, pamphlets, and half-finished chapters. So, to Eddie, to Lori, to Rick, to Jan and Gary, and most of all to Dick, who are almost as happy as we are that the deed is done, we say "thanks" for your patience and forbearance.

PEGGIE VARNEY COLLINS
SHIRLEY WRIGHT COLLINS

INTRODUCTION

W HENEVER a consumer faces the decisions involved in the purchase of an item of home furnishing, the magazines flourishing in the field admonish him to "consult with your own decorator." For vast numbers of prospective buyers far from major metropolitan centers this means a friendly chat with the salesman down at the town's one furniture store or a day-long excursion (or two, or three) to the nearest small city and an over-abundance of confusing information and misinformation from "experts" in several department stores or other manufacturing outlets.

Even advice from an experienced decorator, however, is not a talisman against bad or imperfect judgments in the purchase of articles for the home. Nor can one volume contain all the basic considerations necessary to make intelligent choices in all areas.

The reality is that carpeting salesmen long in the field may be consulting pages ripped from a trade magazine and stapled together as a reference on various fibers and loom terms. Master upholsterers have few textbooks and have learned most of what they know about the construction of durable soft goods as apprentices to master upholsterers before them and from subsequent years of experience. Government publications that do not have widespread circulation within the trade may contain information on paints and their application that painters themselves have learned partly from trial and error, partly from talking to other painters, and partly from advice given at the paint supply stores from which they buy their materials.

In other words, the information necessary to make good personal choices in the area of home furnishings and materials is a mixed bag and for the average consumer a grab bag, at that. Before painting the kitchen we can't apprentice ourselves to a painter to learn which finish and type of paint will give the best and longest service. Only after years of actual upholstery work could most of us be expected to understand the intricacies of construction involved in making a really good sofa.

Currently we consumers must take our information catch as catch can, wherever we can get it: from books, publications, folders, by word of mouth, from retail salesmen trained to sell only their own products, and from behind-the-scenes folklore passed from generation to generation of craftsmen and not always readily available to potential buyers. The problem is further complicated by the fact that we have little opportunity to build up experience in the field, as the purchase of a major upholstered piece or the painting of the family kitchen are widely spaced events and different considerations are involved on each occasion.

This book is an attempt to bring together this widely dispersed and unorganized information on the actual construction and capabilities of home decorating and furnishing materials. Some areas have never been researched except by individual manufacturers to sell their particular products, and some information has been unavailable to people outside the craft or trade involved. Other material comes from excellent government publications or from pamphlets issued by the trades for use by potential buyers or for general public relations purposes.

Our purpose is to synthesize this material and put it together in a readable, clear, concise style aimed at helping the 130 million potential consumers (68 million of them women) in nearly 70 million households throughout the country to become better educated and thereby to support the book's philosophy: that a well-informed consumer is a better consumer.

Article Number One in our Buyer's Bill of Rights is the right to ask intelligent questions, followed closely by the right to receive intelligent answers. A consumer has the right to ask, "Will these cushions hold their shape?" or "Can I depend on this carpeting not to spot easily?" The kinds of stock answers with which this diligence may be rewarded include such double-edged nothings as: "Yes, with proper maintenance"; "Oh, definitely, with normal usage"; "It *should* wear well—in an average household"; "It's the *newest* product on the market"; or that granddaddy of them all, "We've never had any complaints."

Everyone has a right to know what the manufacturer anticipates proper maintenance to be: washing down with a garden hose semiannually, or daily hand polishing. It is not neurotic to wonder if monthly cocktail parties for business clients can be considered normal usage, or whether one organic gardener, a potter, two elementary-school-age children into Little League and cut-and-paste, one Siamese cat, a large Airedale, and two parakeets constitute an average household.

Salespeople as well as editors in the home fashion media and manufacturers will rely on formulas that have worked before. This is not a deliberate attempt to fool you, but rather a lack of communication on several levels: from researcher to manufacturer to salesperson to consumer. Consumers who take the time to examine their life-styles, ask the right questions, and insist on clear and informative answers will force salespeople to get better information from the manufacturers.

Reputable manufacturers, dealers, and designers are aware of the need to inform their customers. The members of the Southern Furniture Manufacturers' Association, in cooperation with the North Carolina Cooperative Extension Service, have prepared and distributed a series of excellent small pamphlets on furniture construction and more recently have undertaken the establishment of the Furniture Industry Consumer Advisory Panel (FICAP) to mediate consumer complaints. These and other industry efforts, plus legislation for safety and product control, and research from various levels of government have begun to bring about better relations between the home-furnishings industry and the consumer.

When we began compiling this book, we were convinced that it was our duty to provide consumers with every bit of information needed to buy home furnishings. Gradually, however, as we worked toward becoming specialists, knowing more and more about less and less, we realized that we ourselves were not able to assimilate all the material we encountered. We realized, however, that what *is* important is to know how to find information, how to judge what is good information, and how to use it well. We developed the philosophy that the good consumer is not only an informed consumer but one with options, and to this end we developed the strategy outlined in chapter 13, so that instead of having to know everything at once, you will know when you need more input, how to get it, and how to use it.

It's simple economics, really. What the home-furnishings industry can't sell won't be manufactured. So we, as buyers, will get what we're willing to put up with.

PUTTING IT ALL TOGETHER

A Consumer's Guide to
Home Furnishings

1

Fibers and Fabrics

O discuss fibers first is to begin at the beginning, for this is the basis of good wear, the first (but certainly not the only) concern of the intelligent consumer. An unwise selection of fabric for a basically well-constructed piece of furniture can ruin the image of an otherwise reputable manufacturer or that of its textile supplier, not to mention the traumatic effect it will have on you.

This chapter is intended to answer the question "Which fabric is the 'ideal' one for my specific needs?" "Ideal" is in quotes because there is no perfect fiber, full-page color ads notwithstanding, and no fabric is perfect in all situations and for all time. Remember this well, for it will save you time, money, and disappointment and will encourage you to be very selective.

The three basics of fabric selection are:

Fibers—the source of wear, the "thread of truth" running through all fabrics
Construction—the added dimension, providing a usable surface; how it all hangs together
Processes—postconstruction "extras," providing non-built-in properties or features, such as color and design, soilproofing, and other finishes

Understand these and you will understand what goes into wise fabric selection. If what you really want is a degree in textile science and not just an appropriate covering for your sofa, consult the bibliography for guidance to more complete information. *Fairchild's Dictionary of Textiles* (the fifth edition was published by Scribners in 1974), a compendium of thirteen thousand definitions of fabrics, fibers, and finishes, is a good place to start.

Fibers

Fibers are either natural or man-made and fall into two categories:

Staple: fibers of limited lengths (from ¼ to many inches); these are made continuous for construction (weaving, etc.) by being twisted together. All natural fibers except silk are staple fibers.

Filament: long, continuous fibers used in one of three ways: (1) alone for single-strand yarns (monofilaments); (2) two or more twisted together (multifilaments) to create stronger yarns and/or blends; (3) cut into staple lengths, then twisted together to resemble natural fibers. All man-made fibers are filament; the only natural filament fiber is silk.

Natural Fibers

Natural fibers have been around for a long time and thus have withstood the test of time. Lots of prime time and space-advertising dollars have been devoted to extolling the newer synthetics, but considering the various raw-material shortages, it is reassuring to know that no test tube has yet produced a fiber more lustrous than silk, softer or more washable than cotton, warmer or more resilient than wool, more absorbent or more lasting than linen.

Fibers of natural origin can be divided first between vegetable and animal (protein) sources. Cotton and kapok are seed-related vegetable fibers. Linen, jute, ramie, and hemp are derived from the stems of plants. Two other vegetable sources are the leaf (from which, for example, abaca, sisal, and Philippine piña cloth are obtained) and the fruit, a very limited source of fiber not used in any widely available textile.

Animal fibers derive mainly from three sources: the silk of silkworms, the wool of sheep, and the hair of certain other animals, including goats (cashmere and mohair), animals with camel-like hair—the llama, vicuña, alpaca, and the camel itself—and others, including rabbits, horses, and reindeer. (Note: Under the Wool Products Act, however, the fleece of sheep and the hair of other animals are considered wool. See the fiber and fabric section of the glossary.)

Most natural fibers other than silk, wool, cotton, and linen are in limited usage in household furnishings but will occasionally be found in handwoven textiles used in cushions and pillows, area rugs, ethnic wall hangings, or spreads for beds or tables.

For the less commonly used fibers, you will have to depend heavily on care instructions on the label of the article. If no label is available, get detailed instructions in writing from the place of purchase, preferably from a known dealer where you have recourse if you have problems. Anyone caught up in the excitement of dickering about price over a cup of tea in a Turkish bazaar will have to understand that the story of the purchase may hold up better than the article itself, especially if instructions for its care get lost in translation.

In the fabric showroom or the local yard goods store, however, you will more often be dealing with natural or synthetic fibers about which you can know quite a bit.

LINEN

The high cost of hand processing makes it difficult for linen to compete with the synthetic fibers, but its durability, absorbency, and strength, added to its natural luster, keep it very much a part of the home-furnishings industry. Natural or unbleached linen is the strongest and is used for backing on many fine fabrics (some expensive velvets, for example). When dyed through (watch for a colorfast label), it can serve long and well in upholstery or draperies. Used as a warp, linen is often woven with another fiber (such as spun rayon) to make reproductions of fine French silks. The intricate patterns and stripes are produced by the the other fiber in the combination.

Irish linen has one of the longest traditions of quality; only that from Belgium surpasses it in beauty and fineness.

The very crispness that gives linen its clean, fresh look necessitates special care when storing table coverings, since the fiber tends to break when folded for a long period of time. Wrap table linens around cardboard rollers (from carpeting or linen yard goods) or drape them over dowel-type poles in special linen closets. When using linen as an upholstery covering, it is wise to have the welts made in another fiber, one that is less prone to breaking.

Linen's faults—poor resistance to mildew, to sunlight, to wrinkling, to soil, and to fire—limit its use, but there are many treating techniques that help improve its wash-and-wear qualities or wrinkle resistance. Linen can be washed, tumbled dry, dry cleaned, and bleached, although continued bleaching will weaken the fibers. Concentrated mineral acids and alkalies injure the fibers, but weak alkalies (ammonia, borax, and laundry soap) do not. Iron linen at 400 degrees. The natural luster can be enhanced by ironing damp and on the wrong side. Spot clean with soap and water or special foams under pressure. A ring should not occur unless there is sizing or a special finish to be considered. Linen ignites easily and is not self-extinguishing, and treatments developed so far to make it fire resistant result in some loss of durability. *Read your labels.*

WOOL

Wool has no peer for combined elegance and durability, but it would be foolish to expect that it—or any other fiber—is indestructible. However, nothing yet produced has displayed the long life and true beauty of an oriental wool rug, not alone for the intricacy of the handcraft involved but also for the richness of color and texture and the resistance to wear ensured by the fiber.

Wool's virtues are many. It is not only resistant to abrasion, but also wonderfully resilient, with a quick recovery rate from the pressures of heavy furniture. It is less sensitive to acid than cotton and has a good affinity to dyes in a wide range of colors (as the heirloom orientals prove). It does not wrinkle easily, has low static, is slow to soil and even slower to show its soil. It is excellent for draperies and upholstery if protected from perspiration.

Slow to absorb wet stains, wool will respond to a quick mop-up operation, but subtler soiling requires careful treatment at regular intervals. Wool will reward the effort of this periodic and seemingly unnecessary cleaning by returning to its previous almost-new brightness of color. And by removing hidden soil, which can eventually destroy any fiber, you will increase the life span of the wool.

Another virtue of this fiber is that it is not readily ignitable and tends to be self-extinguishing.

But even such a good and faithful servant as wool has its drawbacks. For one thing, it is not impervious to chewing animals, be they moths or dogs. For another, wool can be practically destroyed by alkalies—a spilled bottle of ammonia-base household cleaner or an indiscreet pet. It has poor wash-

and-wear qualities (although there are a few "wash-and-wear" wools now on the market) and will lose its shape if allowed to become excessively wet. Wool should be professionally cleaned except for occasional spot cleaning. Because felting (a matting together of fibers) occurs when wool is subjected to both moisture and mechanical action, iron it gently with a cool iron. And finally, good and faithful servants—wool included—do not come cheap these days. If some of the synthetics don't do the job nearly as well as wool, they often do it for a lot less money.

If you are one of those persons highly allergic to wool this whole discussion may be academic. In that case, turn to the section on olefin (the most wool-like of the synthetics) before you break out in a rash or start sneezing at the mere thought. But if you're still with us, we'd like to help you deal with one of the problems facing a potential purchaser of wool: vocabulary. As early as 1939 the Wool Products Labeling Act was passed to deal with the confusion, and a lot has happened since; so, before you go out on a wool-buying spree, turn to the glossary for such terms as *wool, reprocessed wool, reused wool, virgin wool, woolen,* and *worsted.*

SILK

Silk has come a long way since the twenty-seventh century before Christ—all the way from China. The trade caravans brought to the rest of the world the gift of nature's finest fiber and the only natural continuous filament, a fact that makes silk the strongest of the nonsynthetic fibers, next in strength only to nylon for its size, yet with the same type of elasticity that wool, a staple fiber, has.

Although silk also resists mildew and insects and is not easily ignited, it is cherished most of all for its elegance, its beauty, its luster. Elegant though it is, being associated with royal garments, with the Qum oriental rugs, with the fine silk velvet seen on museum-quality furniture, it is not truly fragile, since it is resistant to soil, shrinking, stretching, and wrinkling. It will last many years (as the costume and fine furniture collections testify) if not subjected to its enemies: abrasion, heat, perspiration, sunlight. Treat your great-great-grandmother's Empire chair with just a little of the respect it deserves (you don't have to sit there after a warm eighteen holes on the golf course), and it will continue as a family heirloom in its current silken attire.

Because few people are sitting around unreeling two thousand feet of silk from a cocoon today, there are a lot more people choosing continuous-filament nylon than its natural ancestor. But if you do make the uncommon

choice, you will be getting qualities of beauty that have never been duplicated in a test tube. Silk's fine dyeability allows for a superb and extensive
color range.

Silk can be hand washed, but test for dyes that may bleed. White silk may
be bleached with hydrogen peroxide or sodium perborate bleaches, but
chlorine bleaches should never be used.

COTTON

Cotton, in its place, is truly a universal fiber. It is soft, strong when wet or
dry, low-cost, easily washable for stain and spot removal. Unfortunately, in
direct sunlight, it is neither colorfast nor durable and therefore must be
either blended with other, more sun-resistant fibers or protected from the
rays of a southern or western exposure by linings of another origin (in
draperies) or by window coverings that cut out direct sunlight (for rugs or
upholstery). Its high absorbency is both a bane and a boon, for it absorbs
both spots and such finish improvers as crease-resistant solutions (to
counteract its wrinkle factor) and fire-resistant treatment (to offset its high
flammability), and it dyes well to create a wide and excellent color range.
The process of mercerizing not only extends the color range of cotton but
also adds strength and a luster similar to that of linen.

Wall-to-wall carpeting is out, but cotton in movable, washable, low-traffic
(low-abrasion) "masses" is a highly usable fiber. Untreated cotton is easily
wrinkled but easily ironed, providing you are willing to spend the time and
energy and the "mass" isn't too massive. Throw it in the washing machine,
scrub it thoroughly on bended knee, work it over with a shampoo machine,
bleach it with chlorine or peroxide (testing first for yellowing caused by some
finishes), and it will probably revive some of its old spirit. But you'll have to
clean it often.

Keep this in mind when you're thoroughly enchanted by ads showing you
what you can do to an economically depressed area in your home with just a
few bedsheets in the latest colorful designs. Keep it in mind when you're
about to upholster (rather than slipcover) a piece of furniture in a busy room
frequented by dogs, children, and weekend gardeners.

Cotton blends well with other fibers and is willing to take on many of its
companion's attributes. Combined, for example, with polyester in a 65/35
(65 percent polyester, 35 percent cotton) to 50/50 combination for lightweight uses such as draperies, it becomes more durable and will wrinkle less.
At the same time it "breathes" for the polyester and accepts richer colors
when dyed.

But blends have their problems, too. As with any crossbreeding for improvement of the "line," consideration must be given to faults and virtues on both sides of the family. While cotton and polyester together do in some instances offset each other's negative points, some problems of each fiber will remain. Polyester's propensity for absorbing oily stains must be taken into account, either by preventing the stain in the first place or by using special agents to release it once it occurs.

Synthetic Fibers

Synthetic, or, as they are called in the industry, "man-made," fibers make up the bulk of fibers used in the home-furnishings industry. They have served us well, but sometimes the chemical industry puts a new fiber on the market before it is thoroughly developed. We agree with chemists who work in testing labs (such as for state and federal agencies) who say that most, if not all, synthetic fibers have been marketed much too soon. The chemical companies seem to plunge with great vigor into developing "improved variations" of a fiber only *after* the public has bought it, taken it home, and found it fraught with problems that might have shown up under more rigorous testing. So far, much to the frustration of state and federal home-economy advisers, the chemical industry has hesitated to conduct the bulk of its tests in homelike professional laboratories.

RAYON

The idea of using some sort of vegetable substitute for the protein fiber produced by the silkworm was considered as early as 1664 in England, but the actual simulation was not developed in this country until the early twentieth century (1910). This "artificial silk" was the first of the synthetics.

Today rayon can be made to resemble not only silk, but also wool or cotton, and it is the most commonly used fiber in the home-furnishings field for upholstery, drapery, and curtain fabrics because it combines well with practically all other fibers, adding its versatility to the final blend. In the era of natural-resource depletion and multinational machinations, rayon also has the advantage that, being made from cellulose, it is not so subject to the whims of an erratic economy as are the synthetics that depend on petro-products as raw materials for their manufacture.

Rayon can be used everywhere: from the most elegant, look-but-don't-touch setting to an all-purpose family room. Because of its low cost it is often termed "cheap," but its grade depends upon the quality of the fiber in the first place and the ultimate use to which it is put. Some of the most beautiful and expensive cut velvets, for example, incorporate high percentages of rayon.

Rayon is lustrous and can be produced in a brilliant color range, has good resistance to sunlight (good for lining other drapery fabrics that do not), and is resistant enough to abrasion to be used in moderate wear areas. Although it does not have the static buildup of many other synthetics, it is not used extensively for carpeting because it lacks the ability to withstand heavy traffic.

On the negative side, this fiber ignites easily and is subject to shrinking and stretching unless properly treated, either by you or by solution during manufacturing. But it provides beauty at a reasonable price and, being a sharing fiber, can be treated to overcome its negative qualities such as wrinkling, susceptibility to mildew, and poor resiliency.

ACETATE AND TRIACETATE

Acetate is an important word in your home-furnishings vocabulary but should not be prominent on your home-furnishings shopping list. Except for possible use in good low-cost draperies, bedspreads, and throw rugs, it has enough negative qualities to be a penny-wise-pound-foolish investment. Closely related to rayon (but separated from it by a Federal Trade Commission ruling of 1952), it is manufactured from cellulose and acetate and offers a silky, lustrous effect at low cost. It drapes well, holds its shape (if dry cleaned), is resistant to insects and mildew, and (if solution dyed) is especially resistant to sunlight, perspiration, and air pollutants. (Non-solution-dyed acetate may be subject to atmospheric fading—that is, certain colors may change or fade because of airborne smoke and fumes.)

On the less positive side, acetate is not a strong fiber, does not wear well in abrasive circumstances, wrinkles, ignites easily and must be kept away from heaters, cannot be pressed with anything but the coolest iron, and should be dry cleaned rather than washed. If you buy it at a low price, any saving may be offset by cleaning bills or a short life. Read the label on that silky-looking sofa upholstery—the nice low price tag may mean it's made of acetate.

Additionally, acetate is often used in bedrooms and baths (two favored products: attractive brocade or taffeta bedspreads and small colorful area rugs), and it is in these two areas that it will often meet its deadliest enemies: nail polish remover and perfume. (If you've ever made the mistake of using an acetate rag to remove paint dribbles, you'll understand what acetone does to this fiber: holes begin appearing as the acetate dissolves.) Some acetates can be gently hand washed but should never be soaked. Iron with a cool iron when damp.

Triacetate is an improved version of the fiber. Used most successfully for draperies (such as damasks and brocades), it has greater heat resistance, wrinkles less easily, launders more easily, can have wash-and-wear qualities, and can be ironed at higher temperatures. Its best use is in high-humidity areas, either geographically or in the home, where price is important. You'll probably find just what you want to curtain the bedroom, bathroom, and kitchen windows or your rented apartment in ready-made, moderately priced selections.

NYLON

First of the true test-tube fibers (rayon is developed from cellulose, a vegetable material), nylon has come a long way since it was developed by Du Pont and announced in 1938. Whatever terrible tales you have heard about nylon are probably true, since it was put on the home-furnishings market before full knowledge of its performance was obtained. Now, however, years of development have made it the strongest, most durable, and most widely used of all the synthetics.

Full-bodied pile materials, such as carpeting, can now be made from nylon at less expense than from the yarns that are spun from short staple fibers. But, even more important, nylon in continuous filament is now much more resistant to soil. Now you can afford the strength, durability, and softness of texture that nylon offers by itself or in blend with other fibers for upholstery, draperies, and carpets, especially if the nylon fibers have been treated to offset their less enchanting qualities.

For example, nylon's durability will serve well if its low resistance to sunlight has been counterbalanced. Treated to resist the destructive rays, it becomes an excellent material for draperies or sheer curtains, outdoor-furniture coverings, and umbrellas. Or you can use it in a blend to counteract one of its failings: rayon with nylon, for example, provides the strength of nylon with the low static-electricity buildup of rayon.

Nylon's low absorbency rate means you're more likely to find it hanging from a curtain rod in the bathroom than from a towel rack. For the same reason, it makes a great floor covering in humid settings where other, more absorbent fibers would develop a dank, dungeony odor, but you may not want it as a bathmat if you dislike standing in puddles while drying yourself.

Nylon can be spot cleaned, dry cleaned, machine washed, and tumble dried at low temperatures. As with natural fibers it is best to wash whites separately from colored fabrics. Fabric softener added to the final rinse will cut down on the static-electricity buildup. Bleach only with chlorine bleaches. Nylon generally requires little ironing; set the iron at about 300 to 350 degrees, depending upon the type of nylon. Check the label for care instructions.

In tightly woven hard or smooth finishes this fiber works well as bedspreads or upholstery fabrics which will survive attack by your youngsters, for nylon is both perspiration and abrasion resistant and slow, though not impervious, to soil.

Nylon is not inherently flameproof, and while it does not ignite, it burns, melts, and drips, particularly when combined with other fibers. The industry is currently developing a nylon, still in the test stage and more expensive, designed for high-risk areas.

ACRYLIC

Versatility is the name of the game for acrylics, but it's a game in which you could become a big loser unless you know the rules.

Woven tightly into uncut low-pile carpeting, an acrylic fiber presents its finest wearing qualities and is more likely to melt than to "flash over" in case of fire. These carpets obviously lend themselves well to commerical use, but acrylics can also be found in high-grade home carpeting and will stand up to hard wear in high-traffic, low-care areas like country clubs and resort homes because they will resist attack from spiked golf shoes or muddy ski boots, as well as from hungry insects.

But woven into the popular soft, finely textured, and furlike weaves (warm, cuddly blankets, for example), acrylic fibers become less durable and are highly flammable unless treated. (See chapter 12.) Construction and special treatments such as flameproofing are then as important as the fiber itself in consideration of ultimate use: you may want acrylics on the floor of your ski cabin but not in the blanket you bundle in by the same cabin's crackling fire.

Acrylic fiber has poor absorbency, a characteristic that isn't going to make it the greatest towel in the world, but it serves well for carpeting and upholstery where spilled liquids will often sit on the surface long enough to allow them to be wiped up without staining. It is not harmed by common solvents, bleaches, dilute acids, and alkalies and therefore is easy to clean with whatever is available at the moment you notice the spot, an important fact if you're an impulse cleaner. It is also resilient and resistant to both mildew and wrinkling. Its resistance to deterioration from the ultraviolet rays in sunlight make it in an excellent choice for draperies and curtains, as does another virtue of the fiber—its potential for a good range of colors if solution dyed. It is a very versatile fiber (it can be spun into a variety of textured yarns) and is more resistant to sunlight than nylon, but not as strong or as durable. Acrylics can be machine washed, dry cleaned, and tumble dried at low temperatures. Static-electricity buildup can be reduced by adding a fabric softener to the final rinse. Iron, if needed, at low temperature: 300 to 325 degrees.

MODACRYLIC

When acrylics are modified through a heat process, as in such products as Dynel and Verel, the fiber is much more resistant to flame but, ironically, less resistant to the heat of, say, an iron; the fibers melt and stick together if any but the lowest temperatures are applied.

The lovely, dense, furry fabric that results from modacrylics can provide the warmth and beauty of natural fur without endangering the species it imitates: leopard, wolf, red fox, mink, to mention only a few. Therefore, this fiber may be used wherever lower cost and low flammability are desired along with the exotic or elegant touches of fur in pillows, bedspreads, and upholstery or with the fuzzy warmth of wool in blankets and afghans.

As a drapery fabric, modacrylics (especially Verel) are at their finest, for they are strong and inherently flameproof; they hang better than glass fabrics, can be washed or dry cleaned, are quick to dry, and in a hanging position are not subject to abrasion.

Look for this fiber also on the labels of carpets and other fabrics in blend with other more abrasion-resistant fibers, where it is included as a fire deterrent. Care is about the same as for acrylics, but check labels for special instructions. Iron at a lower temperature, 200 to 225 degrees.

OLEFIN

Olefin (polypropylene) is the perfect example of the fiber placed too soon upon the market. Even with continuing developments, there is still much to be learned about this remarkable fiber, of all the synthetics the closest to the natural qualities of wool.

On the virtue side is the fact that olefin is the lightest of the fibers yet has excellent insulative qualities, that it is nonallergenic (a bit of one-upmanship on its model, wool), that it resists abrasion and is one of the few fibers that doesn't pill, and that it is resistant to sunlight, mildew, perspiration, and aging. Some of these plus points make olefin an obvious choice for indoor-outdoor carpeting, for furniture coverings that are to be exposed to outdoor use, and for use in high-humidity or high-traffic rough-and-ready areas such as a beach house or the family room.

Olefin's greatest virtue is its worst vice: its low cost. Because of the attractive price tag, the unwary consumer may be blinded to its faults. While the fiber resists oils and stains, once it has been spotted, the fabric (especially the older Herculons) may become difficult, if not downright impossible, to clean. This problem has been partially solved by treatment with low-static solutions to eliminate attraction to soil. Solution dyeing of the fiber has solved previous dyeability problems of poor coverage, bleeding, and muddy colors.

Still another "yes, but" applies to olefin's response to heat. Yes, it doesn't ignite easily (a wool-like quality), but unlike wool it melts at an extremely low temperature. Charts can be misleading by giving the impression that 130 degrees is really pretty hot—which it may be if you're sitting on an iceberg, but not by the fire in the comfort of your cozy den.

Just how much of a problem this can be is illustrated in a case on record with the Consumer Division, Home Furnishings Bureau, of the State of California. A woman called to complain that she had had a chair, upholstered in cotton, sitting near her hearth for several years without incident. The trouble began when she reupholstered it with olefin. One day the complainant's daughter, enjoying this cozy setting, reached down along the side of the chair and was shocked to discover it hot and all the fabric on the side nearest the fire melted away.

Methods to eliminate such problems are still being perfected, but it is wise to avoid exposing olefin-upholstered furniture to high temperatures and to keep olefin-filled pads and quilts out of clothes dryers where temperature buildup could bring the fibers to the kindling point. All commercial gas and laundromat dryers should be avoided. Check labels carefully to see if the filling fiber has been treated with a wash-resistant antioxidant to combat this problem.

Olefins can be machine washed and tumble dried at low temperatures. Use fabric softeners in the final rinse to reduce static-electricity buildup.

Pure olefins should not be ironed but blends can be; follow the instructions on the label.

POLYESTERS

Polyester fibers have gotten a bad name because their first uses in the home-furnishings industry spotlighted their faults rather than their virtues. Anyone who is considering using any fabric made from this fiber should check carefully to verify that improvements have been made to counteract the problems.

Early carpets made of polyester in a range of lovely colors soiled, matted, and pilled so badly that all but the most uncaring salesmen refused to sell the product to eager customers looking for a pretty "miracle" floor covering. The miracle was that polyester got on the market without anyone's finding out how badly the fiber failed in the role.

But things have been happening to improve the fiber's performance: antistatic solutions have been added to the formula, making polyester less attractive to soil. While pilling, particularly in spun yarn, continues to offset its long-wearing qualities, the many new fabrics with improved at-home care features bring polyester into greater consideration for window coverings and other low-abrasion uses.

In the past, polyester was hard to wash or dry. Special agents have been developed to release oily stains, but polyesters still pick up colors and lint from other materials during washing. Antistatic agents can be added to the final rinse to eliminate lint pickup. Since you can't get a sofa into the washer, you may be stuck with this lint attraction problem. You should check carefully for labels specifying added features (such as antistatic) and the care needed for the object's ultimate function and long life. Properly pampered, polyester does have sterling qualities that you should not overlook: it is strong wet or dry, doesn't wrinkle easily, ignores threats from moths, mildew, and perspiration. It also shows off to advantage in companionship with other fibers, especially cotton.

It provides its resistance to wear (this time without pilling) and its best wash-and-wear qualities when blended with a natural fiber. Follow care labels.

At the moment polyester cannot be flameproofed because the process causes the fiber to stiffen and lose its body. Although polyesters alone do not ignite easily, once ignited they melt and drip. They will, however, burn readily if blended with the cellulose fibers (i.e., linen, rayon).

GLASS FIBER

Glass fiber offers its greatest and most practical contribution to home furnishings as a material for flameproof draperies. If you are hesitant about the cost of having large expanses of them washed commercially—very few homes have the facilities for washing and hanging them to dry—you can be reassured by the long life of your initial investment, since they do wear well in nonabrasive settings. They are resistant to a long list of potential enemies of fibers: chemicals, heat, mildew, insects, sunlight, salt air, wrinkling, atmospheric changes which cause swelling and contracting. And improvements are coming along all the time: Beta yarn, the newest and most manageable at present, is more elastic and stronger but still subject to glass fiber's greatest fault: shedding, which can produce a skin rash for susceptible persons. The limited color range has been extended with printed colors.

Glass can be hand or machine washed (agitate gently) and drip dried. Rehang drapes on rods to complete drying. Do not spin dry, twist, or wring glass fabrics. Dry cleaning is *not* recommended.

SARAN

Better known to thrifty homemakers as a clinging, airtight wrap for leftover food, Saran as a fiber has been touted in recent years for use in a variety of home furnishings, both indoors and out. Unfortunately some of its recommended uses are questionable, since there are other fibers that do the job better. Indoor/outdoor carpeting and garden furniture are two examples; resistant as Saran is to fading and weathering, it does yellow in direct sun and will also soften, or even melt, in hot weather. Keep in mind the destination of your chaise lounge: sunny desert patio or fogbound seaside deck. Saran fares much better in blends, giving fire-retardant qualities to upholstery and drapery fabrics since it does not support combustion. It is washable, but do not use water much above body temperature.

VINYLS

First developed in 1929, vinyl chloride resins have made a place for themselves in many areas, but no one appreciates them more than the harassed homemaker—the blessings of a vinyl-covered sofa are enjoyed in family rooms across the country.

Rough and ready though they are, these fabrics need care, too. Advertising to the contrary, vinyls are not impervious to all dyes, stains, and chemicals, and where those from petroleum products are concerned, you'll need to be quick to get the stain before it gets to your sofa. A little alcohol or cleaning fluid should do the trick, but your favorite household cleansing powder will remove not only the potential stain but some of the finish to boot.

Vinyls can be laminated (bonded) to a layer of foam, polyester, or canvas or used in a single sheet. Some are called "breathing" vinyls, meaning they are more porous for air flow and therefore more comfortable. A great masquerader, vinyl chloride can be produced in an infinite variety of textures and often must be submitted to the sniff test to be distinguished from real leather. Only your cat may know, for he'll not be tempted to sink his claws into anything but the real thing—a rather unusual plus for using vinyls, if you're a pet lover.

Vinyls fake magnificently as wall coverings, too. While some of the romance may be gone when you discover that that beautiful "grass" cloth isn't really, you may thank your practical self later for buying it anyway, when you're following that trail of dirty handprints down the long hall to the children's bedroom with nothing more than a damp cloth and a little soap.

The uses for vinyls are limited only by your imagination, if you can accept such obvious drawbacks as the lack of soft feel, drapability, and body comfort of fabric made from woven fibers. Because they are nonabsorbent, vinyls fit well into places where spills and wet bottoms (from beaches, baths, and babies) are everyday occurrences. The opposite side of that coin is that on a warm, sultry day, after sitting on even a "breathing" vinyl without an absorbent terrycloth buffer between you and the nonporous surface, you may find that you have developed your own wet bottom without benefit of beaches or cooling dips in the swimming pool.

But a caution: while polyvinyl chloride (PVC) is great at self-extinguishing small fires such as that from a cigarette on the family room sofa, if untreated filling or some nearby material should catch fire, that same PVC will give off a toxic gas, chlorine, which can kill more quickly than fire and which, if allowed to travel through the house, can explode in all parts of the house simultaneously. Chapter 12 contains suggestions from professionals on this subject.

Fabric Construction

As we said earlier, the fiber is only one aspect of a fabric. When you understand some of the characteristics of individual fibers, the next consideration is the way those fibers are constructed into fabrics. Fabrics may be woven, knitted, twisted, felted, and what is termed nonwoven, and the secret of satisfactory home furnishings is the correct fiber in the right construction. Consult the chapter pertaining to your potential purchase: chapter 6 for window treatment, chapter 8 for upholstering, chapter 2 for carpeting.

Weaving

Woven fabrics are constructed by interlacing, at right angles, two systems of threads known as warp and weft/filling. The warp runs lengthwise and may go over or under the weft, which runs crosswise. There are six basic weaves that are used individually or in combinations in making fabrics for home furnishings: plain, twill, satin, pile, leno, and jacquard.

PLAIN WEAVE

This is simply one yarn running over and under the other, one yarn at a time. It is strong and dimensionally stable. Muslin, basketweave, and monk's cloth are a few of the many varieties of plain woven fabrics.

TWILL WEAVE

Twill is produced when the filling yarn (the one that goes across the fabric) "floats" or skips over some of the warp yarns (rather than weaving in and out, over and under, each yarn) diagonally to form a tight regular pattern that looks like raised welts: denim, gabardine, and serge are examples of this weave. Because of twill's compact construction it tends to resist soil better and to wrinkle less than plain weaves.

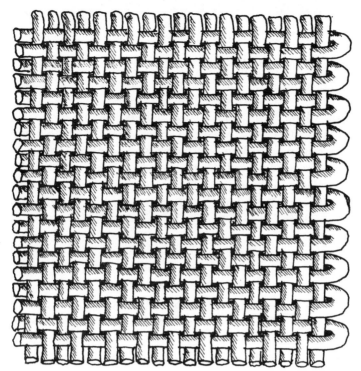

Plain weave

Twill weave

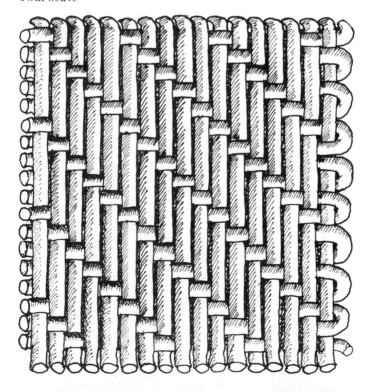

SATIN WEAVE

In satin the filling yarn "floats" back and forth across the warp in a less regular design; at times, the warp may even "float" over the filling yarns. This process creates a smooth and lustrous surface that reflects the light when silklike threads are used. Damasks, antique satin, and satin are some of the fabrics woven in this manner. This weave has a natural luster and can be strong or delicate, depending upon the fiber used and the tightness of the weave.

PILE

Pile is formed by loops that stand up from the flat-lying warp and filling yarns. When the loops are not cut, the fabric produced is the terrycloth type; when cut, the result is velvet or plush. Hi-lo pile gets its name from the process of cutting some of the pile loops and leaving others uncut to create textured surfaces. Patterns, ranging from watered effects to intricate floral designs, can be produced by weaving yarns of different thickness or color into pile. Unless it is made of a soil-resistant fiber, cut pile with its exposed

Satin weave

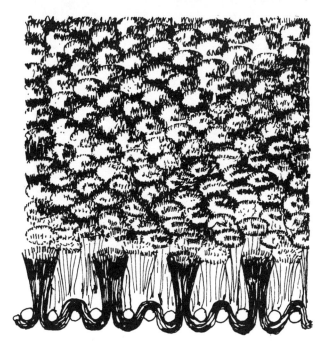

Pile weave

fiber ends provides a very attractive surface upon which to record the grubbier aspects of your life.

LENO

Sheers in drapery fabrics are often produced by leno weaving (sometimes called doup weave), an interlocking of the warp yarns in a figure-eight effect around the filling yarns, creating an open, delicate appearance that belies its strength. This method produces bold, open, loosely woven designs, as well as the small weaves of marquisette and similar porous fabrics in which pattern is not easily discernible.

JACQUARD

This weave takes its name from the loom upon which it is made. The term *jacquard* is applied to the loom, the technique, and the resulting fabric. Simple to complex in pattern, the tightly woven fabric is decorative and as serviceable as the fiber from which it is constructed. Brocade, high-relief brocatelle, and tapestries are among the products coming from the jacquard loom.

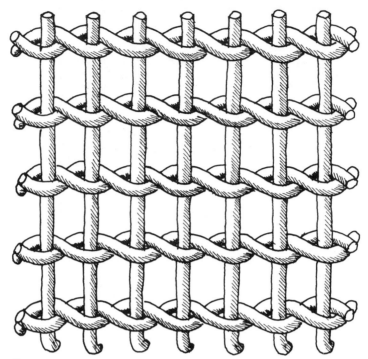

Leno weave

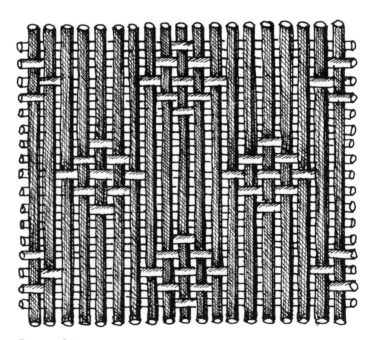

Jacquard weave

Knitting

Knitting is a technique whereby a pattern is produced with a needle or series of needles interlocking yarn into a series of connecting loops with resultant plain, purl, or rib stitches. Since knitting machines, because of the simplicity of the stitches, can work at much higher speed than weaving machines, they are being used more and more in the fabric industry. By combining new fibers with new techniques, interesting and decorative fabrics that are dimensionally stable (they hold their shape) are now being developed.

Some open-weave, fishnetlike drapery material is being produced as a knitted fabric rather than by the twisting technique used by prehistoric fishermen. Sometimes these "fishnet" fabrics are given added stability with a backing of sheer, very stable nylon net.

Twisting

Twisting is the centuries-old method by which lace and net have been made. Here also new fibers and modern machines, using thousands of bobbins simultaneously, combine to speed the manufacture of a high-quality product. Thus lace and net in innovative patterns and designs can be used widely in home furnishings.

Nonwoven Fabrics

The earliest process of fabric construction used by man, felting, is basically a matting together of fibers with moisture, pressure, and sometimes heat to achieve a compact, somewhat fuzzy material. Originally felts were made of wool, but fabrics made by a similar process from Dacron or viscose are now available for draperies and other uses—a far cry from the old concept of felt. Nonwoven fabrics may ultimately be the answer to a demand for lower-cost construction, by eliminating spinning, cutting, and sewing, and perhaps even by spraying fiber onto forms. Vinyls are among the nonwoven fabrics, being either pressed, bonded, or applied by a heat process.

Selecting Construction

Tight weaves are the most durable and resistant to abrasion (wear), pulling (snags), or stretching. Made with narrow or small compact yarns, these can be smooth, like sheeting which is a plain weave; firm, like a jacquard tapestry fabric; or rough, like a true denim which is a twill. The same weaves, made looser and of softer, thicker yarns, provide almost as good wear with a softer "hand" (feel to the touch).

The more a weave is opened up, however, the less strength and dimensional stability (ability to hold its shape) it will have. Open-weave drapery fabrics are a perfect example. They must be hemmed twice, once when they are hung and once more after they have hung for a while. A well-constructed open weave should eventually reach a point when it will stretch no more, preferably before the draper becomes a permanent member of the family.

Knitted or twisted fabrics should be tight and firm; you should not be able to "pull" the design out of shape.

Felted fabrics should be smooth and firmly bonded. You should not be able to see light through the fabric, and it should be of uniform thickness.

Vinyls with small perforations are "breathing" vinyls and are the most comfortable for upholstery. A tricot or woven backing creates a softer feel. You should be able to bend the fabric without causing cracking. (Vinyls can dry out, so be careful of this.)

Fabrics with a pile, such, as velvet, should have tightly woven backs made of strong fibers. The pile surfaces should be dense and cover the backing evenly and completely.

Processes

The last step in fabric manufacture, processes can be applied to add color, pattern, or qualities intended to improve the fiber's performance. This is an admirable goal but often unrealistic because treatments can have the effect of exchanging one set of problems for another. Linen towels are an example: despite the fiber's natural high absorption and fast-drying qualities, "100% linen" on the label does not ensure a thirsty dish towel like those Grandma treasured in her hope chest. Printed patterns which improve the appearance of the product may interfere with its ability to soak up moisture.

Ideally the fabric should have a label giving the dye process, how it was printed, any treatments applied, and how to care for the fabric that is the result of these manipulations. There are groups at work to bring informative labeling to the consumer, but until that happy day arrives, ask questions and more questions of the supplier.

Dyeing

Dyeing fibers and fabrics can be done in a variety of ways. Since dyeing is one of the most complex phases of the fabric industry, a little knowledge can be dangerous. Dyes, at their best, are subject to fading and deterioration. The most satisfactory performance comes from solution dyeing done early in the fiber process because then the dye better permeates the entire fiber of yarn. Dyeing piece goods is the least satisfactory, and poor jobs can be recognized by the bits of uncolored thread in the cloth, especially in linen, which is a difficult fiber to dye under the best of circumstances.

Crocking, the rubbing off of dye from the surface of the fabric when friction occurs, indicates either a poor dyeing process or incorrect selection of dye for the particular fiber. To avoid purchasing fabrics in which crocking will take place, rub the material against itself, or better, against a lighter-colored fabric, to detect how stable the dye surface really is.

In solution dyeing of synthetic fibers the dyes are put into the solution before the fibers are spun by extrusion (a process by which the liquid is forced through the tiny holes of a device called a spinneret). Natural fibers are dyed in solution (also called "stock dyeing") before being made into yarn.

The next-best dye process is vat or hank dyeing, a technique by which hanks of yarn are dipped into vats of dye before being made into cloth. In another type of vat dyeing, vat dye of a type especially resistant to light and to washing is applied in soluble form, the color "taking" when oxidation occurs. These vat dyes are used widely on vegetable fibers such as cotton, rayon, and linen, but because they are applied in an alkaline bath which is harmful to animal fibers they have been used only in a limited way on wool and silk. New processes are being developed to counteract this problem and to make possible even wider use of vat dyes which provide brilliant color and an almost unlimited range of shades.

Printing

Another way to introduce color and pattern to fabric is to print it. Methods of printing are so numerous, varied, and detailed that we recommend consulting the bibliography or your local library for books on the subject.

Most printed designs can be distinguished from woven or knitted patterns by looking at the back of the fabric. Woven or knitted designs go through to the back, as they are part of the fabric construction, while most printed designs sit on the surface of the cloth. Because of this basic difference, when the design is actually woven or knitted into the cloth both the design and the cloth will obviously wear better.

However, it is not always easy to determine whether or not a fabric is printed. In heavily backed fabrics such as velvets and cut velvets, a woven-in design could be covered with backing, making it impossible for the uninitiated to differentiate between weave and print. Duplex printing, on the other hand, may produce a pattern on both sides of the fabric, which may then be confused with woven goods. If in doubt, ask the salesperson with the hope that enough questions by enough customers will nudge him/her to be ready with the answer.

While prints provide a great range of colors from bright to the subtlest tone-on-tone and a variety of designs limited only by human imagination, they do require special care if they are to retain their original beauty. At the time of purchase ask for the instructions that apply to your print fabric, for harsh soaps, bleaching, and in some cases cleaning solvents can attack the dyes and dull or destroy them.

Fabric Finishes

Each fabric finish has been developed to improve a given fiber or fabric and/or add to it a quality or qualities it does not naturally possess. This is an admirable but sometimes unrealistic goal, since no one fiber or fabric can be all things in all situations. And meeting the challenges of the fabric in a given setting by application of a performance-improving chemical may create a whole new set of challenges involving the finish itself. For example, chemical polymers used to impart greater body and better drape to otherwise limp and soft fabrics can cause the fabric to change color or yellow. In addition, such chemicals can be diluted and finally dissipated by washing or dry cleaning, resulting in loss of crispness or other finish.

Disclosure is a continual communication problem between the manufacturer and the consumer. Ideally, reading the label would tell you what finish or finishes were applied and how to care for the finished fabric to ensure continued service. Unfortunately, this labeling information is not always complete, nor does the manufacturer's tag warn you of new problems that you may have been given along with the solution of the old. Anything newly concocted by the fabric industry will need time before all the "test" is taken out of the test tube. The miraculous new finish which turns a certain difficult fabric into a thing of beauty and a joy forever may also make it highly susceptible to flames. Obviously, a label can't tell you something the manufacturer doesn't know—and might be reluctant to disclose if he did. We see no answer to the complex problem of new product control except better research methods on the part of the industry, forced by legislative pressure, if necessary, and by consumer reluctance to jump on the bandwagon of each new "miracle" in the marketplace.

Be careful, also, when you order a special finish or apply one on your own. Most householders, for example, do not know that the best-known stain-resistant finish provides only a *resistance* to staining and not a guarantee against it. If some of the treatment finish has worn away or if a spot-producing substance has been allowed to lie on the fabric until it soaks through, the stain will sink beneath the surface and spread out under the applied finish, making removal difficult, if not impossible. That's just one of the things that labels on cans, tags on fabrics, or glowing advertisements about finishes don't tell you. There are others you'll pick up if you listen to other consumers, ask a lot of questions, insist on honest and up-to-the-minute answers from people who have had wide experience with the product or products you're concerned about.

Most finishes are best applied by professionals. However, when finishes are applied by the homemaker rather than by the manufacturer, a little more control is in the hands of the consumer, so he/she must read the label carefully before the first application and follow the directions absolutely. Cautionary statements on the can are put there by law to protect the user, especially those warning against inhalation of fumes or against getting the substance near or in the eyes. Even if it means wearing a face mask or protective glasses, it is wise to remember that one is dealing with toxic materials. Further care should be exercised to store cans in a cool place where the temperature cannot possibly build up to 120 degrees (not, by the way, an unusually high mark on a summer day in a closed place subject to direct sunlight). When disposing of used or, for that matter, unused cans, always puncture the container and make sure it is out of the reach of children.

Even when properly applied, most home-applied finishes wear off or wash out and should be tested periodically to see if they need retreatment. Check also to be sure the spray is doing what the label says it will do. A stain repellent, for example, should make the fabric less absorbent, and this can be checked by waiting until the test spot is dry and then dropping water on the fabric to see if moisture beads up and sits on the surface. If not, another application is immediately in order.

Finishes can be a boon—unless you expect miracles. You must still be sure to treat the fabric according to its fiber content, its weave, and its color or pattern, with the finish standing guard against small invasions. Defense against major assaults is the job of the fabric and its fiber, and a few brave salvos with a spray cannot ward off all evil forces.

The following is a list of different textile finishes and their varied uses. It is neither a complete listing nor a recommendation.

TEXTILE FINISHES

Purpose	*Trade Names*
Absorbency To increase the ability of fabrics to absorb moisture and permit more rapid evaporation	Fabulized, Nylonized, Sorbinol, Sorbtex, Telezorbent, Zelcon
Antiseptic To reduce tendency for growth of bacteria and retard absorption of odors by fabrics	Dowcide, Eversan, Permachem, Permacide, Permaseptic, Puritized, Sanitized
Antistatic To prevent accumulation of static electricity	Bounce, Cling Free, Downy
Crease (wrinkle) resistance To resist creases and wrinkles; fabrics are impregnated with synthetic resins; may improve draping qualities but could weaken fibers and wash out; dyes may become more permanent; shrinkage is reduced in spun rayons, cottons, and linens; bonding to foam or tricot also gives wrinkle resistance	Aerotex, Bradperman, Bradura, Casual Care, Dela Shed, Disciplined, Drismooth, Fresh-Tex, Martinized, Norfix, Resloon, Sanforized Plus, Stazenu, Staze-Rite, Superset, Tabelized, Unidure, Vitalized, Wrinkle-Shed, Zeset

Purpose	*Trade Names*
Crease retention	
To maintain pleats and creased edges	Koratron, Si-Ro-Set (applied to woolens)
Crispness	
Permanent sizing that should not wash out	Apponized, Bellmanized, Cellin Everglaze, Heverlein, Ice, Re-si-Perm, Sabel, Saylerized, Stabilized, Stazenu, Trubenized, Unisec, Vitalized, Vitolast, Wat-a-Set
Durable press	
To help a garment or fabric to retain its initial shape, flat seams, pressed-in creases, and unwrinkled appearance during use; precure or postcure treatment; similar to crease resistance	Burmi, Coneprest, Dan Press, Koratron, Never Press, Primatized, Reeve Set, Super Crease
Fire repellence	
Depending upon the treatment, certain fabrics can be made fire- or flame-retardant or -resistant; check label carefully	Aerotex, Anti-pyros, Banflame, Ellicote, Erifon, Fire Chief, Flamefoil, Flame Retardant, FR-1, Permaproff, Pyroset, Pyrovatex, Saniflammed, THPC, X-12
Mildew resistance	
To retard or prevent the growth of mildew; antiseptic finish	Aerotex, Ban-Dew, Dowcide, Fresh-Tex, Permaseptic, Puritized
Mothproofing	
To make fabrics moth repellent (not permanently mothproof)	Amuno, Berlow, Boconized, Eulan, Larvonil, Mitin, Moth Snub, Woolgard
Shrinkage resistance	
To reduce shrinkage of finished fabric; the degree may vary from 1 to 2 percent	Aerotex, Apponized S, Avcoset, Avcosol, Bradura, Cyana, Definized, Delta-Set, Dylanize, Evershrunk, Facility, Fiverset, Harriset, Kroy, Lanaser, Permathol, Perryized, Protonized, Redmanized, Resloom, Rigmel, Sabel, Sanco 400, Sanforized, Sanforlan, Sanforset, Saylaset, Schollarized, Shrink-Master, Stazenu, Teblized, Tub-Allied, Unifast, Wat-a-Set, Zeset

Purpose	*Trade Names*
Stain resistance To resist soil and stains and/or make fabric less absorbent; resin finish	G. E. Silicones, Repel-A-Tized, Scotch-gard, Xylmer, Zepel
Thermal or insulation To keep body heat in (coat linings) and reflect sun's rays (drapery linings); metallic finish	Milium, Temp-Resisto, Thermalgard
Waterproofing To prevent the passage of moisture or air through coated fabric	Beautanol, Koroseal, Reevoir
Water repellence To resist water but permit passage of air through the fabric	Durable: Cravenette, Druasec, Four Star, Hydro-Pruf, Lovely-On, Norane, Norfixn, Nortex, Permel Plus, Silicone, Unisec, Zelan Renewable: Aqua-Sec, Aridix, Dry-dux, Impregnole

Other Finish Processes

Beetling. Pounding linen and linenlike fabrics with steel or wooden mallets to give luster. The process greatly reduces moisture-absorption qualities.

Calendering. Pressing fabrics between rollers to give smooth finishes and high-glaze sheens embossed with moiré, crepe, and other patterns. Also serves to tighten the weave.

Glazing. Adding resins to give a more or less permanent smooth, lustrous finish that resists soil and improves drape.

Mercerizing. Treatment applied to cellulose fibers (cotton and rayon). When done under tension this increases strength, luster, absorbency, and dyeability; when the fibers are in a slack state, it causes them to swell and contract, which increases the crimp of the yarn and its stretchability.

Glossary of Fabric Names

Now that you know something about fiber and construction and how they are (excuse the expression) interwoven, you're going to be sensitive to the names of fabrics with which you are likely to be confronted in the marketplace. Don't panic if the term isn't familiar. Check the glossary at the back of the book for a list that is arbitrary, by necessity incomplete, and subject to changes in fashion and technology. If you find something new, ask questions.

Resources

Books

Faulkner, Ray and Sarah. *Inside Today's Home,* 3rd ed. New York: Holt, Rinehart and Winston, 1968.

Linton, George E. *Natural and Man-Made Textile Fibers.* New York: Duell, Sloan, and Pierce, 1966.

Miller, Edward. *Textiles—Properties and Behavior.* London: B. T. Batsford, 1968.

Moncrieff, R. W. *Man Made Fibers.* New York: Wiley Interscience Division, John Wiley & Sons, 1970.

Wingate, Isabel. *Textile Fabrics and Their Selection.* Englewood Cliffs, N.J.: Prentice-Hall, 1955.

Encyclopedia Americana. New York: Americana Corporation, 1964.

Fairchild's Dictionary of Textiles, 5th ed. New York: Charles Scribner's Sons, 1974.

Organizations

Chemical Fabrics and Film Association, 453 Route 211 East, Middletown, N.Y. 10940. Pamphlets.

Credit Union National Association, Inc., Box 431, Madison, Wis. 53701. Pamphlet: "Durable Press."

Department of Consumer Affairs, Bureau of Home Furnishings, State of California, 3401 La Grande Blvd., Sacramento, Calif. 95523. Howard Winslow, Chief; Thomas Cushman, Head of Laboratory. Script of movie *Unfurnishing Your Home*; Lab Report SP-71-1.

Man Made Fiber Producers Association, Suite 310, 1150 17th Street N.W., Washington, D.C. 20036. "Guide to Man Made Fibers" (1969); "Man Made Fiber Fact Book" (1974).

Manufacturing Chemists, 1825 Connecticut Avenue N.W., Washington, D.C. 20009. Consumer Information (NHFL Conference Bulletin) 11/69.

U.S. Department of Commerce, National Bureau of Standards, Consumer Information, Washington, D.C. 20230. Series 1, "Fibers and Fabrics," by Josephine M. Blandford and Lois M. Gurel; available from U.S. Government Printing Office, Washington, D.C. 20402.

Vinyl Fabrics Institute, 65 East 55th Street, New York, N.Y. 10022. Pamphlet: "Vinyl Fabrics."

2

Floors and Floor Coverings

THE first rugs were no doubt the skins of hapless saber-toothed tigers that wandered too close to the caves of prehistoric peoples, who seized the opportunity—and the tiger—to add warmth and comfort to their dwellings. The selection of floor coverings today is sometimes almost as haphazard and only slightly less dangerous.

Because they cannot be discarded as readily as the lamp or small table or chair that was "never quite right," floorings are a major consumer purchase. This chapter is devoted to the many choices confronting the potential buyer, for once a flooring material or floor covering is down, the consumer is literally stuck with it.

Homework

As with any major purchase, do your homework before shopping. Some of the questions you will need to ask yourself are:

Where is the flooring to be put and what are the options?
Are you covering subfloors or poor existing floors, or are you covering or accenting existing quality surfaces?

What are the comparative maintenance problems?

What are your realistic personal housekeeping attitudes?

How much traffic will the floor have and what kind?

Who is going to use the area and for what activities?

Must there be special considerations for the very young, old, allergic, or handi-
capped?

Do you have animals?

Will certain surfaces offer special features associated with hobbies or other
leisure uses?

What kind of comfort factors are important to you and your family?

Have you considered using the floor covering for soundproofing?

What is the relative cost of the original purchase and installation, continued upkeep, and eventual replacement?

How durable are the products you are considering?

How permanent is your place of residence?

Do you use that residence year-round?

Are you dealing with excessive heat or cold and the added problems that accom-
pany such situations?

What are the aesthetic considerations regarding color, space, style or period,
and personal preference?

Carpets

The terms in the carpet and rug industry are probably the most confused
jumble of all the areas of home-furnishings consumer information. In this
section we discuss carpeting as a continuous woven or tufted floor covering
in various standard widths, as opposed to area rugs, which may also be
woven, either by machine or by hand, or may be of other materials such as
plant fiber or fur.

Quite often the carpet ads you see are actually advertising a fiber from a
specific chemical manufacturer and not the final product from a carpet
manufacturer. It is of the greatest importance that you know the fibers from
which carpets are made and their comparative characteristics. As we said in
chapter 1, good wear begins with the fiber. In carpeting, it is the quality of
the fiber, the kind of fiber (wool, nylon, etc.), and the amount per square
foot measured by weight. Not all fibers wear the same under all circumstances. When you have decided where you are going to use carpeting in your
home, select the fiber that is best suited to that use.

Materials

Material used for continuous carpeting is made in a very wide variety of fibers from animal, vegetable, and chemical sources; this group includes wool, nylon, the acrylics, polyesters, and polypropylene (olefin). Cotton is not satisfactory in wall-to-wall carpeting, as it soils easily, is difficult to clean, and mats down under heavy traffic. It is, however, quite satisfactory in area rugs which can be washed in the machine or braided rugs whose tight multicolored construction resists or hides soil.

WOOL

The pacesetter, the model that all the synthetics attempt to emulate, is wool. It is durable, soft, resilient, lustrous, has an excellent color range, and resists soil, but it must be mothproofed, can be damaged by alkalies (a consideration if you have babies, pets, or both), is difficult to clean once soiled, is allergenic and expensive. Wool can be used in high- or low-traffic areas but should be kept away from high-risk food preparation areas. It is poor economy to buy a cheap reclaimed wool carpet; save your dollars by purchasing a quality carpet in a less expensive fiber or by cutting corners with some other part of your household furnishing budget.

NYLON

The strongest of all the fibers and the leading synthetic, nylon is extremely durable, resilient, nonallergenic, and easy to clean. Some nylons even "hide" soil by their reflective qualities, but the fiber builds up static electricity if not treated and tends to pill in some inexpensive carpets such as single-loop piles made from monofilament yarn or cut piles from short-staple fibers. Nylon soils easily in light, bright colors, but it is impervious to alkalies and therefore can be used in situations involving animals and children.

ACRYLICS

These include the modacrylics, which are generally woven with other fibers to incorporate nonflammable qualities. Used alone, the modacrylics are fine for scatter and bath rugs but do not provide the durability needed for wall-to-wall carpeting in high-traffic areas. Acrylics have light-reflecting colors; in tight commercial one-level loop weaves they have soil-hiding qualities; they are nonallergenic and crush resistant, but they are neither as strong as nylon nor as resistant to soil. They also pill and build up static electricity if not treated. In tightly woven, low-level looped carpets, acrylics are at their best in any traffic situation, but the high, fluffy piles are best kept in low-traffic areas. In high piles they are also more susceptible to fire than in tightly woven low construction. (See chapter 1.)

OLEFINS (POLYPROPYLENES)

The olefins are nonallergenic and durable, but they crush easily in high pile and melt at low temperatures. They resist soiling but once soiled are difficult to clean. Indoor/outdoor carpets in tightly woven, low-pile weaves in these fibers have proved quite successful, because, besides resisting abrasion, they are not easily damaged by moisture and retain their bright colors. Being highly susceptible to oil-based stains, they should, however, be kept out of food preparation areas.

POLYESTERS

Extensive changes have occurred since these materials first came on the market for carpeting. At that time they pilled and crushed so badly that some carpet salesmen refused to sell them. Now the polyesters are more durable, have an excellent color range, are crush resistant in some weaves, and are nonallergenic, but they still pill and build up static electricity. They do well in areas subjected to only moderate traffic.

Carpet Problems

A word about static electricity and carpeting: this is a small electric charge that is built up by friction caused by walking and atmospheric conditions, especially on synthetics. This buildup can give you a mild shock that is annoying but not dangerous. Of more importance to the consumer is the fact that static electricity attracts and holds dirt on the fibers of the carpet. The industry has made great strides to correct this situation, so ask your salesman whether a specific product is naturally antistatic or has been treated to combat the problem.

Pilling, another carpet problem, occurs when some fibers give off small amounts of fuzz that form into balls and cling to the surface. A leading carpet manufacturer, who otherwise provides helpful information to its consumer public, has suggested that these be clipped off by hand. This sounds simple but could turn into a full-time job with certain carpets. Check with your salesman for pilling information about the carpet you are considering.

Pilling is not to be confused with shedding. Any new carpeting has some loose fibers which have been caught in the pile during manufacture, but the shedding of these should diminish in time and should not mar the beauty of the carpet.

Construction

All carpeting is woven, tufted, knitted, or needlepunched. Weaving, which is the oldest process, is the method whereby the pile and backing are woven together simultaneously. The term *broadloom* originated with the development of looms wide enough to weave the 9-, 12-, and 15-foot-wide materials used today for "seamless" carpeting; it has nothing to do with quality. *Axminster, Wilton,* and *velvet* are loom terms for woven carpets and denote specific types of weaves. Axminsters are woven in one direction and must therefore be carefully cut and laid when installed to be sure that the nap on all pieces falls in the same direction. Wiltons and velvets provide cut pile effects through weaving rather than tufting.

Even though the tufting power equipment has been developed only in the past twenty years, there are today far more tufted than woven carpets. There is little difference between good woven and good tufted materials in wearability; the only differences are in construction and cost of production; tufted is considerably less expensive than woven carpeting. Tufted carpets are made by stitching tufts of carpet fiber through the backing material, after which latex is applied to the back to bind the stitches more firmly. The number of tufts per square inch is a guide to quality construction unless the carpet is a very long shag with density provided through length rather than spacing of the yarn. (See Shopping Hints.)

The use of knitting machines is on the upswing and has given a greater selection of modestly priced carpeting, but at present knitted carpets comprise only a small segment of the carpeting market.

An even smaller percentage of the industry is devoted to needlepunching done by machines on which thousands of needles work simultaneously to interlock a fiber core and layers of loose fibers. Modestly priced, these compact, feltlike carpets are backed with latex. Generally sold for indoor/outdoor use, their wearing qualities depend predominantly on the fiber from which they are made. These products should not be confused with the complex, custom-designed needlepunched area rugs which lie at the other end of the cost spectrum. They have nothing in common in either appearance or price tag.

Textures

Fashion determines the popularity of a particular texture at a given time, but certain textures have greater wearing qualities than other, more luxurious ones. Decide what your traffic is—high or low; be realistic and you won't be disappointed.

VELVETS

These carpeting materials (also called plush, frieze, splush, and cut pile) are the velvety-looking cut piles, all one length, that give a "cushy" feel when you walk on them. The shadowing from footprints is considered a design plus. They do tend to show soil more than other textures and may show the backing when wrapped around stairs. Good in formal, low-traffic areas.

RANDOM SHEAR

This is a surface of cut and uncut loops. When the loops are all at one level, random shear is not quite as smooth as velvet and is more durable. When the loops are multilevel, they create a sculptured look. Good for high-traffic areas and stairs.

TWO-LEVEL LOOP

This has a surface of cut and uncut loops at different levels, giving a patterned look. Depending upon the difference in the height of the loops, this can look even more sculptured than a random shear. It is also good for high-traffic areas and stairs.

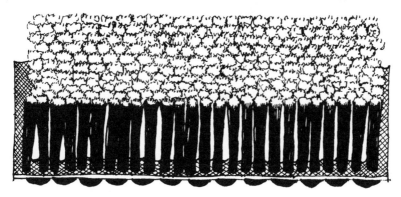

Velvet pile

Random shear, one-level pile

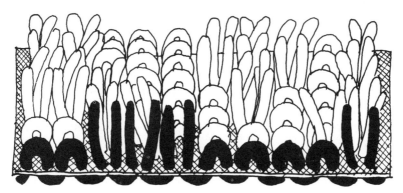

Random shear, sculptured multilevel pile

ONE-LEVEL LOOP

This texture is formed of the low, tightly woven uncut loops often seen in commercial carpeting. Indoor/outdoor carpeting is generally woven in this texture as it withstands water very well. Excellent for high-traffic areas and stairs.

SHAGS

These come in varying lengths up to 6 inches and are intended to look like turf. If they have a dense amount of yarn that is twisted tightly, they can be used in high-traffic areas; otherwise, shags should be limited to areas of moderate traffic. The backing may show when shags are wrapped around stairs; the back should be dyed to match the yarn to help disguise it when exposed.

Backing

Good backing will add years to the life of a carpet. Almost always made of jute, backing is an integral part of the carpeting and should be tightly woven and/or firmly constructed. It should provide dimensional stability, which means that the carpet will hold its shape and not creep or wrinkle. Because of several variables (political unrest, climatic conditions, labor supplies, and so on in the countries of origin) leading to fluctuations in the supply of jute, manufacturers are beginning to investigate the use of man-made materials in the mass production of backing. Some but not all of these same variables apply, however, to the petrochemicals being substituted as raw materials, forcing the home-furnishings industry to consider the development of new sources of jute production.

On tufted carpeting a secondary backing is needed for additional stability and wear; this is made of jute, a synthetic material, or foam rubber, which is bonded to the first, or primary, backing. Woven carpets do not require a secondary backing because the yarn is woven with the primary backing.

Recently a backing called "unitary" has been developed, a combination of the primary and secondary backings bonded into one layer and made of sponge rubber or vinyl foam. There are also new woven and nonwoven backings made of polypropylene. These synthetic backs are all mildewproof and nonallergenic. Carpets with the unitary backing are usually expensive and

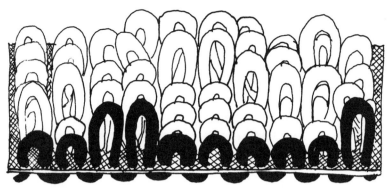

Two-level loop

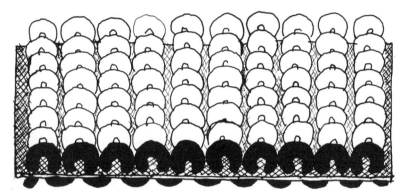

One-level loop

Shags

durable and are not to be confused with the cheap rubber-backed carpeting that is available. This is a case of getting what you pay for.

Sometimes, to reduce the cost of a carpet, the secondary backing is omitted, reducing the wear quality of the carpeting enough to make it a dubious saving.

Pads

Pads are a must, adding to the life of your carpeting by protecting it from impact damage caused by footsteps and furniture pressure.

Remember that padding is not generally included in the price of the carpeting. There are many types, and as the quality varies, so does the price. Good cushioning will be provided by a 40- or 50-ounce jute and hair combination, with a truly luxurious feel being offered by 80- to 90-ounce rubber. The materials commonly used for padding are hair, latex, foam rubber, sponge rubber, urethane, and combined hair and jute; most have some kind of pattern such as waffling to keep them from slipping.

Hair provides the most classic cushion under carpeting and has good resistance to impact and to wear. Since hair pads are not mildew resistant, they should not be used on damp or below-grade floors, but they do very well over radiant-heated floors. In good commercial installations, 50-ounce hair is quite often the standard pad. It cuts down on friction from the latex backing and does not break down under very heavy traffic as rubber would.

Foam "rubber" pads are synthetic and therefore nonallergenic and resistant to mildew. They come in 1/16- to 7/16-inch thicknesses and are priced accordingly. Foam rubber absorbs sound and conducts heat from radiant-heated floors better than any other pad.

Sponge "rubber" is not the same as foam rubber; it is more porous and can be either natural or synthetic, blown into a very soft, springy cushion.

Urethane can be purchased in solid or bonded forms (bonded is firmer) and is graded for firmness per cubic inch much like foam for mattresses. Grades of 5½ to 6½ pounds are acceptable if they are at least ⅜ inch thick. Urethane is mildew and insect resistant.

The least expensive pad you should buy is a hair and jute combination; the more hair, the better the quality.

An all-jute pad is unsatisfactory, as are the paper-thin sponge, foam rubber, or shredded urethane pads. These break up and cause wear spots in the carpet.

Measuring and Installation

HOW TO MEASURE FOR CARPETING

Rooms

Measure the length of your room. Measure the width of your room. Multiply the length by the width. Divide by 9. The answer will be in square yards.

Stairs

Figure ¾ of a linear yard per step. Multiply by the number of steps. (The average home stair tread is 10 to 12 inches deep and 3 to 4 feet wide, with a 7½- to 8-inch riser.)

Because carpet comes only in specific widths, you will probably have to buy more than you need. Always take with you the measurements of the room and a floor plan if possible (verify the measurements on the plan). Have the salesman give you an estimate. If it varies too much from your yours, have him do it again; he may be cheating you or he may have made an honest error. You should rely on the professional carpet estimator's measure, for he is then responsible for any errors and can place the seams in the least obvious places. If he does measure wrong, don't let him piece the goods; ask for a new piece of whole carpet. A reputable dealer will treat you fairly and professionally.

Installation should always be done by professional carpet installers. The investment in the carpeting and the padding warrants proper installation.

Care

Carpeting should be vacuumed regularly, about twice a week for an active family. After a new carpet has been installed, remember to empty the sweeper bag after each cleaning for about three months to keep the loose fibers from clogging the machine. Daily touchups with an electric broom or carpet sweeper throughout the life of the carpet will increase its wear, since dirt and stains not only are unsightly but destroy the carpet fibers. When the necessity arises, have your carpet shampooed by a professional if possible, for his equipment can "deep clean"; if you want to do it yourself, you can buy or rent the equipment. Just how often shampooing is needed depends on many of the variables discussed in this chapter, but every six months is a good average. If you have shag carpeting, invest in a "carpet rake." This will help bring the dirt that has gotten down into the shag to the surface for easier cleaning.

Shopping Hints for Carpets

1. Take along your measurements and plans (if you have them). Compare the measurements with the estimator's, and if there is a great difference, have him explain why. Because of the widths carpet comes in, you will have to buy more than you need, but a good estimator can come very close.

2. There is a saying in the industry, "The deeper, the denser, the better," which is a good guide when buying carpeting. Long shags cannot be too dense because the yarn needs to be able to fall in scattered directions to give the "grass look." You can check the denseness by folding the carpet and revealing the backing. The yarn should be close together and in even rows. Check for the tightness of the backing material.

3. Weight (amount of fiber per square foot) is directly related to wear. (If the label doesn't record it, ask the salesman.) Nylon, for example, in 20- to 24-ounce-weight residential carpets will last as long as eight to ten years. Commercial-grade nylons range from 20 to 28 ounces and will probably outlast your interest in the pattern chosen.

4. If the carpet is tufted, find out if it has the secondary backing.

5. Check the label. The Federal Trade Commission requires that the following information be on every carpet sample and rug label:

    A. Name of manufacturer or distributor
    B. FTC registration number or manufacturer's name
    C. Generic names of all fibers in the carpet
    D. Percentage of each fiber
    E. Country of origin of imported carpet or rug

Your wall-to-wall carpeting roll will not have a label when it arrives, but the invoice should include the same information that was on the label of the sample from which you ordered and on your conditional contract.

6. Find out what is included in the purchase price:

    A. Pad?
    B. Installation (stairs are always extra)?
    C. Metal stripping for thresholds?
    D. Below-grade installation charges?
    E. Sales tax (on materials only—not on labor—in states where tax is applied)?
    F. Warranty on restretching? This may be needed to correct buckling from movement of the house, from heavy furniture being moved over the carpet, or from atmospheric conditions. Usually there is no charge for

this service up to one year from installation. If the problem involves the backing (if it comes loose from the top layer, for example), your dealer should handle this promptly. A mill representative is called in, and you should be offered either replacement for the affected area (if the bedroom carpeting is faulty, the manufacturer will not replace the carpeting in any other rooms unless it shows signs of the same problem) or a cash settlement. We recommend taking the replacement.

7. Ask who will install the carpet.

8. Look at the sample on the floor, not on the rack. Step on it with the pad you are considering under it.

9. Compare wool to wool and nylon to nylon, and so on. Compare textures the same way.

10. Look at the twist on the strands of yarn. A puffed look indicates a carpet that will not wear well. Multiple strands of yarn, tightly twisted, wear the best. Uncut loops wear better than cut loops.

11. Check the guarantees the store is willing to give. The length of time a store stands behind its merchandise shows its faith—or lack of it—in the product.

12. Find out whether the installers will take up your old carpet and dispose of it and how much this will cost.

13. Before you buy extra carpet to "hide" so it can be moved down on stairs to accommodate the extra wear, check the price of doing this and whether your particular carpet can be installed this way. (There is some discussion as to whether this is a valid way of installing carpet; we have our doubts.)

14. Record the date you purchase the carpet in a place where you keep special records so you can check the kind of wear you are getting.

15. Ask for the leftovers.

Rugs

Rugs can be large enough to cover an entire room or so small that they provide only an accent to a beautiful expanse of floor. If room size, the rug should leave a 12-inch border in a large room and slightly less, 8 inches perhaps, in a smaller one.

You can buy area rugs made from the same carpeting material used for wall-to-wall installations or one of the many variety rugs on the market today. Be sure that the edges of the rug are carefully bound by the dealer. If you prefer, for a reasonable price he will add fringe as a decorative touch.

Every country in the entire world has some kind of floor covering, and it sometimes seems that the American consumer is exposed to both good and poor examples from all of them. This is a situation where a reputable dealer is invaluable. It might be fine, for example, to have a throw rug from Afghanistan, but if it isn't properly cured, the odor will probably offend Yankee sensibilities more than it would those of an Uzbek tribesman. For this reason, you should be happy to let your dealer in ethnic rugs judge the bargains in quality floor coverings for you.

The same is true with oriental rugs. Finding a dealer who has been in business in the same location for thirty to forty years is a fair assurance that he'll be around tomorrow. Actually, it's even a pretty fair assurance that his sons will be around thirty or forty years from now, since oriental rug dealers tend to pass their knowledge on like an inheritance. It's certainly a lot safer than attending an auction advertised in the newspaper for next Sunday afternoon in the Gold Room of your local hotel.

Oriental rugs are a good investment since, properly chosen and properly treated, they do not diminish in value. Even more important, they can be enjoyed as objects of art for the fine workmanship involved in the hand-knotting process, for their age and geographic background, for the deep, rich colors and their symbolism, for the intricacy of their designs. Lots of homework is going to be involved, however. Learn values. (*Everyman's Money*, in the spring of 1974, stated that a prospective buyer could expect to pay $20 to $100 per square foot for a good oriental rug.) Study design and places of origin. Learn the differences between the rugs of various geographic areas: Persian (Iranian), Turkoman (Bokhara), Caucasian, Anatolian (Turkish), Indian, Chinese, or other.

Before going out on your oriental adventure, do spend enough time on your homework to know the difference between the Dhiordes knot of the Turks and the Senneh knot of the Persians, for example. A good book might be E. Gans-Ruedin's *Connoisseur's Guide to Oriental Carpets*. In addition to this volume of over four hundred pages, Tuttle has published several other authoritative texts on oriental carpets, including those by Charles W. Jacobsen.

The Metropolitan Museum of Art has published a learned but expensive volume on the subject; you can catch some of the flavor of their specimens, however, in an issue of *The Metropolitan Museum of Art Bulletin* devoted exclusively to the topic of Islamic carpets and featuring examples from the outstanding Joseph V. McMullan Collection. As thin as the Gans-Ruedin is thick, this little issue, lovingly reproduced in Munich, captures some of the beauty of the carpets and rugs with McMullan's own descriptions of the samples from his collecting experience. Begin reading and then go out and begin to visit dealers and look at the rugs themselves to learn how to recognize your own magic carpet when you see it.

Even with a dealer you trust, you should spread a rug out and look at it for flaws, for uneven edges, for wrinkles. Irregularities in color or worn places may not keep you from buying, but you should know by careful inspection just what you're getting and decide how much you are willing to pay. Don't rush. A rug that's a good buy today will be a good buy tomorrow. Even, probably, just a tiny, tiny bit more valuable, since given two rugs of equal excellence, the older will bring the better price. In the East, rug dealers "age" their rugs by placing them where they will be subjected to use in order to enhance their value. Wear from the street traffic of people and camels brings up the luster and softens the fibers of some wool orientals (though not silk or silk and wool combinations).

Special care must be given these lovely floor coverings. Although they do increase in value with use, there are things you will have to learn not to do with them: better to brush or sweep them than to vacuum them; avoid placing heavy furniture on them or walking on them with deck shoes.

American Indian rugs also should be chosen carefully—after study of the various origins, from a reputable dealer, and after careful inspection. (See chapter 11 for sources of Indian arts and crafts.) Many modern reproductions of Indian rugs are on the market; these can be a welcome addition to your home for color and design, but do not be deceived about their collector value.

Imported rugs made from fibers such as sisal and hemp should be carefully examined for import tags stating country of origin. You should have the assurance of the dealer that they have been passed by customs and therefore sprayed for insects which could not only destroy the rug but also infest your home.

Shopping Hints for Rugs

1. Buy pads for area rugs. They increase the rug's life and reduce the slipping problem.

2. If you buy a "valuable" imported rug, get a signed receipt for insurance purposes.

3. If you are buying a piece of carpeting to use as a rug, determine whether the price includes binding the edges. How much does fringe cost?

4. Check for a label. The FTC requirements are included in our shopping hints for carpets.

Resilient Floors

Early sea captains often painted, or had painted, patterns on sailcloth to provide floor coverings for their ship's cabins. From this idea came, later, felt-base materials and, still later, in the nineteenth century, linoleum. Eventually the rotogravure process revolutionized pattern printing, and from that, in the past decade or two, experiments have led to dramatic changes in the industry.

Resilient flooring is one of several terms applied to a group of floor coverings, not all of which are actually resilient. Another term, *hard-surface floors*, covers too broad an area, embracing wood, ceramic, and other hard-surface materials as well.

Resilient floors are available in tile, as sheet goods, and as semipermanent loose-laid "rugs." Also in this category are resin and laminated floorings.

Do not lay any resilient flooring on damp subfloors, unsecured wood floors, or surfaces where paint is in poor condition. Any hollows, bumps, chips, or lumps will show through the flooring, so take the time to sand and seal the floor before installation.

Tiles

Tiles are sold by the box. The most common sizes are 9 by 9 inches or 12 by 12 inches. They are simple for the do-it-yourselfer to put into place; when installed professionally, they require more handling than sheet goods and consequently are more costly to install. Tiles have the distinct advantage of being removable if one area is worn more than another or is damaged in some way. On the negative side, the seams may present such problems as collecting dirt or curling because of improper installation or too much water during cleaning.

The most widely used tile is vinyl asbestos, which combines the qualities of asbestos and vinyl to make a product less durable than asbestos but more resistant to moisture, grease, and alkalies. It is priced moderately, between low-cost asbestos and expensive pure vinyl tiles. For the do-it-yourselfer, adhesive-backed tiles are available and easy to install.

The much maligned and least expensive asphalt tile is in reality a very durable product for heavy traffic areas and enjoys widespread use in public buildings. It has a limited color range because asbestos does not "take" color as well as products containing vinyl. It should not be used in food preparation areas because of its poor resistance to grease.

Natural cork tiles have been improved by the addition of resins, which create a product that retains the natural beauty of cork while offering an excellent wear surface. Cork has the plus of soundproofing.

Pure vinyl tiles are the most costly and the most durable. The very best have patterns or colors which run all the way through the tile and consequently will not wear away. The so-called pure vinyls in whatever form—tiles or sheet goods—develop the brightest and clearest colors of any of the resilient floor materials and, therefore, offer a wide color selection from which to choose.

Sheet Goods

Sheet goods are available in widths that range from 6 to 15 feet and are marketed in large rolls. Not all types or patterns come in all widths, so check for this problem early in the selection stage.

VINYL SHEET GOODS

Vinyl sheeting comes in two forms: with filled-vinyl wear surfaces and without. The filled surfaces are the most expensive and the most durable because the vinyl (including any chips of vinyl in the pattern) runs through the entire material. These will bear the heaviest furniture loads before showing dents or depressions, and the pattern, being part of the sheet goods itself, does not wear away.

In the unfilled type the color or pattern is printed or embossed onto the vinyl surface and then coated again with vinyl. Although vinyl is a tough material, this product may eventually show signs of surface wear.

Special attention to seams is particularly important in the installation of the newer cushioned vinyls, which are backed by a layer of foam; the services of an expert may be required in getting a well-laid product. Cushion vinyl manufacturers recommend the use of a seam sealer. Be sure your installer follows the manufacturer's specifications.

FELT-BASED SHEET GOODS

Another product almost replaced by vinyl, the felt-based sheet goods—linoleum, for example—still has a limited market because of its low cost. However, the expense and time involved in installing a product with so poor a wear surface, comparatively speaking, make this an unwise choice for permanent flooring. Felt-based products such as linoleum are, however, often available as semipermanent loose-laid flooring. Despite its less sturdy wearing qualities when compared to pure vinyls, linoleum is a wise choice when price is a consideration and a movable product is needed. Caution should be exercised in placement and care of linoleum rugs to keep them dry, since the backs are often absorbent material easily damaged by moisture.

Resin Flooring

The very newest flooring is also one of the oldest. Poured resin floors with many small pieces of pure vinyl in them present a tough and attractive surface. Years ago, if the resin did not "set up" in a specified time, it never did. The resultant mess had to be scraped up and the process started all over again. The product on the market today no longer seems to have this problem.

Laminates

For a price, you can have the very youngest and most innovative member of an already extensive family: the laminates—wood, fabric, or wall coverings impregnated with pure vinyl. Caution: since laminate floorings are made from the finest vinyls and will wear a long time, this should be taken into consideration when the pattern is selected. If you choose flooring to match your kitchen curtains, it will be difficult to change your color scheme whenever the mood comes upon you.

We have put into chart form the various types of resilient flooring that have evolved and are now commonly available, listing their characteristics and where each can be used, along with some maintenance tips which will help not only to maintain the product over a longer life but also to assist in making a flooring selection in the first place.

FLOORING CHART

Material and Size	Composition	Areas of Use	Durability	Maintenance
		Tiles		
Asphalt tile 9 by 9 standard	Asbestos fibers, fillers, pigments, resin binders	On wood or masonry subfloors and below or above grade	Good. Over radiant heating, temperature must not exceed 85 degrees. Generally greaseproof. Can be dented by furniture or cracked by sharp impact.	Soaps weaken the tile; solvents and oils attack it. Use only synthetic detergents and water-emulsion resin finishes and waxes.
Rubber tile from 9 by 9 square to 18 by 36 rectangular	Rubber, fillers, curing chemicals	Above, on, and below grade; on-grade concrete	Good. Resistant to denting. Some not greaseproof.	Seriously affected by oils, solvents, strong soaps, and alkalies. Use waxes or polishes made for rubber floors.
Vinyl asbestos tile 9 by 9 standard	Comparable to asphalt but with vinyl resin binders	Above, on, and below grade; on concrete, wood floors, metal, plywood, or Masonite subfloors, and over radiant heating	Excellent. The most widely used tile. Resistant to grease, moisture, alkalies, acids, denting, and chipping.	Wash with detergent and wax with water-emulsion waxes. Some are coated with silicone to resist water and this may have to be removed before a water-emulsion resin finish can be applied.
Vinyl tiles 9 by 9 standard	Flexible vinyl, plasticizers, pigments, fillers, and stabilizers	Above, on, and below grade	Excellent. Resistant to grease, moisture, alkalies, acids, denting and chipping.	Same as vinyl asbestos. Some are treated and do not need waxing.

FLOORING CHART—Continued

Material and Size	Composition	Areas of Use	Durability	Maintenance
Tiles				
Cork tiles 9 by 9 standard, 12 by 12; some rectangular available	Cork curlings and granulated cork compressed with resin binders and wax	In light traffic areas according to manufacturer's specifications and on walls; do not install on grade, if floor is concrete, or below grade	Good, but must be sealed and finished when installed. Can become porous and deteriorate when finish wears off.	Damp-mop and/or sweep. Reseal according to manufacturer's instructions.
Vinyl cork tiles	Vinyl added to cork to increase durability	In moderate traffic areas and on walls, according to manufacturer's specifications; installation areas are the same as for cork tiles	More resistant to grease, dents, dirt, and wear than standard cork	Damp-mop and/or sweep. Reseal when needed according to manufacturer's instructions.
Sheet Goods				
Linoleum 9 by 9 standard in tile, 6 to 15 feet wide in rolls	Wood flour and/or ground cork, pigments, oxidizer oils, and resins, generally applied to burlap or felt back	Suspended concrete properly seasoned, smooth troweled, and dry; suspended wood underfloors, solid and free of all foreign matter	Good. In quality grades resists denting better than asphalt but not as well as vinyl asbestos or pure vinyl.	Do not flood with water as water seepage can eventually destroy floor from beneath. Highly susceptible to alkali damage. Wash with mild detergent and wax with water-emulsion wax. Do not use varnish or shellac finishes.

FLOORING CHART—Continued

Sheet Goods

Material and Size	Composition	Areas of Use	Durability	Maintenance
Vinyl sheet, unfilled surface 6- to 15-foot widths by roll	Wear surface of clean unfilled PVC; back of resin-saturated felt in cheap varieties, polymer-impregnated asbestos sheeting in the most commonly used, and vinyl backing on the expensive	Polymer and vinyl backs can be used anywhere; felt back on suspended floors only	Excellent. Patterns and colors are printed under the wear surface to prevent pattern change from wear. Resistant to grease, denting, acids, and alkalies.	Wash with detergent and wax with water-emulsion wax. Some types do not need waxing.
Vinyl sheet, filled surface 6- to 15-foot widths by the roll	Vinyl resins in granular form, plasticizers, stabilizers, pigments, and fillers	Same as vinyl unfilled	Excellent. The solid vinyl filling ensures good wear and forms the pattern. Same wearing qualities as vinyl unfilled, sometimes better.	Same as vinyl unfilled

Shopping Hints for Resilient Flooring

1. Take plans of the area you wish to cover with you. Check the measurements carefully before shopping.

2. Measure the same as for carpeting: length times width, divided by 9 for square yards. Find out the widths your particular goods come in.

3. If you plan to install the material yourself, check the type of adhesive you should use.

4. Determine what is included in the price.

5. Be sure to order extra tiles and ask for the leftovers from sheet goods. You just might be able to cut and piece if need be. Also, the extra pieces make great shelf liners.

6. Find out if the supplier will take up your old tile and dispose of it and how much he will charge for this.

7. Don't forget to check guarantees and their duration.

Natural Hard Surfaces

Long before wall-to-wall carpeting or resilient floorings were manufactured, the householder had to rely upon other hard surfaces—woods, both hard and soft, ceramic clay tiles, cement, or stone-type materials such as aggregate, terrazzo, marble, brick, slate, and quarry (natural stone) tiles. Ceramic tile, bricks, and pavers are made, and stone, slate, and marble are quarried. Natural materials have inherent faults that sometimes cannot be corrected, whereas the manufactured materials are subject to greater control.

All these products have withstood the test of time (even the soft woods with their greater maintenance challenge), and either in their traditional state or as improved by modern technology they continue to be appropriate in many household settings.

Wood

Wood flooring material is available in a variety of squares, blocks, and strips to create a seemingly infinite number of designs and patterns. Some patterns are even prearranged in squares and secured to a cheesecloth backing, ready to be laid into larger floor designs. Wood flooring is sold both by the unit and by the square foot; estimate by determining the square footage of the area to be covered.

In addition, you must remember to measure the depth of the area to be covered. Is it lower than, higher than, or flush with the adjoining floor surfaces? Some woods may be as thick as ¾ inch, requiring either subflooring adjustments or building a threshold to bridge the height differential. You might also be able to use the thinner wood blocks available for just such circumstances. Usually prefinished, some of these even have preapplied adhesive which requires only the removal of the protective backing before direct application to the prepared subfloor. Special tools may be required for cutting.

Hardwoods, which include oak, walnut, and maple, have fine grains and are expensive. Their long-term qualities of beauty, tradition, and wear are considered by many homeowners to be a worthwhile investment.

The soft woods such as pine can be effectively distressed (given markings to simulate long, heavy use and to create rustic effects) and any additional signs of wear will only serve to enhance this look. Softwoods lend themselves especially well to provincial and country furniture for this reason.

Wood floors can be finished in a number of ways, depending upon where the floor is, the traffic it will have to bear, and your personal preference. For an unusual and soft patina finish you could bleach, tint with a colored water-based stain, seal with a paste wax, and buff. For a "slicker" look you can use oil-based stains in either wood tones or colors and finish with a moisture-cured urethane. We suggest an expert to apply the more unusual finishes and colors. If you do it yourself, read labels and our chapter on paints and stains to be sure the materials you are using are compatible.

There are four different finishes that may be used to protect wood floors: paste wax sealers, urethanes, varnishes, and shellacs. Of the four, the urethane finishes are the most serviceable, needing only waxing and buffing to give the desired shiny finish. The distressed and wire-brushed woods with their rustic look do not even need the additional waxing and buffing care.

Urethanes, such as Verathane and Dura Seal, have opened up the entire house, including kitchens, bathrooms, and play areas, to wood floors at minimum maintenance and in a range of finishes, mat to satin. The moisture-cured urethanes must be applied professionally, but the oil-modified urethanes are available for home application. Once applied, the finish must be kept intact and checked periodically, since even the most durable applications eventually wear through.

As water is the enemy of wood, wax is its friend. Dust wood floors with a treated mop or cloth and keep them regularly waxed and buffed. Use a paste or liquid type of wax, not the water-based kind or the self-polishing waxes, which are made from acrylics and can damage some floor finishes. Consider the solvent-based cleaner waxes which clean and wax at the same time, leaving a film which you buff away. Old wax buildup can be removed with mineral spirits or naphtha.

All wood must be protected from moisture (including high humidity), grease, oils, and excessive traffic. Wood flooring should not be placed in areas where moisture exposure cannot be controlled (i.e., below grade) and should be sealed and the seal kept intact. With proper care, your wood floors will serve you well and beautifully.

Ceramic Tile

Ceramic tiles and bricks are probably one of man's oldest building materials, having been used for about seven thousand years. The evidence of ceramic tile's durable beauty can be seen in the Alhambra in Spain and the Taj Mahal in India. They are excellent in hot, humid areas and where minimal upkeep is needed. Ceramic tiles are used extensively in hospitals, food preparation areas, dairies, and hotels; but their use in the home does not have to be limited to utility areas. On the negative side, their very durability can be a problem as anyone who has dropped something breakable on a tile floor knows.

Glazed tiles are available in a dazzling variety of colors with both mat and glossy finishes and with patterns either incised or printed. Since the designing of ceramic tile is still an art, take advantage of the custom-designed tiles whenever possible. The shapes and sizes range from delicate 1-inch mosaics to 1-foot squares.

Unglazed tiles have been developed to a point where they are resistant to acid, grease, oil, bacteria, and alkalies. These are known as extruded quarry and brick tiles, not to be confused with natural quarry and bricks. Although these were developed for commercial use, they are great for kitchens, entryways, and patios. They are expensive but will last indefinitely with minimal care.

Grout is the soft, fine-grained mortar material which is used to seam tiles together and which hardens to hold them permanently in place. The industry has passed on to the public the new acid-resistant grout first developed for commercial needs. These new grouts are excellent and some come in pre-blended colors to complement or match the tile.

Stone

The stones that are most commonly quarried are the clay tiles called quarry tiles, which are fired just as they come from the earth and are rust, rose, brown, or slate blue in color. Slates are either the Virginia, which are black, charcoal, or blue-green, or the Vermont, which are red, green, or purple. Marble comes in a variety of colors; it is becoming scarce and is therefore expensive. Included in the marbles are the travertines. Terrazzo is a floor made from small chips of marble set in cement and polished.

Pavers can be made from a variety of clays or cements. They are generally uneven and can be found in colors running from tan to red to charcoal. When buying clay pavers you should determine whether they have been sun or kiln dried. If kiln dried, they are stronger and easier to cut and, unlike the sun dried, can be sanded down if the surface is too rough and uneven. The molded cement tiles and pavers can produce any effect the manufacturer desires, including "raccoon tracks" on some of the more poetic pavers. The resins that are put into the cement create a strong and nonporous product; cement can be colored or have small stones embedded in it to create an aggregate floor.

Ceramic tiles, glazed and unglazed, need occasional damp mopping with a synthetic detergent and soft water. Soap and hard water may leave an insoluble scum. Natural quarry tile needs to be protected with a vegetable oil–based sealer and then cared for as tile. Slate floors have to be sealed, and, if you want a shiny look, an acrylic sealer may be used.

Terrazzo and marble should be protected from waterborne stains by sealers. Bricks and pavers of the glazed type need no special care, but the unglazed need either a masonry silicone or liquid acrylic sealer applied.

Shopping Hints for Wood, Ceramic, and Stone

1. Take plans of the area to be covered and carefully recheck measurements.
2. Know the floor structure over which you will be working. Your subflooring must be able to take the considerable extra weight of these floorings.

3. If you wish to do the job yourself, tell the salesman so that he can direct you to the floors made for this. Ask your supplier if he has installation tools you can rent or borrow.

4. Have an expert install anything other than "do-it-yourself" tile. Be sure to have a professional installer for stone unless you have specific experience in setting stone.

5. Find out what the price includes:

For wood: thresholds, staining, finishing, and/or sealing are generally extra.

For ceramic tile: if you are going to incorporate a design, check how much is involved for the extra labor. Be sure you know whether you are being charged by the square foot or by the tile.

6. When buying stone check with the dealer for the specific sealer needed for the particular stone you are buying. And be faithful about keeping the seal intact, for once the more porous materials are stained, they might be permanently marred.

7. Find out if there are any guarantees, what they are, and how long they last.

Resources

Books

Gans-Ruedin, E. *The Connoisseur's Guide to Oriental Carpets.* Rutland, Vt., and Tokyo: Charles E. Tuttle Co., 1971.

Magazines and Newspapers

Christian Science Monitor: "Buying a Carpet," March 11, 1975; "Caucasian Carpets as an Investment," July 16, 1974; "Oriental Rugs: Demand Cuts Quality," May 19, 1976.

Consumer Research, "How to Choose a Carpet," April 1976.

Everybody's Money, Box 431, Madison, Wis. 53701: "Oriental Rugs," Vol. 14, No. 1 (Spring 1974); "What's Afoot in Carpeting?" Vol. 12, No. 4 (Winter 1972–73).

House Beautiful, September 1971.

Los Angeles Times, Home Section, May 18, 1975.

The Metropolitan Museum of Art Bulletin, Vol. 28, No. 10 (June 1970).

Organizations

Armstrong Cork Co. "A Guide to Easy Care of Armstrong Carpet," CD 2-273-B; Care manual, Acrylic F3-60M.

Bigelow-Sanford Inc., 140 Madison Avenue, New York, N.Y. 10016. Booklet: *Everything You've Always Wanted to Know about Carpet but Were Afraid to Ask.*

Ceramic Tile Institute, 700 N. Virgil, Los Angeles, Calif. 90029.

General Services Administration, Consumer Products Information, Distribution Center, Pueblo, Colo. 81009. "Carpets and Rugs," CIS 12.

Monsanto Advertising, F8-AC; F6-Q073; F9.

U.S. Post Office Department, Washington, D.C. 20260. "Floors/Care and Maintenance," Series S-3 (rev.).

3

Wall Coverings

THE first wall adornments were probably the mysterious paintings on the walls of prehistoric caves like those at Altamira, Spain. Scholars still ponder why man first adorned his home, and salesmen continue to be confused as to what people will buy for wall coverings and why.

Whatever the mysteries of choice, effective use of today's wide variety of wall coverings can bring about some of the quickest, most dramatic changes available to the home decorator, and, approached intelligently and with imagination, the whole matter can be great fun. Unfortunately, the average householder is ill prepared to work his or her way through the myriad bits of information, if any, concerning materials and adhesives and to cope with the installation peculiarities of the final choice. If you define your situation and investigate the products available, however, you should be able to set out upon your shopping trip with only the problem of getting what you want for the price you are willing to pay.

Homework

1. Do you need the wall covering to do something besides look good:
   Hide poor walls—cracks, rough or uneven surfaces?
   Provide extra-hard wear—in hallways, children's rooms?

Hide structural problems—for example, pipes, walls, space broken by ill-placed or poorly designed cabinets?

Offer soundproofing?

2. How permanent is your home—rented, long-term leased, owned?
3. Who will use the area most?
4. Do you intend to do the work of installation or application yourself? Do you have the talent, the time, the training, and the tools?
5. What effect do you want to create—open, cozy, airy, bright, cool, calm?
6. What options are available for this setting:

Wallpaper and related coverings?

Wood paneling?

Other surfaces, such as ceramic tile?

Wallpapers

Given a stack of wallpaper books in the local paint and paper shop or "Wallpaper Salon," one tends to set to with a great goodwill which can erode rapidly when assaulted by the enormous variety of colors, patterns, and materials. Knowing about the various materials will help quite a bit; being realistic will help even more. Is that delightful pattern in the perfect shade of orange the hard-wearing vinyl which you decided, in the calm and protection of your home, is really what you need? Meditate. Visualize the perfect orange covered with fingerprints, the delightful pattern rubbed away by constant scrubbing.

Wallpaper selection can be made much easier, less painful, less of a drain on one's psychic energy, by applying the SEM approach we outline in chapter 13. This method will protect you from trauma by providing calm and rational alternatives when those funny and almost inevitable things happen to you on the way to the paperhanger's: the Perfect Choice will not hold up in the bath; the pattern is stocked in the regional warehouse two states away (and your paperhanger is waiting in the living room—order the paper and *then* schedule the paperhanger); that very popular pattern has just been discontinued. If you have followed our directions well, you will calmly order your next choice, because you know what you want and you know several ways of achieving it.

If you know exactly what any given home furnishing should do for you and how a given choice will best do it, you have one foot in the stirrup and are ready to take off at a full gallop. We have a client who retains a special place of favor in our memory; asked, during the selection of wallpaper, what kind of impression he wished to convey to his friends as they stepped into his hall, he responded instantly, "I want them to think I'm rich." *Both* feet in the stirrups, that man.

Before You Shop

Wallpaper can be inexpensive or very, very expensive. Beyond a certain point, you will discover, the materials from which the paper is made cannot be any better and what you are paying for is the design, and possibly the exclusiveness of that design. In other words, after the customer has been given the best paper, the best rollers, the finest screens, the most talented workers, the most modern factories, what then? The most expensive wallpapers (exclusive of truly hand-applied designs) are not necessarily gold embossed, for example, but are simply the products of the latest fashion output in the field.

Whatever its price, wallpaper is priced by the single roll but is rolled and sold by the double or triple roll. (This guide does not always apply to the purchase of imported papers. Double rolls from abroad sometimes contain less footage than our domestic doubles, so check with your salesperson and/or the front of the wallpaper sample book.) By paying a "cutting charge," you can sometimes, but not always, get a single roll if you need an odd number of rolls. If you think you can get by with six rolls, but might need seven, order an extra double or triple (depending on how this paper is rolled) and arrange to return it if your paperhanger has not cut into it. Establish carefully what the return conditions are and record them on your receipt; there could be handling charges and/or time limits.

Since papers can have a great color variation from run to run, you must get the "color run number" (which is recorded on the wrapper) in case you have to order extra rolls. Many "grasses" and similar weaves come from villages of the Orient and are subject to so many variables that the actual material received may look, at best, like a distant cousin of the sample seen at the time of order. It is always wise to avoid matching paints and fabrics to wall-covering samples before the arrival of the actual working material, but with the grass-cloth types of covering it is imperative.

Measuring

Although there are traditionally 36 square feet in each single roll (S/R) of wallpaper, you can depend upon only 30 because of a certain amount of waste in cutting and fitting. The linear footage needed will vary according to the width of the paper.

Square-foot system (this is "safer" but has about a 20 percent waste factor):
1. Multiply width of wall by height
2. Deduct 1/2 S/R for each large opening (door or window)

Linear-foot system (this does not allow much margin for error):
1. Measure around edge of room for number of widths of paper needed (depending upon paper selected, the trimmed width will be from 18 to 36 inches)
2. Multiply by the height of the room (in feet)

One professional paperhanger we know saves his clientele a lot of money by his measurement technique. He measures around the edge of each room (skipping doors and large windows) as if he were hanging 18-inch paper and then multiplies by the number of feet from floor to ceiling for running (linear) feet. Since few wallpapers are as narrow as 18 inches, the extra width of the actual paper provides the "waste" to cover walls above the openings he's skipped over. For him this works beautifully, leaving very little unused paper to pay for, but we don't recommend it for the do-it-yourselfer who has had less experience at measuring and still less at hanging.

Another factor with which the uninitiated must cope is the mystical drop match. This measurement of the design's repetition frequency should be recorded on the back of the wall covering; it can in some instances double or even triple the amount of paper required. This not only increases the cost of materials proportionately, but also requires a more professional—and therefore probably more expensive—hand to apply it.

Since paper must be cut with 3 inches extra at the bottom for trimming and filling, 3 inches of a repeat design (drop match) is lost on every length, and in order to match the pattern on the next strip, more paper must be cut away (again allowing an extra 3 inches at the bottom). Obviously, the greater the distance between repetitions of the design (the larger the drop-match number), the more paper lost in the cut. A 33-inch drop match, for example, works ideally on a standard 8-foot-high wall, since three repeats of the pattern (99 inches) will provide 96 inches of linear coverage plus the 3 inches for trim. In comparison, a 38-inch drop will mean the loss of 15 inches of "extra" pattern on each length hung. Multiplied by the number of widths required, this could mean running short on the last length or even needing several additional lengths. This, in turn, could mean ordering a specially cut single roll or breaking into a new double or triple roll with the resulting costs in time, money, and inconvenience. Consumer refusal to purchase impractical drop matches (some reach extremes of 56 inches) may eventually deter their design and manufacture.

This, we hope, will be one of the items on the agenda of the Wallcovering Manufacturers' Association, an organization formed in 1974 to provide better communication within the industry and with governmental agencies and other interested bodies and to set standards of quality for wear and color.

Options in Wallpaper

1. Machine prints on paper. These are generally inexpensive and not washable.
2. Hand prints on paper. These are delicate silkscreen prints, usually done on fine paper, and are moderate to expensive in cost.
3. Flocks, silk, laces, fabrics on paper. Laminated on paper, these are among the most delicate of wall coverings, with the exception of nylon flocks on vinyl, which are washable and more durable. The papers are moderate to very expensive and not washable.
4. Vinyl-coated papers. These can be either machine- or hand-printed papers which have been "sealed" with vinyl to make them more resistant to soil. These are washable but not scrubbable.
5. Pure vinyls. These are made of polyvinyl chloride which has been applied under pressure in one of three ways and can be made to resemble any texture—silk, glass, wood, cork, or whatever. The heaviest or commercial weight is extremely durable, but even the light weights are generally good for five to ten years of wear. The strongest and most durable of the wallpapers, these can all be scrubbed and, when being replaced, can be stripped to their backing, which will provide a base for the next hanging. Varieties are vinyl laminated onto paper backing, vinyl coated onto cloth backing, vinyl laminated onto cloth backing.
6. Foils. These are metallics laminated onto a paper back. Although expensive, they can be maintained with careful wiping.
7. Natural textures—grasses, burlap, woods. Laminated to paper, these range in price from moderate to very expensive. Natural materials generally cannot be washed, although a few will survive gentle wipeups.

Hanging

Installation begins with preparation of the walls. This means removing any old peeling or cracking paper or paint, and for this you can rent a steamer, accompanied by ample instructions. Even wallpaper in good condition should not be left on the wall if vinyl is to be applied, since the wheat paste involved in paperhanging will develop mildew under the nonporous vinyl cover; because of this mildew problem and the heavier weight pull of vinyls, they are applied not with paste but with special adhesives.

Where an especially good surface is required, as with hand prints, grasses, silks, and other delicate wall coverings, blank stock, a special paper without design, is hung as a base to cover any wall imperfections that might show through. If hanging is to be done on walls painted with a gloss or semigloss coat, the surface must be sealed before applying the paper or blank stock. Sealer must also be used on raw wood or unpainted plaster walls, and greasy spots should be touched up with clear shellac to seal them. As time-consuming as this preparation may be, it will save you the time and aggravation of repasting papers that keep coming loose, or of counting the bumps and lumps that show through.

"Prepasted" and "pretrimmed" papers, put out by the industry for the convenience of the do-it-yourself market, are just what their names imply. Usually the prepasted products come with a container for water into which the paper is dipped before hanging. If the adhesive material is old or improperly applied to the paper, there will be difficulty in getting a good bond with the wall surface. Despite this and the fact that there is no substitute for traditional pastes applied on the spot by paperhangers who know what variables to expect and how to cope with them, the nonprofessional may still want to buy prepasted papers. They offer quick decorative changes for the householder who does not want the extra expense or inconvenience of buying and mixing wheat paste and renting or borrowing equipment with which to do repasting.

Pretrimmed paper is a definite convenience for the do-it-yourselfer, its main disadvantage being that it comes in a limited range of patterns, since the high-fashion (i.e., more expensive) wall coverings are not trimmed before being put on the market. One step, cutting for proper length before hanging, cannot be avoided with either prepasted or pretrimmed papers, and the householder about to do his own paperhanging will do well to prepare for this both in calculating his paper needs and in providing a surface, a cutting tool, and a straightedge measure to facilitate the all-important task.

Prepaste and pretrim are not the only options picked up by homegrown hangers. A report in the *Christian Science Monitor* (March 26, 1974) says that one-half of all the people purchasing vinyls are hanging their own; since vinyls represent 80 percent of the wallpaper market, a great deal of paste is being applied by unseasoned hands. To rent the equipment necessary (or to get it on loan from your paper dealer) may require an appointment; plan ahead for that exigency.

If you have decided you will, after all, employ the services of a professional paperhanger, there is still work to be done. First of all, get a bid in advance, asking for a breakdown of costs for the job: sanding, sealing, patching, blank stocking, papering. Be sure this is a firm bid and not an estimate. Many paperhangers dislike the nitty-gritty of wall preparation, and you may wish to discuss with yours what the saving would be if you undertook this task yourself.

Be prepared with information (and a large sample of the wallpaper you wish to hang). Ask your hanger for an estimate of the number of rolls you will need; if his figure differs radically from yours, determine why. Too little paper means trying to locate more of the pattern in the same color run, which can cause considerable delay and perhaps having the hanger return to complete the job. At worst, you may not be able to find more of the pattern at all, in any run.

Too much paper means having to return the extra at a service fee or being stuck with the surplus. Actually, there are worse things than having an extra roll of your dining room pattern. If an accident occurs before the paper has been in place long enough for obvious color fade, the extra roll may serve a very useful purpose.

After you and your paperhanger have determined the amount of paper required, run, don't walk, to your friendly neighborhood paint and paper shop (where you have previously established that: no, the pattern has not been discontinued and, yes, the paper is readily available) and order same before it is (1) discontinued or (2) out of stock. These things happen, more often than not, in the wallpaper industry. (Always remember: keep workable options.) If luck and the gods of home furnishing are with you, you have established an order and a reasonably firm delivery date. Then gamble again. Call your paperhanger and set an installation date.

Wood and Wood Paneling

Besides the obvious beauty of wood, this material can, as a wall covering, provide a good measure of soundproofing and, in some cases, fireproofing. Wood is available prefinished or raw (ready for stain or paint) and by the panel, board, or block. It can be obtained not only in solid woods but in the form of veneers, plywoods, hardboard, and laminates. Measure for wood paneling by determining the height and width of the wall area to be covered. In some circumstances and with some materials, it will be necessary to buy the next larger size paneling unit and cut it to fit. Areas must be cut out for light switches and plugs, so be prepared with the tools to do the job properly. When covering walls with planking, measure the same way as for paneling, and let your lumber dealer calculate the number of board feet needed.

Solid wood should be kiln dried and straight. Its advantages over bonded woods are that it can be carved and/or turned to create intricate patterns, that you can sand down an area that has been marred and refinish it, and that it will not peel or come apart, as poorly constructed plywood or veneers sometimes do. Its drawbacks are the expense of really beautiful matched wood for paneling and the possibility of warping, swelling, or shrinking.

Thin blocks of solid woods (¼ inch thick) are available ready to install, like wall tiles, by merely removing a protective paper from the preapplied adhesive backing.

The so-called man-made woods have sometimes been considered inferior to solid wood, but this is not true. Available as veneers, plywood, laminates, and hardboard, they have nearly all the attributes of solid wood with few of the negative features.

Veneers are thin slices of wood either glued or bonded to many other thin layers of wood or used as a fine wood top layer on a less elegant but stronger wood or hardboard core. Veneer can also be laminated to paper to be hung as wall covering. Modern adhesives have eliminated the earlier problems of peeling veneers, and the process is widely used today to offer the beauties of fine wood with savings in both cost and wood supply.

Plywood, available in a much greater variety of widths and lengths than solid wood, is made either of a series of veneers pressed together or of a center core of hardboard sandwiched between veneers. As a wall covering, plywood can have a veneer of fine wood for interior use only or a textured surface that can be used both indoors and out. An example of the latter is V-grooved paneling, or Texture 1-11, widely used and loved by architects. Exterior plywood is weather- and waterproof and can also be used quite effectively in kitchens and baths where moisture would be a problem for some woods.

Wood laminates are plywoods that can be used to create curved surfaces. While this feature is applied more often to furniture, it is occasionally used in problem or unusual wall-covering situations.

Hardboard is made by reducing solid wood to fibers and bonding these together to form everything from unglamorous particleboard to products resembling cork, glass, tile, or fine-grained hardwoods. It is sold by the panel.

Other Surfaces

The variety of materials that can be used for wall coverings is as limitless as the consumer's ability to think of things that can be made to adhere to walls. Here we will limit our discussion to the products other than wallpapers or woods that are most commonly sold and used.

Wood laminates, mentioned earlier, should not be confused with the laminated plastics which sell under such trade names as Formica and Micarta. These, like many other materials, were originally used only for countertops, and the first patterns ranged from gold flecks to gold shells with little between. Now these products have become so sophisticated in color and pattern that many lend themselves to wall use. Since the patterns are duplicated photographically, there is no "class distinction" and you may choose barn wood or rosewood at the same price. The pattern surface is a thin sheet which is laminated to plywood for wall installation. Once in place it can be washed and is virtually impervious to soil and stain. It is expensive but is one of the most durable of wall coverings.

Cork can be purchased by the square in its natural state and is also available laminated to wallboard or to paper. The natural squares vary from the dark chocolate brown lower-grade refrigerator cork to exotic cuts of lighter natural-toned and textured cork bark just as it came from the tree. Cork is fragile and has poor resistance to stains but is beautiful and an excellent source of soundproofing. It has never been inexpensive, but prices have reached record heights in the last few years. However, compared to fine hardwoods, cork may prove to be an even better choice for your money.

Ceramic tiles for walls come in various sizes from the tiny mosaics to 12-inch squares. If they are thin (¼ inch) and therefore light in weight, they may be applied to the wall without the traditional wire mesh bed that the ½-inch, ⅝-inch, and greater thicknesses require. The services of a professional tile setter should be secured for any but the simplest projects. Commercial improvements in this home-furnishing material have been passed on to the consumer, who can enjoy the advantages of the same colored and nonstaining grouts (thin mortars) that are used to apply floor tiles. Be sure to ask your tile salesman about these options and specify them for your tile wall installation.

Any mirrors other than the self-adhesive squares should be measured and installed by a professional glazier. Keep in mind that any cuts for wall switch plates will be an extra charge. Get a firm bid for the work and have a design drawn from which the installer can work, with measurements both of you have decided upon.

Stone is generally limited to fireplace walls and dividers. It reflects sound and is expensive to install but does add durable, unchanging beauty.

If you are considering other, less common wall-covering materials, we advise you to make your own thorough investigation. Always do your homework. Always explore options.

Shopping Hints

1. Take with you a list of all pertinent measurements and your material calculations.

2. Establish the availability of materials you are considering *before* you take samples home. You may need to consult your SEM options (see chapter 13).

3. Determine return policies.

4. If you are doing the work yourself, check on rental equipment. If not, ask for the name of an installer and schedule an installation date. If you do not know the standard labor cost, get two or three bids and recommendations. Reputable installers will be happy to give you an estimate, but don't waste their time.

5. Know the condition of your wall. You could get started on the preparation work while waiting for your paper to come.

6. When you order, record a firm delivery date on your receipt.

Resources

Informative booklets on the subject of wall coverings can be obtained from the following organizations:

American Hardboard Association
20 North Wacker Drive
Chicago, Ill. 60606

Ceramic Tile Institute
700 North Virgil
Los Angeles, Calif. 90029

Douglas Fir Plywood Association
1119 A. Street
Tacoma, Wash. 22283

Masonite Corporation
29 North Wacker Drive
Chicago, Ill. 60606

4

Paints and Stains

BECAUSE the paint industry is a highly developed, innovative business, its workings can be confusing to the nonprofessional whether he is planning a do-it-yourself project or calling in a paint contractor. Every manufacturer has his own product to sell and is interested in telling the consumer only the virtues of his paint or stain and not those of another material that will do the job better. Labeling is so difficult to understand that we suggest you read some of the books listed under Resources in this chapter in order to clarify the subject.

Homework

In what setting will the coating material be used—formal or otherwise?

What kind of wear does the area receive?

Are there children, animals?

Is there moisture nearby—from either the outside (air, adjacent lake or ocean) or inside (baths or kitchens)?

Would stain do the job better?

What kind of tools will you need?

Paints

Types of Paint

Despite the confusing labels, you will find that the material you are using can easily be assigned to one of three basic categories: solvent-thinned, water-thinned, or catalytic coatings.

SOLVENT-THINNED PAINTS

Oil-base paints have been used over the years for both interior and exterior work but are applied today primarily by professionals and usually for exterior surfaces. They are slow drying, have a "paint" odor, and must be thinned with turpentine or mineral spirits. They can be applied with brush, roller, or spray equipment; the tools must be cleaned afterward with some type of solvent. The room must be well ventilated to combat the toxic fumes.

Alkyd paints, which also are available for interior and exterior surfaces, are easy to apply and dry faster than oil-based paint. Since they are almost odorless, thin them with an odorless thinner like mineral spirits. They can be applied with brush, roller, or spray gun, in a well-ventilated room for your own safety. Tools must be cleaned in some type of solvent.

WATER-THINNED PAINTS

Used inside and out, latex paints are today the most popular because they are easy to use, dry quickly, and can be applied over damp surfaces. A second coat can be applied within an hour; alkalies in new masonry do not harm the paint; it can be touched up, since the fresh paint blends easily with the first coat; and the tools can be cleaned with water. Latex paints can be brushed, rolled, or sprayed.

Any bare wood or chalky surface must be primed with a special latex sealer. Do not apply latex while temperatures range below 45 degrees, and, even though these coatings can be applied over damp surfaces, do not undertake an outside project if rain is expected within a few hours after the painting is to be completed. These products will seal off moisture but are unstable during the drying stage. Paints in the latex category are rubber, acrylic, and vinyl (PVA or plastic).

Water-thinned paints also include emulsion and linseed-oil emulsion paints, which are easy to use, can be applied to chalky surfaces, and often, but not always, cover in one coat. Bare wood must be primed. Clean tools with water.

CATALYTIC PAINTS

"Set up," or hardened, by chemicals rather than by the evaporation of solvents and thinners, the catalytic paints provide the toughest and most durable finish available, with maximum adhesion and high resistance to water, acids, solvents, and abrasion. They can be applied to wood, masonry, plastics, tile, metal, and fiber glass. They are called epoxy, urethane, or polyurethane coatings and can be applied with brush, roller, or spray gun.

On the negative side, they are difficult to handle and expensive, and until they set up (in a few hours) they are toxic and emit irritating fumes. They tend to chalk and fade when exposed to hard weather, but since the protective coating is not damaged, they are used extensively in marine work. They can be applied over old epoxy but not over other paints. They cannot be stored for long periods.

Paint Uses

Another way of categorizing paints is to divide them into groups according to the work they do.

EXTERIOR PAINT

Paint designed to resist weather and sun. It has a different balance of pigments and resins or solvents to make it tougher and therefore more expensive than is necessary for interior use.

INTERIOR PAINT

Paints designed for the various surfaces inside buildings; they should not be used for exterior work.

FLOOR PAINTS

Special enamels, varnishes, and sealers designed to hold up under heavy wear on floors and decks.

MASONRY PAINTS

Paints designed especially for masonry. Many ordinary paints can be used on masonry, however; check labels for recommendations by the manufacturer.

MARINE PAINTS

Paints designed specifically for boats. The added expense is considered a saving by wise boat owners. These paints are also excellent for outdoor furniture and where a high gloss and/or tough finish is necessary.

Paint Finishes

Paints, undercoats, and primers are designed to work together in what is called a paint system. Using all of the products from one manufacturer is one way to provide a compatible system, but you can assemble one yourself by deciphering the label and/or checking with the paint dealer to be certain that the materials you are getting will work properly together.

When selecting paints, consider what area is to be covered and the finish you need. Finishes are flat, gloss, semigloss, eggshell, and textured.

FLAT PAINTS

Generally wipable but not scrubbable. They give less wear than enamel, but their non-light-reflecting qualities and ease of application make them a good choice for large wall expanses that receive minimal actual wear.

SEMIGLOSS, GLOSS, AND EGGSHELL

Enamels provide the best wear surfaces for the home. They perform well on doors, molding, and in areas where frequent scrubbing is required. Because they are applied best with a brush, the extra labor involved in application has limited their use on very large wall surfaces. Consider choosing eggshell enamels (the least glossy) for children's rooms and hallways in addition to their traditional use for bathrooms and kitchens.

TEXTURED PAINTS

Good for cracking walls and for brick or concrete surfaces. They can either have a "sand" finish or be put on thick enough to be manipulated with brush, trowel, or other device to create a texture on the newly applied surface. Spanish-style textured walls are a good example of this technique, the effect of adobe or stucco being troweled onto the paint.

Coverage

How much area will your material cover? This is a good question, but one that unfortunately has many answers.

First, your calculations will depend upon the condition of the surface to be covered, upon the size of the area involved, and upon the kind of material you will be using for cover. For example, a gallon of epoxy primer for use on concrete and cinder blocks will cover, according to one manufacturer, about 75 square feet, while you can get about 225 square feet of coverage from the more expensive epoxy enamel that is applied over the primer.

Paints generally cover more area than stains because stains are absorbed into the wood (more on stains later). A gallon of acrylic latex exterior stain might be expected to cover a 200-square-foot area, whereas a like amount of acrylic latex house paint will spread over 450 square feet of surface. Most labels will help you determine what the expected coverage is. Keep reading those labels.

To estimate for interior painting, measure the surface to be covered. Take the height times the width for walls, the length times the width for floors. Multiply these two numbers and you have the number of square feet. Because you should use an enamel on the doors and on window trim, measure them separately from the walls to be covered. Treat even the windows as though you were going to paint them solid (multiplying the width times the height, as before, to establish the square footage). You may have a little enamel left over on the window estimate, but you'll be surprised how close you'll come, since the additional bumps and crevices of windowsills and frames need as much paint to cover as would the wall surface displaced by the window opening.

To measure your house for exterior painting, take the perimeter and multiply it by the height of the house. If your house is gabled, you can add 2 feet to the total height. (We know painting dormers isn't exactly home furnishing, but we thought you'd like to know.)

Note what surface is to be covered and its condition. Masonry takes more paint than sealed wood, and shingles require more paint than smooth wood does.

Are you changing colors? If so, the job will probably require two coats unless the colors are similar.

Caution

Some paints are more toxic—that is, they give off poisonous fumes to a greater degree—than others. You can't tell the difference between the harmless ones and the lethal ones by the odor, as many odorless paints are very dangerous. Read labels carefully. Always paint in a well-ventilated area, just in case, and wear a mask or inhalator when working with spray equipment. Children, animals, and persons with respiratory problems should be kept away from paint projects.

Lead content is another hazard. Federal law requires that lead content be recorded on the labels of paint products. Until some new agent is found, lead remains an almost indispensable ingredient for good coverage. In children's rooms and on children's furniture, low-lead paints or one of the new totally lead-free paints (which must be so labeled) should be applied, but you may need two or three coats to get the necessary coverage.

Tinting

The coloring process always used to be done in the paint store, and for unusual colors we recommend that you stick with the experts. A series of all-purpose colors has been developed, however. These come in tubes and can be added by the amateur to either water- or oil-based paints. You can start with white as the base paint or begin with a color close to your final choice—for example, if you want medium or dark blue, use clear pale blue as the base.

Mix the paint in large batches and record your formula very carefully, in case you have to remix. First add the colorant to a small amount of the base paint and mix until it is thoroughly blended, then add this slowly to the base until you achieve the color you want. Since paint dries lighter, make test swatches and dry them with a small hand drier so you can see the true color. Check labels for lead content, as colorants will add to the percentage of lead in your final coating material.

Stains

Stains are designed to protect wood, color it, and enhance its natural grain and texture. Unlike paint, which coats the surface, stains are absorbed into the wood. Some stains must be protected by a finish such as shellac, varnish, or lacquer. You cannot make a stain by thinning down paint. The special oils in stains are far more penetrating than thinners.

There are oil-, water-, and alcohol-based stains. Unlike oil-based paints, the oil-based stains are the easiest and best to work with, while the water- and alcohol-based stains need a professional hand. Varnish stains do the job of varnishing and staining in one application but do neither job very well. These are really good only for areas where all you want to do is get a sealing job done quickly (in old buildings, for example).

Oil-based stains have been used for many years and are now enjoying a new and deserved popularity, especially for exterior surfaces. Oil-based stains are either clear or opaque (pigmented). Clear stains add color to the wood but do not conceal the grain. Opaque stains cover more of the grain and look a little like paint but do not obscure the wood texture.

For small areas, such as fine furniture, you will get the best results by applying stains with a brush or a clean cloth. The wood should be clean and sanded smooth unless you are dealing with a textured surface; then it should be clean and free of loose splinters.

One coat is sufficient over old stain, but you will probably need two over raw wood. Stains can be used over paint only if the paint has nearly weathered away. Otherwise, the surface must be sanded or sand-blasted free of paint in preparation for the stain application. Oil-based stains take about twenty-four hours to dry.

Always test the stain color you have selected on a piece of the wood you are staining. Brush it on or use a clean cloth, let it dry, and apply the finish if there is to be one. You will then be able to see what the final color will be like. It is better to apply the stain as sparingly as possible while still covering well than to apply it too heavily. You can always apply another coat if you want a darker color, but once a stain has penetrated, it has to be bleached (a difficult process) or sanded to lighten the color.

If the sample is blotchy or the wood does not absorb evenly (hard spots in the grain can cause this), use a very thin white shellac first as a sealer.

Other Finishes

These materials are generally clear and are used over paint, as a base, or by themselves to seal surfaces. They are not as durable as paint or stain for exterior surfaces. There are many, but the three most commonly used are varnish, shellac, and lacquer.

Varnish

There are many types of varnish and all have specific individual purposes. No single one does everything. The most durable varnishes are spar varnish (marine) and urethane varnish, both of which can be used inside and outside. Because there is a definite way that varnish should be applied, we suggest that you either read *How to Paint Anything* (see Resources) or consult your local paint dealer for direction. Varnish is slow to dry, and care must be taken to keep the area dust-free while the drying takes place.

Shellac

This material dries in about fifteen minutes and you can apply the second coat in two hours. Check the label carefully for dating. If the shellac doesn't dry correctly, return the can. Because shellac loses its drying properties quickly, it should not be stored longer than six months and can even begin to weaken in three months. You can tell by checking the color, since it begins to darken as it loses its strength. All shellac cans are dated by the manufacturer, as we indicated, so return the merchandise if it begins to darken in less than three months. And buy freshly dated shellac immediately before starting the project you have in mind.

Shellac forms a good base for other covering material to seal knots and resinous woods, especially pine, and is used as a finish for fine furniture. Shellac finishes should be kept waxed.

Lacquer

Lacquer is fast-drying and forms a hard, glossy finish. It is available either clear or with color. As it acts as a paint remover, it should not be applied over paint, but it can be used as a base for paints. Lacquer is highly flammable and should be used and stored with care.

Painting furniture as opposed to painting walls and woodwork is an entirely new ball game. Besides the Grotz gem mentioned in Resources, we call your attention to the excellent article by Gena Thomas also listed there and written especially for those who are interested in furniture finishes.

Shopping Hints

1. Record measurements of areas to be covered, condition of the surface, and what it is (masonry, wood, interior, exterior). The paint salesman can tell you how much material you will need, or you should be able to get a good idea yourself by reading the coverage estimate on the label.

2. Take samples of colors in the room to be matched. Then take the color chips (manufacturer's samples) home to look at them in the light of your own rooms. Lights change color; check chapter 5 on lighting.

3. Remember that light-colored paints get lighter and deep-hued paints more intense in large areas. Large expanses of color will reflect on the entire room. (Yellow will make it yellower and pink, pinker, and so on.)

4. Take a piece of the wood you are staining or at least the kind of wood (pine, fir, or whatever) and get the salesman to show you what a stain will look like on "your" wood. The stained wood color samples look great in the paint store but the salesman sometimes forgets to tell you what kind of wood was used and how old they are (if he knows). Many a decorator has been fooled by stains on redwood when the wood to be stained was fir.

5. Remember to ask about tools needed and tarps to protect furniture. Can they be had on loan or is there a charge?

6. If you are doing the painting or staining yourself, don't forget sealers, undercoats, and finishes. Which ones are needed and which ones go with your paint?

7. If you are having a professional do your work, he should tell you the brand of paint he uses so you can get color chips of that particular brand. Discuss what kind of paint he is using, where, and why. Get a firm bid for labor and materials and a time estimate.

Resources

Cobb, Hubbard H. *How to Paint Anything*. New York: Macmillan, 1972. A very complete and readable little volume that will be helpful to those interested in a broader knowledge of paints and stains.

Grotz, George. *Staining and Finishing Unfinished Furniture and Other Naked Woods*. Garden City, N.Y.: Dolphin Books, Doubleday, 1973. One of a series by "The Furniture Doctor," who is as delightfully entertaining as he is instructive.

Thomas, Gena. "S-T-R-E-T-C-H Your Furniture Dollars with Paint and Add Color Too." *Consumer Research,* February 1976. Single copies are available for $1 each from *CR*, Bowerstown Road, Washington, N.J. 07882. Residents of New Jersey may obtain the extension bulletin from which this article was excerpted by writing to Rutgers University Cooperative Extension, Cook College, New Brunswick, N.J. 08903.

Paint and Painting, Consumer Information Series No. 2. General Services Information, U.S. Government Printing Office, Washington, D.C. 20407.

5

Lighting

PLANNING the use of lighting in our homes as carefully as it is planned commercially will not only conserve our resources but also provide more comfortable homes. Illuminating engineers have found that the proper light for a given task can relax and refresh while poor or incorrect lighting causes fatigue and irritation.

Our homes and apartments are proof of the lack of planning for lighting other than for decoration. Lighting outlets are placed with little real thought for their use in everyday living. The consumer is left to elevate the profits of the "swag chain" manufacturers by having to drape light fixtures to the needed area. We would like to see at least two outlets on each wall and two on the floor of all rooms, and a switch by every door to control some light upon entering. This would enable the home furnisher to establish a balance among the three major types of lighting: task lighting (reading, sewing, working), general lighting (which balances the light in a room), and decorative lighting, which can add to the general lighting.

Homework

What activity must be lighted?
Who will use the light—old, young, a group?
How often is the light needed?
Is the light necessary for safety—stairs, dark halls?

Light Bulbs

For years people have been buying light bulbs by wattage when they should have been buying them by lumens. Lumens are a more efficient measure of light than watts; illuminating engineers use lumens when planning light for specific purposes.

One lumen is equal to one foot-candle of light per square foot. A watt is equal to one ampere under one volt of pressure. In other words, lumens are a measure of light, and watts are "about" energy, two equally important considerations when planning proper, energy-saving lighting.

The Federal Trade Commission ruled that as of January 1971 all household-type bulb packages should state watts, lumens, and average life of a bulb. We use a General Electric three-way bulb package as our example.

	Low	Medium	High
Watts	50	100	150
Average life (hours)	1,500	1,200	1,150
Lumens (average light output)	580	1,640	2,220

Here is a tip to remember as you compare watts to lumens while shopping for bulbs. Long-life bulbs (such as GE Twice the Life) have twice the average life expectancy of ordinary bulbs, while giving off fewer lumens per watt than standard bulbs. The comparison varies from wattage to wattage, and you may need the next highest wattage to achieve the light level you need if you want to use long-life bulbs. Example (GE bulbs):

	Standard	Long-life
Watts	75	75
Average life (hours)	750	1,500
Lumens	1,170	1,075
Watts	100	100
Average life (hours)	750	1,500
Lumens	1,710	1,585

The following is a limited and general list of lumen recommendations for certain rooms and activities, to help you establish lighting needs for different-sized areas. Multiplied by the room square footage, these figures should provide the range of lighting needs in various living areas.

	Lumens		Lumens
Living room	40–80	Bedroom	40–70
Dining room	20–45	Hallway	10–45
Kitchen	40–80	Laundry	40–70
Bathroom	30–65	Detail work	100–200

(Since there are some differences of opinion about lumen requirements, this list is arbitrary. A more detailed list can be had from the Illuminating Engineering Society; check Resources for the society's address and other information about lighting.)

The estimates on the chart are based on the needs of young eyes (20-20 vision) and are guides only. The figures are also for light from balanced sources; if only recessed lighting is used, the figures must be doubled. To determine the number of lumens to meet your room needs, figure the square feet in the room in question (length times width in feet) and multiply that number by the recommended number on the chart.

Good light illuminates the task area without glare. General lighting balances the light in a room by providing light from different sources, and decorative lighting provides either selected task lighting (table or floor lamps with three-way bulbs) or gracious touches, along with light control (such as a dimmer on a dining-room chandelier).

Light can be controlled by reflection also. Light-colored walls and ceilings reflect a lot of light (example: light cream, 75 percent), while dark colors absorb light (dark green's reflective power is only 7 percent). Shiny or high-gloss paints can create glare; glare also comes from too much light, from poorly placed fixtures, or from bright light coming only from one direction.

The recommended reflection percentages for major surfaces are:

	Percent
Ceilings	60–90
Floors	15–35
Walls	35–60

(If you would like more information, consult an excellent book with easily understood charts: *Electricity in the Home* by Emanuele Stieri; see Resources.)

The color of a light source is important. Warm light flatters people and enhances colors. Cool light opens up areas and defines objects. The two kinds of light are produced by two completely different types of bulbs. There are many varieties (see *Electricity in the Home*). Incandescent bulbs are the source of warm light. They do not flicker or hum. Most home lighting fixtures are designed to accommodate these bulbs. Fluorescent tubes are the source of cool light. They produce three to four times as much light as incandescent bulbs for the wattage used and last about ten times as long. They produce less glare and cover a larger area. Fluorescent tubes can be affected by radio and television waves. A combination of incandescent and fluorescent lighting is the most balanced and economical system. Fluorescent bulbs can be used for the close task lighting needed in kitchens and workshops, and they can be combined in ceiling fixtures with incandescent bulbs for the warmer, softer light.

The direction of light can be controlled by the size, shape, and color of shades, and by placement. Shades on reading lamps should be light in color, translucent, and broad enough to allow the light to fall on the reading material and the area around the reader. The bottom of the shade should be even with the eye level of the reader. The best position for bulbs is low in the shade but not exposed. Shades on hanging fixtures can direct the light up, diffuse it over a broad area, and/or direct a beam to one spot.

Lamps with shades higher than eye level should be placed at the rear of the reading area and to one side. Desk and sewing lamps should cast light from the side opposite the working hand. Much more can be said, and has been, by experts.

When buying any electrical item made in the United States, look for the "UL approved" tag. Standards have been set by the Underwriters' Laboratories, and if an electrical item (lamp, cord, toaster) does not meet these standards, it is refused the label. The UL approval is an assurance of safe, proper construction and is well worth demanding. If you are building a new home, you may not be able to pass electrical inspection if you do not have UL-approved materials.

Other precautionary measures to be observed: (1) Know the type of material from which ceilings and walls are constructed, if you are mounting light fixtures. (Hanging lighting from radiant-heated ceilings presents an additional problem and hazard.) (2) Do not hang fixtures directly from electrical wiring (use special brackets, chains, canopies). (3) When working on special installation problems, find and turn off your master switch.

Interaction of Light and Color

Besides varying in reflective qualities, different colors respond to light in different ways. Technically, objects do not have color; their color is determined by their surface ability to absorb or reflect light. In simpler terms, the reason that lovely blue-green sofa looked yellow-green when you got it home was that the store probably had fluorescent tubes and you have incandescent bulbs. To give you an idea of the properties of color, we suggest you read two interesting books listed under Resources: Munsell, *A Grammar of Color*, and Halse, *The Use of Color in Interiors*.

Light and color can also be used as an art form—mobile color, kinetic color, lumia. If you wish to look into this method of lighting, start with a fascinating book, *The Art of Light and Color* by Tom Douglas Jones, which may well light up a whole new world of color for you.

Shopping Hints

1. Make a list of the kinds of light fixtures you need, the total number needed, and their specific purposes.

2. Consider lights that can be turned on inside a garage before entering, floodlights that can be turned on from inside, light for stairways, both top and bottom, and dimmers for bedrooms in times of illness.

3. Take the "desired" height measurements of lamps needed for certain tables. (Measure the table height also.) Table height plus height to the lower edge of the lampshade should equal the eye level of the person using the lamp. Each child should have at least one place to read or study that is designed for his/her eye level.

4. Calculate the number of lumens or watts needed in your rooms, how you intend to divide that number among various fixtures, and whether you want incandescent or fluorescent bulbs and/or a combination of both.

Resources

Books

Alexander, Mary Jean. *Designing Interior Environments.* New York: Harcourt Brace Jovanovich, 1965.

Allphin, Willard. *Primer of Lamps and Lighting.* Reading, Mass.: Addison-Wesley, 1973.

Halse, Albert O. *The Use of Color in Interiors*. New York: McGraw-Hill, 1968.

Jones, Tom Douglas. *The Art of Light and Color*. New York: Van Nostrand Reinhold, 1972.

Munsell, Albert H. *A Grammar of Color*. New York: Van Nostrand Reinhold, 1969.

St. Marie, Satenig S. *Homes Are for People*. New York: John Wiley & Sons, 1973.

Stieri, Emanuele. *Electricity in the Home*. New York: Barnes and Noble, 1962.

Magazines

The January 1967 issue of *Consumer Research* magazine reports on the testing of light bulbs to establish comparative costs of various types. By breaking down the costs of bulbs by lumens and watt and voltage rates, *CR* concludes that there should be no price difference between short- and long-life bulbs. It's a good article to read, even if it is a bit technical.

Organizations

General Electric Residential Lighting Specialist. Nela Park, Cleveland, Ohio. *The Light Book*. Although this booklet uses watts only, it is very specific about placement. Send for a copy.

Illuminating Engineering Society, 345 East 47th Street, New York, N.Y. 10017.

6

Window Treatment

U NLESS you live on the top floor of a skyscraper (assuming peeping window washers or friendly skywatch pilots are not a problem) or deep in a wilderness where your only neighbors are quick brown foxes, window coverings are a matter you must deal with.

Privacy is not the only reason for covering windows. Noise control, architectural problems, avoiding glare, protection of colors from strong sunlight, and the economy of reduced heating or cooling bills are other important considerations.

Homework

What kind of window are you covering?
Do you need to open it?
Is it a sliding glass door?
Do you want temporary or permanent coverage?
Do you own your home or rent?

Do you intend to make the treatments yourself?

What is the purpose of the window (light, ventilation, view, access, a combination of these)?

What is the purpose of the covering (to insulate, block light or view, decorate, a combination)?

Curtains and Draperies

Curtains and/or draperies can be purely functional—not interfering with a view—or they can be the "stars" of the show distracting the eye from uninteresting views or unpleasant architectural faults.

The term *curtain* at one time applied to the layer of fabric that hung closest to the window. Now curtains are often used alone and can be placed on traverse rods (rods with pulley mechanisms for drawing the curtain) like draw draperies.

Casement curtains are semisheer or open-weave draw curtains on traverse rods that are sill or floor length. Glass curtains are sheer, hang next to the window, and are not on traverse rods. Draw curtains are either sheer or opaque, hung on traverse rods, and are often called draw draperies. Draperies can be stationary panels at either windows or doorways. Some of these can be closed manually. Stationary draperies can also be divided in the center and decoratively held back with a loop of fabric, cord, or chain which will do what its name implies: "tieback." The fabric can also be draped through a specially designed ring or over a decorative "holdback."

Cornices are bands of fabric, approximately 12 to 24 inches deep, placed at the top of the rod to conceal drapery rods or other parts of the window treatment. Valances are longer, often resembling short curtains. Either can be trimmed and/or cut to a patterned design. Padded and covered boards serve the same purpose of hardware concealment and are called cornice boxes.

The glossary at the end of the book has a more complete list of types of curtains and draperies.

Custom, Ready-Made, or Custom-Made-at-Home

Custom draperies or curtains have the advantage of being made for a specific window or set of windows. The variety of treatments and decorative touches is fairly large and can give your room an individual look. Although they are generally more expensive than ready-mades, you might find the difference is not as great as you imagined. If you can fit them into your budget, we feel custom-made draperies are a must for permanent installations. The draper or the store should let you see the samples in your home (see the lighting chapter). Custom draperies should always be measured by the installer.

Ready-made draperies and curtains come in standard window sizes only. They have the obvious advantage of being ready to hang. Ask for advice on the proper rods for the particular draperies you have selected. The store may have an installation service, but be sure to establish whether there is a charge.

Custom-made-at-home draperies can be worth the time and effort, providing you have a working knowledge of how to go about it. Classes in drapery making at your local adult school or community college are a good resource. Check Resources for an excellent booklet called *Windows Beautiful*. Consult your local hardware or drapery store for the final selection (armed with your own careful considerations) of the rods, brackets, and other installation materials.

Construction

How can you check for good construction? Appearance comes first. The seams should be straight, flat, concealed (very important), and serged (double bound with thread by a special commercial machine) or French seamed (with the seam sewn on the face side of the fabric and then folded back on itself on the wrong side and stitched completely to cover the rough edges). If a seam shows from the front, it is a good (or, really, *bad*) sign of poor construction.

Hems should always be double thickness. This is a poor place to save money, because a single hem hangs badly and will be uneven. Even on ready-mades the hem should be at least 3, preferably 4, inches deep. Drapery weights (flat pieces of metal) should be sewn into the hem on every seam and corner to weight the drapery down for a smooth-looking hang.

The material gathered into pleats at the top of the drape, or the "header," should feel stiff and firm from the buckram or Pellon sewn there. If the header material is limp or not heavy enough, the pleats will droop and hang poorly. These stiffening materials are usually white or natural in color and should never show through the drapery material except with sheer fabric, in which case the underlying header material should blend inconspicuously.

To provide deep pleats, the width of fabric used should be at least double the width of the window to be covered in ready-made draperies, two and a half to three times the measured width in the case of custom orders. In the trade these will sometimes be referred to as 200 percent, 250 percent, or 300 percent fullness, so if your drapery man says that a 45- or 48-inch material gathered or pleated into a 24-inch panel has 200 percent fullness, you may assume that it is ready-made or, at best, minimum-quality custom work. Triple fullness is ideal, if you wish to invest in long-term beauty and are willing to pay for custom draperies. If, however, you are buying ready-mades and the draperies in question seem skimpy (pleats more than 4 inches apart, for example), pull out your retractable pocket tape measure and check the bottom hem to be sure that the width of the panel *is* at least twice the width of the area to be covered.

Thread is important and should be mercerized cotton, not nylon, which can become brittle, dissolve, or unravel.

The hardware should be sturdy and strong enough to hold the weight of the fabric to hang from it. It should be securely attached to the wall, and if it can be "jiggled," complain immediately to the installer. There is a correct weight of rods for corresponding weights of draperies. Get a written guarantee on the installation and hardware. One year for labor and five years for hardware is a reasonable expectation.

Measuring

The following formula is a guide used by some custom drapers when measuring for plain, unpatterned fabric. It may be of assistance when you decide to make your own, when checking a draper's figures (particularly when very expensive fabric is being used), or when you are checking for custom quality features.

Begin by measuring the width of the area to be draped to determine how many widths of fabric will be needed. Add the following measurements:

Hems—Each side requires a 1½-inch hem (allow 3 inches of fabric).

Overlaps—All pairs of drapes should overlap when pulled shut, 2 inches per side (allow 4 inches of fabric).

Returns—Calculate the distance the rod stands away from the wall plus ½ inch. Multiply by two.

Multiply the width of the area to be draped by the fullness desired (two, two and a half, or three).

Add the hems, overlaps, and returns.

Divide that number by the width of the fabric. This will be the number of widths needed. Always round off fractions to the next highest whole number.

Now, measure the height of the area to be draped. Allow for headers and hems.

Hems—The bottom (double) should be 4 inches deep (allow 8 inches of fabric).
Header—Top (double)

Drape length	Header depth (inches)	Amount of fabric (inches)
Short (to window bottom)	4	8
Long (to floor)	5	10
Extra long (extra-high ceilings)	6	12

Add the height, hem, and header (amount of fabric) figures.
Multiply this number by the number of widths.
Divide by 36 inches (1 yard) to get the number of yards needed. You should figure on a little extra yardage here also.

Fabrics and Fibers

Fabrics used for draperies and curtains should, if possible, be resistant to fading and deterioration from sunlight, to heat (sun on glass builds up heat), to mildew (moisture on the inside of windows can create a perfect situation for the development of mildew), to atmospheric fading (from smog, cigarettes), to airborne soil (dirt from smog and dust), and to fire. They also need another important characteristic—dimensional stability.

Glass fiber curtains come close to being "perfect" if you are not allergic to the shedding fibers and can find the colors you want. Fabrics made from Beta yarns are the best.

Cottons are dimensionally strong dry or wet and have an excellent color and print range. They must be treated to resist the sun, mildew, and flames. Cottons should be washed or cleaned often as they soil easily. They must be ironed if not blended or treated for wash-and-wear qualities.

Before washing check for Sanforized labels to avoid problems with shrinking. Be certain that the header material is also washable. Whenever there is any doubt, dry clean.

Linens are stronger than cotton and stay clean longer. They are available in a good selection of colors (remember they must be vat dyed) and prints. Although unbleached linen is resistant to sunlight, all others should be protected from or treated to prevent sun deterioration, as well as mildew and flames. Draperies of linen should be dry cleaned unless the fabric has been treated for wash-and-wear qualities and the mass is not too large. Linens are dimensionally stable dry and wet.

Wools have limited use as draperies because of their high cost. While wool is naturally resistant to sun, soil, and fire, it must be treated for insects. Wools should be dry cleaned unless treated with wash-and-wear finishes. They are dimensionally stable when dry.

Rayons are the most widely used fabrics for draperies and are available in a variety of textures, finishes, and colors. They are dimensionally stable in most weaves when dry. When blended with cotton or linen, rayon lends its natural resistance to sunlight and mildew to the resultant fabric. Conversely, when blended with acetate, the fabric is weak and highly flammable. Rayon must be treated to resist flames, and if not treated for wash and wear it must be dry cleaned.

Nylons are strong, resist soil and mildew, are colorfast, and have excellent dimensional stability. Nylon fabrics must be treated for protection against sunlight deterioration. Nylon does not ignite easily but does burn and melt when ignited. It can be washed or dry cleaned.

Acrylics are resistant to sunlight, mildew, insects, and chemicals and have good dimensional stability. They can be washed or dry cleaned and are available in a wide variety of colors and textures. They must be treated to be resistant to fire. Having a low resistance to abrasion, acrylics serve well as draperies (low wear situation).

Modacrylics are resistant to sunlight, mildew, chemicals, and insects and have good dimensional stability *if* stabilized. Being inherently flameproof, modacrylic fabrics or blends are excellent for draperies. Verel is a highly respected fabric for draperies and is stronger than most modacrylics.

Acetates are resistant to mildew and insects. If not solution dyed they must be treated to resist sunlight and destruction by air pollutants. They must be treated for wash and wear to be washed at all; it is best to dry clean them. They are weak wet and dry. They can be used effectively where a quick splash of color is needed at a low price. They ignite easily but lose some durability when treated to resist fire.

The fibers described are those most often used in draperies. Check chapter 1 for more complete information on all fibers, especially if you are considering a blend.

Weaves and Construction

The weave or construction of the fabric should be dimensionally stable (check fabric construction) and can be checked by pulling the fabric in different directions.

Colors, dyed and printed, should be checked for crocking or uneven spots. Prints should be colorfast if possible.

Finishes

Finishes for drapery fabrics are available to combat sun, soil, washing, and fire. These all deteriorate and are removed a little at a time by cleaning or washing. We would like to see all fabrics flameproof, but that is impractical at the moment from the standpoint of cost and loss of durability in some fabrics. Do select fire-retardant fabrics for children's rooms (or treat them yourself) and for smokers' bedrooms. Fabrics in vertical positions (draperies and curtains) burn much faster than fabrics lying horizontally. See Resources in chapter 12 for the name of a very complete booklet put out by the California Fire Marshal's office for lists of fire-retardant, both inherent and treated, fabrics, materials, and chemicals.

Linings

Linings can double the life of draperies and improve their appearance and hang. The lining can either be sewn to the drapery or made up separately and installed on a rod closer to the window. Milium is a particularly good lining material; it provides insulation against heat or cold and shuts out a high percentage of light. Any lining material should be resistant to sunlight. A lining does not have to look like a lining as long as it protects. A set of modacrylic sheer curtains could be used next to the window to protect a more sunlight-sensitive drapery behind them.

Care

Read all care and material labels carefully. If there is no label, quiz your fabric supplier (or drapery salesman, if he is supplying the fabric) and get his recommendations in writing. Draperies are far too expensive to cut corners with their care. Find out the fiber content and check chapter 1 on fibers and fabrics. All draperies and opaque curtains should be cleaned at least once a year; sheer curtains will probably need more frequent cleaning or washing.

Shopping Hints

1. Take all window measurements with you, preferably on a drawing of the wall. What kind of windows and of what materials—metal, wood? Know the material your walls are made of. It may make a difference in the installation.

2. Take your yardage calculations (include how you got the estimate).

3. If you are doing it yourself, ask about rods. Take a sample of the fabric so the rod salesman will have an idea of how heavy your draperies will be.

4. If you are having draperies custom made, get a definite installation date in writing and guarantees on hardware and labor.

5. Check fabric labels for content, care, and finishes.

Other Window Treatments

Shutters

Shutters provide solid coverage but allow for partial light and ventilation if the louvers are movable. Although they are very durable, their initial cost is high.

Woven Woods and Bamboo Shades

These treatments are designed to roll up like a shade or run on a track like draperies. Some woven woods have brightly colored strips of yarns running through them while others are simply stained wood slats. Similar to the woven woods are the plastic shades, trimmed with olefins and washable (by hand), excellent in high-moisture areas in town or country house. Bamboo and/or wooden shades should be carefully inspected if they are not purchased from a dealer who will give you a guarantee against insects, for if they are not treated properly, you will eventually see little piles of sawdust, and soon after, the shades will disintegrate. Bargains are suspect in this area.

Fabric Window Shades

Fabric shades provide the least expensive way of covering your windows, if they are standard sizes; custom shades can be as expensive as draperies. You can select shades that pull from the top down or on a track from the bottom to the top of the window, depending upon your decorating and privacy needs.

Blinds

Blinds include horizontal venetian blinds made of wood, metal, or plastic. They offer excellent air and light control. On the negative side they collect dirt and are difficult to clean. Vertical blinds of wood, metal, plastic, or fabric also provide good light and air control and do not soil as easily because of their vertical position. Both types are moderate in price.

Shoji Panels and Grilles

Shoji panels are Japanese-inspired screens which consist of simple frames or intricate grillework. The frames are filled with fabric or grass cloth and the grilles can be either open or cloth backed. Very effective, they are generally custom made and expensive.

Resources

Faulkner, Ray and Sarah. *Inside Today's Home*, 3rd ed. New York: Holt, Rinehart and Winston, 1968.

"Consumers Guide to Draperies." Apartment Specialists, Inc., 5221 W. Jefferson Blvd., Los Angeles, Calif. 90016.

Windows Beautiful. Kirsch Co., Sturgis, Mich. Put out by manufacturers of drapery hardware, this excellent booklet is regularly updated and readily available in home-furnishings yardage shops and in drapery/curtain shops or departments.

7

Beds and Bedding

THE bed has been held in high esteem throughout history and reached its pinnacle during the Middle Ages, when the "Great Bed of Ware" measured 12 feet square and stood 7½ feet high. In seventeenth-century France the royal bed was held in such veneration that subjects genuflected before it even when King Louis XIV was not "in residence."

While genuflection is no longer the order of the day, it is an accepted fact in the home-furnishings industry that if one has a limited bank account with which to begin acquiring household items, one should at least provide for a good refrigerator and a good bed.

That good bed will justify its cost, which can be prorated over a ten- to fifteen-year life expectancy. On an hourly basis, there is nothing the consumer can buy for his home that will give as much dollar-for-dollar service and satisfaction, for, as *Consumer's Digest* points out, one can calculate that in fifteen years the average person will spend approximately forty-four thousand hours in bed.

Don't be taken in by the widespread myth that the quality of beds is always directly related to price and that the more one pays, the better the product. We're not disputing the premise that the top of the line of a reputable manufacturer, large or small, is good. What we do question is this: How much better than "best" can the inner materials and construction be? Even quality inner construction, the hidden value of a mattress, involves just so many things: the coils, the padding, the insulator. The extra expenses are in subtle things like more expensive (but not necessarily sturdier) coverings or in latex-coated coils, an absolutely questionable "luxury." The real clue to quality is how the mattress feels when you lie on it, plus the length and depth of the manufacturer's guarantee. Does he promise that a mattress with latex-coated coils will actually last much longer? Read the label carefully for intent as well as content; not every floral-covered mattress promises a bed of roses.

Homework

Points for your bed and bedding checklist should include:
Who is going to use it?
What is his/her height, weight?
Are there special age and health considerations: for the old, the ill, the young?
Are there any allergies to be considered?
What are the sleeping/living habits and preferences?
Will the unit be subjected to special nonsleep use and abuse: jumping children, lounging teen-agers?
Must both day seating and night sleeping be provided?
Is a water bed one of the possible options under consideration?
What about bedding?
Do you need to consider new sheets, pillows, pillowcases, blankets, and spreads in your bed and bedding budget?
How readily available in various sizes and at what cost?
Which size bed will best fit your purposes?
How much space do you have?
What problems will be involved in installation?
Will queen or king sizes have to be brought in over an outside balcony or will they turn the corner, clear the stairs, go through the door, fit in the elevator?
What additional problems of moving or room space will the headboard present?

Mattresses

Common Mattress Sizes

The following list gives sizes that are recognized as standard in many places and by many manufacturers. But remember, measure if in the slightest doubt. Better still, measure even if not in doubt.

These sizes are approximate because mattresses can deviate from labeled size by as much as an inch because of rounded corners and similar construction variables. There are also size differences in pieces designed for eastern or western United States consumption. If you move from coast to coast, you might find yourself unable to buy the proper size linens when you have transported your old bed to its new location. For example, the Eastern King is approximately the width of a pair of Twins (2 × 39 = 78), but it is 5 inches longer and *totally* different from either the Regular King or the California King. The Eastern King is often labeled "King" only; it is important to measure carefully to be sure you're buying the size you want.

Name	*Width* (inches)	*Length** (inches)
Single or Youth Bed	30–34	75
Twin Regular	39	75
Twin King or Extra-Long	39	80–84
Full Regular	54	75
Full King or Extra-Long	54	80–84
Queen Regular	60	75
Queen King or Extra-Long	60	80–84
King Regular	76	75
King King or Extra-Long	76	80–84
Eastern King	78	80
California King	72	84

*If circumstances permit, a mattress should be 6 inches longer than the sleeper's standing height to allow for stretching. Measure carefully to determine exact space requirements, taking into account both length and width additions necessary for headboard, bedposts, and similar attachments.

Before Shopping

Having thought something about mattress size, adaptation to space, and budget requirements, you should consider carefully the several types of sleep surfaces from which you will be making a final selection. Eliminating, for the time being, the special considerations of sleep sofas and water beds, the basic choices of mattress construction will be innerspring, stuffed, or foam. Here are some of the general things you should know about these various types before making a final selection.

Innerspring Mattresses

Most widely used, the innerspring mattress consists of:

1. Covering.
2. Layer of padding: cotton, polyester, polyurethane foam, or a recently developed plastic from Du Pont called Pneumacel.
3. Insulator: a layer of strong, durable material, usually sisal. Keeps the springs from popping through, helps control the "coil feel," and keeps the top layer of padding from getting into the springs, if these are the open-coil type. Two materials not satisfactory for this layer are clear plastic, which breaks and tears, and a flexalator, a wire construction outlawed in at least one state (California) because it does not provide the proper insulation between padding and coils.
4. Coils. Counting coils will not help your sleep, for the number is not as important as the quality of construction. Check the cross section shown at the place of sale, making certain that it represents the model currently being sold. There are several different types of coil units on the market, but the two most commonly used are the Marshall and the Bonnell. Both types are good; your choice should be based on which one feels best when you lie on it, not which one has developed the most persuasive advertising.
   A. Open coil (Bonnell type). It is important to check for high-quality, flexible steel springs with good recovery, a secure system of attaching the springs to each other (either with clips or steel strips), and whether the coils are so placed that they will not eventually rub together and create a noise problem. If properly placed, they do not need to be latex coated but should have a good baked-enamel finish to prevent rusting. They should have a firm piece of steel border wire establishing the edge of the unit. This unit is designed on the premise that the body should sleep *on* the mattress, not in it.
   B. Pocketed coil unit (Marshall type). This unit may be pocketed in muslin or in a cloth made from olefin, which provides strength but is highly flammable. While theoretically each spring works independently of the other, the fact that they are attached to each other tends to restrict independent movement. These units do not always have or need a steel border frame. The premise of this unit is that it conforms to the body contours. The Marshall is generally the more expensive of the two types of mattress.

Stuffed Mattresses

The best stuffed mattresses seem to be about 5½ inches high, containing either high-grade cotton or polyester. This material generally is wrapped with a layer of polyester foam about ⅝ inch thick. Called a "topper" in the

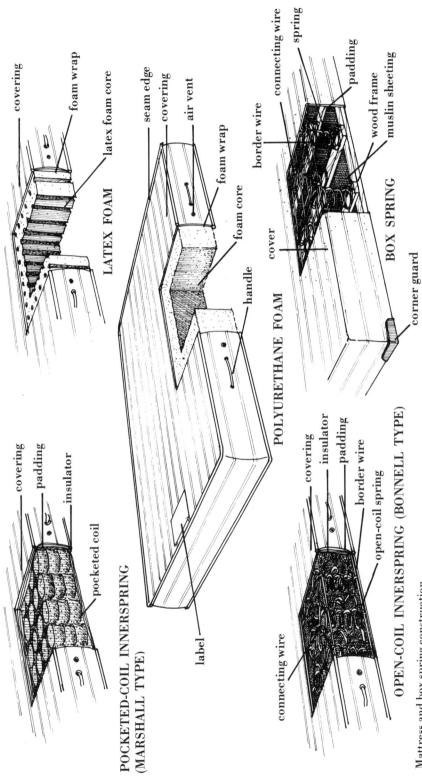

POCKETED-COIL INNERSPRING (MARSHALL TYPE)

covering
padding
insulator
pocketed coil

LATEX FOAM

covering
foam wrap
latex foam core

seam edge
covering
air vent
foam wrap
foam core
handle
label

POLYURETHANE FOAM

connecting wire
spring
padding
wood frame
muslin sheeting
border wire
connecting wire
cover
corner guard

BOX SPRING

OPEN-COIL INNERSPRING (BONNELL TYPE)

covering
insulator
padding
border wire
open-coil spring
connecting wire

Mattress and box spring construction

trade, this foam layer lies under the cover or tick and acts as a fire deterrent when used over untreated stuffing materials, thus enabling the mattress to meet fire standards. In low commercial grades, treated cotton felt is often the top layer, and in the very cheapest mattresses, loose cotton and kapok may be used; all of these have little durability, lose their resiliency more quickly, and produce lumps after a while.

Foam Mattresses

Foam today is almost exclusively polyurethane when used in the manufacture of mattresses or upholstered items in the United States, as most rubber foam does not pass the flammability tests now required. Testing and experimentation to develop an acceptable rubber foam is continuing, and at this writing there is at least one, under the name "Neoprene," giving the reassurance that proper pressures brought to bear do bring results in the form of new and acceptable products.

Latex foam has gone through the same transformation from poor to acceptable quality as have so many other synthetic products. Should the one factory producing quality latex for mattresses be back in production by the time you read this book, you may identify it by the many small, uniformly spaced holes that allow body odors and heat to escape.

During this transitional/developmental period read chapter 12 on flammability problems before purchasing a latex mattress—and make sure to check the label to see whether or not the product was manufactured after the effective date (December 1973) for stricter federal laws. (Keep in mind the problems of latex foam, too, in do-it-yourself projects: pads for platform beds or cushions and mattresses for your camper or trailer.)

Because of the still-to-be-solved problems of fire-resistance standards for some foam products, polyurethane is currently the most widely used foam mattress material. It is generally molded with a solid core and graded at the factory for density by a machine which determines how much weight is necessary to depress a given size disk 1 inch into the foam and have it return to its original shape within a given period of time. The resulting grades are rated accordingly:

pounds	
10–20	Soft
20–30	Medium
30–40	Firm or hard

An unfortunate aspect of this grading system is that it is generally recorded on the foam itself at the time of testing and is covered when the ticking is applied. It is sometimes, but not always, noted on the box in which the foam is shipped to the mattress manufacturer. The consumer has a right to ask for and receive the foam manufacturer's rating expressed in weight, and not by the less definitive terms used by the mattress maker: soft, medium, or hard.

Since urethane tends to recover more slowly than rubber foam, it is wisest to err on the firm side in the selection of a synthetic "weight." It is also important to note that not all foam mattresses have solid-core construction. Buying a shredded-core product is a serious waste of money. To avoid a mattress that will not hold its shape, keep reading those labels.

It is especially important to determine how a foam mattress is finished. One feature provided by some manufacturers to offer greater support is a layer of foam wrapped around the outside rim of the mattress to reduce spreading and sagging of the solid-core form. This, if used, should be held firmly in place by an edging with covered tape, which should also be used to secure the ticking. Avoid foam pads loosely covered or wrapped instead of having tops and borders with defined, piped edges, for improperly secured ticking on foam bases will creep and crawl and twist, eventually producing an unfortunate warp to the mattress form. Like innerspring and stuffed mattresses, foam units have a selection of covers from which to choose and each unit should have built-in air vents in its borders; but even with these vents, foams tend to hold moisture and odors if used in extremely humid settings. This and the fact that they provide less body support may be offset by nonallergenic properties and resistance to insects and mildew.

Children's Mattresses

Mattresses for babies and small children are made in a manner similar to those for adult units. The safest choices are either an innerspring or a nonflammable foam or a treated-cotton-filled product with a cover of nonflammable material such as that used in hospital beds. Bumper pads, when used, should be of flame-retardant cotton. It can be difficult to find the products that meet these requirements, but it may be a matter of life or death for your child.

At the moment, the most commonly used plastic cover is polyvinyl chloride (PVC). This, as mentioned in chapter 1, is safe in case of a small fire, but combined with polyurethane foam in the mattress and the vertical bumper pads (in this position the foam is considerably more flammable), it can become highly explosive if the whole mattress catches fire. Add to this the high flammability of some of the cuddly soft (acrylic) blankets used for children's beds, and the possibilities are terrifying. See chapter 12 for further details; but remember that all materials used on and in children's mattresses should have fire-retardant labels or be made of inherently fire-retardant materials.

Emphasis has been placed upon the importance of good beds for good sleep, but with children the support of a quality mattress is also important to growing bodies. There is a widespread habit of relegating children to hand-me-down cribs and beds from other families or from older members within their own family. Check your child's bed periodically for wear signs (lumps, bumps, and sags).

Shopping Suggestions for Mattresses

Having done your homework on space and money budgets, personal life-style needs, and mattress construction options, you now are ready to choose the precise mattress for your use. The only way to test a mattress is to lie down on it, and you will be less embarrassed if you concentrate on the long-term investment you're making while you bounce a little, turn, and twist to check out how your possible choice responds. Here are some of the things you'll want to check for:

FIRMNESS

Ideally, the more weight that is placed upon the mattress, the firmer the surface should become. Otherwise, the heavier parts of one's body may depress the mattress unduly, leaving the lighter parts (such as the feet) "floating" higher. All mattresses are graded according to various degrees of firmness. This is an arbitrary decision by each manufacturer with no industry coordination. The terms are the same, but the guidelines are not, so that it is unwise to compare grades between manufacturers or between types of mattresses (coil vs. foam). Generally used terms are *soft, medium, firm, extra firm, orthopedic,* and *orthopedic-type* (usually labeled with some trade name that incorporates "ortho" as a prefix or "pedic" as a suffix to give the impression of special healthful properties). In some states, such as California, anything labeled "orthopedic" must be designed by a "member of the healing arts," still a somewhat vague requirement. No such guidelines, loose or not, exist for "orthopedic-type" units, which can become merely a gimmick label for superfirm, sometimes almost rock-hard, mattresses. Actually, any good-quality firm mattress which keeps the spine straight meets the standards reported by J. D. Ratcliff (see Resources) from a consensus of leading orthopedic surgeons throughout the United States.

COIL FEEL

To put it succinctly, there shouldn't be any.

SILENCE

In contrast, there should be lots of this. Bounce a little. Any squeaks? If you don't mind the stares of salesmen and other customers (are you meditating on that long-term investment?), both you and your sleep companion, if you expect to have one, should lie on the mattress at the same time and move about, listening for those telltale sounds of improper inner construction if innersprings and/or box springs are involved.

LENGTH

If possible, as we stated before, select a mattress 6 inches longer than your standing height. Stretch out and see how important length is to you. Think about how close your toes come to the end of the bed and whether they'll be cramped when the sheets and blankets are tucked in.

WIDTH

This is strictly a personal preference, according to your size and normal tossing and turning, and whether you're a cuddler or a stay-on-your-own-side-of-the-bed type.

O.K. Time to get up. Now sit on the edge of the mattress and do some more checking:

EDGE SEAMS

These should be well covered and secure.

GIVE

The border should not give too much or feel too stiff when you sit on the edge of the mattress—no hard wire feel.

AIR VENTS

Vents should be on both sides for best circulation and should be securely attached.

HANDLES

These are needed for frequent turning, required to extend the life of the unit. (Despite what some "experts" say, foam mattresses need turning, too.) Handles should be securely attached to a metal plate inside the mattress cover. This is an area in which otherwise good mattresses are often found wanting.

COVERING (TICKING)

Do not be dazzled by the wide and varied selection of material available for coverings, which quite often increase the cost without necessarily improving the wearing quality. If you get psychic value from knowing that you're sleeping on a bed of roses, fine; but remember that others will not know how well your ticking matches your wallpaper unless they happen to be around when you're changing your mattress pad. Good wear comes from other factors: your cover should be of at least 5-ounce, preferably 8-ounce, fabric, tightly woven to keep out dust and to prevent stretching. There should be no buttons except on stuffed mattresses and certainly no tufting, which makes for uncomfortable lumps and is not an especially efficient way of securing the cover anyway. Covering on borders (sides) of the mattress should be evenly and securely stitched. Rayon or cotton provides the sturdiest covering material; acetate is both weak and flammable, and olefin, while durable, is not fire retardant unless treated. Some red and blue dyes are not only more flammable but tend to bleed when wet and/or crock. (See chapter 1.)

LABELS AND WARRANTIES

Last but far from least, check the product for material content and safety standards. Is it stuffed or padded with new or used material? (With luck your state will require such labeling of contents.) Was it manufactured before December 1973, when the current federal flammability law went into effect? If so, what standards were imposed by the state in which it was made or distributed? Don't be lulled into a false sense of security by presently effective rulings, since the federal laws supersede and control previous state standards, some of which (California's, for example) were stricter than the smolder test now effective. While this federal restriction gives some protection against the major cause of mattress fires, cigarettes, it does not assure your safety if your sleep unit is subjected to the open flame of matches or fires started on other articles in the room or even on the bed. (See chapter 12 if you haven't already memorized it.) Check carefully also to find whether the warranty covers the cost of returning the mattress to the factory. If not, will your store help return it or will you be stuck with a big delivery charge? All warranties are prorated over the expected life of the mattress, so that unless a major fault develops immediately, you will never recover the full cost of the unit.

Budget Shopping Alternatives

If, after checking out several reputable lines of mattress/spring combinations, you discover that your budget will not stretch to include a really top-quality new mattress, consider the possibility of acquiring a used hotel unit (not to be confused with "hotel type" beds featured in questionable advertising). Sometimes large hotels or hotel chains will replace a large number of existing sleep sets at one time and, after sanitizing the old sets to meet state laws, advertise them for sale; check for the identifying American Hotel and Motel Association label to establish that the organization's high standards of construction have been met. As with many other interior furnishings, these commercial lines have incorporated a number of safety and long-wear features not readily available to purchasers of units for residential use at a comparable price.

We challenge the industry to pass on these special quality features to the buying public at a fair price, at the same time that we challenge the consumer to look beyond fancy covers to more important signs of quality. Until the average buyer demands at home the same sleep comfort he expects in a Las Vegas hotel, or the same high standards of safety and convenience found in a hospital room, the manufacturer will continue to produce what his market demands at a price that will bring him profit and volume.

Box Springs

Box springs are technically a mattress foundation with coiled-spring construction resting in a wood or metal frame, upholstered on top with felt or similar material, and covered with ticking on top and sides and with muslin sheeting on the bottom.

This is no place to "save" by getting by with a unit that does not go with your new mattress. Box springs should be purchased at the same time; putting a quality mattress over an old bed spring is self-defeating, since combinations are manufactured with the same life expectancy and are meant to coordinate with each other in providing sleep support. Most manufacturers, in fact, will not guarantee one without the other. These coordinated sets are not to be confused with "matched sets," in which both mattress and box springs must have the same number of coils. Testing is now in progress to determine whether or not this is a necessary standard or merely an expensive extra.

As a standard, box springs are approximately 7 inches high, but foam mattresses may need slightly thicker units to bring them up to a comfortable height from the floor, since foam construction is usually not as thick as innerspring or stuffed models. Some box-spring units have wooden legs screwed into each corner, a practice that can crack and split the frame. A much better means of supporting the unit is provided by a metal frame on casters if your bed frame is not itself built to hold the two units.

The box-spring frame should be made of kiln-dried hardwood, since green wood warps. There should be wood slats supporting *each* row of coils in the box, with a rigid center brace to provide greater strength, or a metal framework that provides the same support. There are units with torsion-bar suspension which use wires bent into square instead of cylindrical spirals. If a demonstrator model is not available, ask questions about this construction; shape is not as important as where the support is placed. In some units, the so-called box springs are not really springs at all but use a slab of polyurethane foam as the core. In testing, *Consumer's Digest* found these to be equal to the traditional box springs when comparing the best with the best.

In box springs the padding on the top should eliminate any feel of the springs inside, and the ticking, which usually matches the mattress, should be of at least 5-ounce, and preferably 8-ounce, grade.

Bed Springs

Bed springs are a layer of springs held in a metal frame to serve as a foundation for a mattress. Obviously not as effective as a box-spring unit, they sometimes, as with bunk beds, provide the only alternative and can function satisfactorily where weight stress is not great, as in small children's beds.

Bed springs should be of high-grade tempered steel (we cannot emphasize this too much) and firm to the feel. If the unit is properly designed, there is no reason for squeaking. Before you purchase this type of spring, be sure to ask how much weight can be supported, and for how long, before sagging begins. Try to get a written guarantee from the store.

Water Beds

Much of the information provided for the consumer by the water-bed companies is primarily concerned with sleep and not with water-bed construction. Many interesting and revealing studies are being conducted on sleep, but so far the scientific reasons for sleeping on a water bed are far outnumbered by the exotic ones. The water bed must stand the test of time, and it should have the opportunity to do so. Like many new concepts, and particularly such an innovative one, water beds have sometimes been presented to the public in a fly-by-night manner, which not only is unfortunate but could prove dangerous.

This makes it necessary for standards to be set for this infant industry—from within (we hope) and from without (definitely). The reputable manufacturer is as much hampered by the not-so-reputable ones as the public is hoodwinked by them. The Department of Consumer Affairs Bureau of Home

Furnishings of the State of California has conducted elaborate testing and has arrived at a set of standards for water beds made in or sold in that state. These are reasonable and good criteria for anyone buying a water bed anywhere. Check the labels; if there are none, find out why. As water beds become more plentiful, states with bedding laws will probably follow California's lead.

Basically, a water bed should have a sturdy frame and a mattress that can safely contain 200 gallons of water and resist simple punctures, be resistant to mildew (this can be helped by using one gallon of ordinary chlorine-type household bleach to one bag of water), and have a separate heating unit (not generally sold as part of the package but considered a necessity, nonetheless). The cord and plug should be of a heavy-duty type with a UL (Underwriters' Laboratory) label on the frame as well. This standard was validated when a faulty unapproved plug on a water bed shorted out, burning the entire room—except the water bed, which was left standing intact.

In defense of the water bed in the "great weight controversy" which rages between water-bed owners and managers of multistory apartment buildings, we would like to state a few facts. An average water bed weighs anywhere from 1,600 to 1,800 pounds, including a simple wooden frame, with this weight spread over the entire bed size (approximately 35 square feet in a queen-size unit). Compare this with the weight of a 6-foot grand piano (approximately 680 pounds) pressing down on the tips of six slender legs, and one can soon see that the argument against water beds doesn't hold water, if you will forgive the pun for the point.

Irving London, M.D., who is given credit for designing the original water beds, filed for and received Federal Housing Authority approval for use of his product in structures covered by the administration's loans, the only stipulation being that the bed stand against one wall, thus giving the support of the strongest wall and floor construction. Since FHA approval is not given without extensive testing, one can be assured that this ruling meets strict standards of safety and prudence.

Other concerns of prospective water-bed owners, cost and use of electricity, have also been studied by California's Consumer Bureau. The bed used in the test was queen size (approximately 60 by 84 inches), filled with water to a height of 10 inches and with the water temperature maintained at 91.5 degrees Fahrenheit and the room temperature at 72. The only bedding used was a quilted polyester bedspread approximately ⅓ inch thick. The cost of operating the 400-watt heater for one month was $1.35 at the then current Sacramento rate of $0.0112 per kilowatt-hour. This means that approximately 120 KWHs were expended to maintain the prescribed water-bed temperature. Look at your most recent power bill or call your local electric company to check your current KWH rate, which may vary considerably from one part of the country to another, particularly with rising energy costs. Multiply your present rate by 120 and you will have a fairly accurate estimate of what it will cost you to operate a similar-sized heater for the water in a queen-sized bed under "normal" conditions for approximately one month. In New York City, where rates have been among the highest in the nation, the pleasures of a heated water bed a year after the Sacramento test would have added better than $10 to your monthly tab.

Since no federal regulations now exist on heaters for water beds, you may find it helpful to send to Howard Winslow, Chief of the Bureau of Home Furnishings, 3401 La Grande Blvd., Sacramento, Calif. 95823, for a copy of the water-bed regulations put in effect in California in 1974 as a result of these tests. Ask also for a copy of the tests to study so that you can operate your water bed with maximum safety and efficiency.

Tests and laws such as these are necessary because a few unscrupulous persons have sought to sell inferior materials. Testing and labeling could provide another protection for the consumer: proof of certified testing could be shown to a potential landlord to calm his nightmares about 200 gallons of water running down the hall and/or 1,600 pounds of water bed crashing through his ceiling.

Sleep Sofas, Studio Couches, and Other Confusions

Spelled out at considerable length, and with supposedly clarifying illustrations, in the text of the mattress standard established by the federal government are the terms relating to various sleep furniture and accessories. The glossary contained in the text, which is available from the Department of Commerce, couldn't be more contradictory if written for that precise purpose, and the accompanying pictorial examples do nothing to clear the confusion. Let us therefore merely mention some of these terms and some of the sleep units to which they may be applied by different manufacturers in different parts of the country. If, for any reason, you find it necessary to communicate with the Commerce Department about your sleep furniture, may Mercury and all the other gods of trade and communication be with you.

Bunk Beds

These are a tier of beds, usually two, sometimes three, one over the other in a high frame complete with mattresses, which are generally of the stuffed variety, smaller than a twin, and resting on a single layer of springs. Be sure the mattresses are of high quality when they are to be used daily, especially since this type of bed is most frequently used by growing children.

Convertible Sofas

This is an upholstered sofa which converts into an adult-size bed with the mattress unfolding out and up from under the seat cushioning (which is removed first and set aside). This is the most commonly used type for both day (sofa) and night (bed) use. The mattresses are usually high-grade solid foam or an innerspring unit especially made for this type of sofa, being thinner than a regular innerspring and capable of being folded. The seat pillows can fit at the back of the sofa unit to fill the gap left when the unit is converted, and the mattress rests on a layer of metal bed springs rather than on coiled innersprings. This frame should have not only the obvious front legs but also back legs for proper support, and they must be made of high-grade steel. The design may vary, but you can feel for good support by having the mattress pulled out (better still, pull it out yourself) so that you can lie and sit upon it to check for firmness and steadiness. Also check to see how well the mechanism which converts the unit operates: does it move smoothly, noiselessly, without undue exertion on your part?

Sofa Beds, Drop-Arm Love Seats, and Similar Units

Many names cover the variations on the units which have backs and arms and convert in such a way that you sleep on the upholstered unit rather than on a mattress and with your body parallel to the wall (instead of head to wall as in the convertible sofa). Some of the terms you will hear applied to variations on the sofa bed, sometimes upholstered as a unit, sometimes with the back and seat upholstered separately, are *sofa lounge, sleep lounge, pressback lounge, push-back sofa,* and *jackknife sofa.* In some models the back is pressed down to the level of the seat to form the sleeping surface; in others the back remains upright and the seating surface alone is extended into a sleep-width unit.

Another similar unit, in which the sleeper rests on the upholstered seat surface, is the drop-arm love seat. When the side arms are in a vertical position, this piece is, as suggested, a love seat, but the adjustable arms can be lowered to one of four positions from chaise lounge to single sleeper. The vertical back support always remains upright and stationary. This has limited use as a sleep unit but is good for occasional guests, especially where space does not allow full-length day seating.

Since each of these upholstered sofa beds has a different name and a different means of conversion to nighttime use, consult with your dealer about the various types available in your locality. And test. Having checked to see that the converted unit will fit not only your needs but your room space as well, lie down to see if it meets your other standards.

High-Risers, Studio Couches, Divans

Here again, confusion of terms reigns supreme, but basically we are talking about parallel-to-wall sleeping on a portable sleep cushion or mattress (occasionally on a back cushion or cushions laid flat), sometimes upholstered, sometimes slipcovered. Some of these become single sleeping units by removing bolsters or loose cushions to widen the sleep surface, while others convert to twin or double beds by lifting the loose top sofa/sleep cushion onto a high-riser or glide-out unit. The term *high-riser* is sometimes applied to the sofa rather than the converting unit, but basically this is a frame of sofa seating height with two equal-size mattresses without a backrest. The frame slides out and pops up to provide a single layer of springs to support the top cushion when it is moved onto it.

In contrast, the glide-out or roll-out unit does not pop up and the twin sleep surfaces are much lower than that of the appropriately named high-riser.

Terms you're apt to encounter include *studio couch, studio divan, twin studio divan,* and possibly even *day bed,* although the latter may differ from the others in having coil rather than flat springs and usually arms or an equal-height headboard and footboard (possibly decorative) but no back. In hotels and motels or in residential locations where convertible units are needed and space is at a premium, corner groups similar to studio couches are sometimes used. Two twin-size bedding sets on frames, usually slip-covered and with slipcovered bolsters, are placed at right angles abutting a corner table.

Never mind what these units are called. Consider whether they do what you want them to do in your room and provide the kind of sleep comfort the situation demands.

The trundle bed doesn't really quite fit into either of the two preceding categories. It is really a bed with a stuffed mattress and single-layer (flat) springs, tucked under another bed. Sometimes it incorporates a high-riser unit, but the bottom unit may be simply a slightly shorter- and lower-than-standard frame on wheels, ready to roll out all made up with pillow, sheets, and blankets for instant sleep accommodations. These are popularly used in small children's rooms and/or small rooms for children.

Questions about Convertible Units

All along we've been saying, "Check for comfort, check for quality," just as you would with any sleep surface. But just once let's go over some of the questions you'll need to think about carefully only in the very special area of sleep units used both day and night.

1. Do you need everyday sleeping and seating or occasional?
2. How much room will your unit need when it is fully opened/converted? Are you allowing for walking and bed-making space, for moving coffee tables or other furniture aside? How heavy are those "movable" pieces of furniture? Measure exactly.
3. Does the fabric have to take a lot of wear and how much care are you prepared to put forth when you fit it into your life-style?

Bedding

Having made your bed, you'll have to lie in it, so we leave the matter of bedding, such as sheets, pillowcases, and blankets, to your own personal choice. However, there are some aspects that need special consideration.

Mattress Pads

Since it is impossible to clean heavy soil and built-up body odors from mattresses, a mattress pad is an absolute necessity. The best pads are quilted, made of cotton or polyester fabric, and filled with polyester fiber, with fitted sides like a fitted sheet. The cotton-filled versions shrink and break down more easily, resulting in poor fit and lumpy surfaces. Check for labels: mattress pads are controlled by the same flammability standards as mattresses.

Electric Blankets

Electric blankets must be treated as an appliance rather than merely as another piece of bedding. This product is simply an electric "sandwich," with the wires being the filling between layers of traditional blanketing material. We agree with the Consumers' Association of Canada, which suggests that the unit should be constructed with a very firm surface (fluffy surfaces are more flammable) of durable, washable, flame-resistant fabric, with interior padding to conceal the bumps of the thermostats and wires. Since all electric blankets sold in the United States must have Underwriters' Laboratory approval, the internal wiring will have waterproof insulation and a series of thermostats to prevent overheating. If you do not see a UL tag on the electrical cord of the blanket, beware.

The UL also requires the following to be printed on every box in which an electric blanket is sold or on an enclosed card: "Read carefully, before using the blanket, all the instructions for handling and caring for this blanket; DO NOT use an electric blanket on an infant, helpless person, or anyone insensitive to heat; DO NOT tuck in the wired areas; keep the control away from an open window; do not use pins in the blanket; be sure to use this blanket only with the current and voltage recommended by the maker; turn off the electric current when blanket is not in use; to avoid excessive heating, avoid folding the blanket when in use."

In addition to the guidelines for use established by the underwriters group, the National Fire Protection Association urges that you not sit on the blanket or allow children to jump and play on it. The wiring is sturdy and safe but not designed to be bent or crushed.

From the U.S. Department of Agriculture comes further advice. Check all connections and make sure the plugs fit securely both at the wall and on the blanket; be sure the signal light works properly when turned on; and when the blanket stops working or the cord becomes frayed, DO NOT attempt to repair it yourself. Take it to an authorized dealer (this should be on your warranty) and be prepared possibly to wait several weeks in case it must be sent to the factory for repairs.

Above all, DO NOT dry clean an electric blanket, as this can ruin the insulation on the wiring and endanger your personal safety. Wash according to the manufacturer's instructions, usually on the gentle cycle of a washing machine, and then tumble dry at a low temperature.

Since the UL warns you about tucking in the wired area of the blanket, check to be sure that the blanket has enough unwired area to make the bed properly; 8 or 10 inches should be fine.

Pillows

Some of the most satisfactory bed pillows are those filled with down or feathers from waterfowl (geese or ducks), for these have more resiliency than the feathers of land birds such as chickens.

A good pillow can be judged by its bulk in comparison to its weight. A well-filled, standard size, 21- by 27-inch pillow of goose down (the most expensive) should weigh about 1½ pounds. The same-sized pillow filled with duck down could weigh twice that, since generally the down used is from ducklings and not from the mature birds used by the meat industry. The younger fowl produce a good down, smaller and less expensive than that of the older ducks and much more subject to packing down and therefore weighing more than that of either geese or mature ducks.

There are grades on all plumage products, so if you are comparing live plucked down with meat industry down, you can be sure the live plucked down will be worth the extra cost. But if you are comparing American down with imported down, it behooves you to check the place of origin. The finest down is exported from Poland, but beware of imports from the Orient, as their processing is often of dubious quality.

The contents should be stated on a label attached to the pillow. Some pillows have a combination of feathers and down, and with poultry-product fillings it is always wise to hand test the pillow, feeling for quills while testing for resiliency. To test for a good feather pillow, press down in the center with your hand; the more quickly the pillow springs back into place when you remove pressure, the better quality the feathers or down used and the longer the pillow will hold its shape. Comparative shopping will help you to observe differences in quality.

Foam pillows are either polyurethane or latex foam. No flammability law exists in this area of the bedding industry, so remember the high-risk potential of the latex product. Foams in pillows, like mattress material, will be graded as soft, medium, or firm. Here, too, shredded foam should be avoided; solid foam provides a product that has greater comfort and wear.

Another very popular filling for pillows is Dacron polyester. These pillows should be filled to a compact fullness and have no lumps; too little makes for a skimpy pillow and too much creates an uncomfortably hard pillow. Those allergic to feathers now have a choice among foam, treated feathers, and Dacron polyester.

Good pillows need two covers: one to contain the feathers, down, or foam and a pillow cover that can be zipped off to be washed. This does not replace the pillowcase. It is most important to keep the material inside a pillow from becoming wet and/or impregnated with body oils. Frequent airing and "fluffing up" are necessary to retain the body of a good pillow, and some people routinely augment this by tossing their bed pillows into the clothes dryer on the air cycle for a quick fluffing on the day they change bedding.

Having exhausted you with all this information, we wish you pleasant dreams—on a firm, long-lasting, flame-retardant mattress, of course.

Shopping Hints

1. Compare equivalent units from different companies for quality of construction and price.

2. Read labels. If you don't understand them or if there are none, ask questions.

3. Get guarantees in writing.

4. Establish who delivers, when, and if delivery is included in the price (get it in writing).

5. Lie down (with your partner, if you plan to share) on mattresses, sit on sofa beds, open them up and lie down. Remember: don't be shy about testing; this is one time when a good consumer should lie down on the job.

6. Take your list of measurements for beds, sofa beds, and the required bedding, as well as information about the areas where they will be placed.

Resources

Books

Hardy, Kay. *How to Make Your House a Home.* New York: Funk and
Wagnalls, 1947.

Magazines and Newspapers

Consumer Reports, May 1973.
Consumer's Digest, January-February 1971.
Reader's Digest, "I Am Joe's Spine," by J. D. Ratcliff, M.D., March 1971
(available in reprint).
San Francisco Chronicle and Examiner, "How to Choose a Mattress," June
23, 1974.

Organizations

Dayton's Consumer Service, 700 on the Mall, Minneapolis, Minn. 55402.
Memo No. 6, "Bedding."
Department of Consumer Affairs, Bureau of Home Furnishings, State of
California, 3401 La Grande Blvd., Sacramento, Calif. 95823. Howard
Winslow, Chief; Thomas Cushman, Head of Laboratory. Script of
movie *Unfurnishing Your Home*; Technical Bulletins 105, 106, 115; Lab
Report SP-71-1; copies of the Home Furnishings Act, Law Labels, the
Furniture and Bedding Inspection Act, and Water Mattress Regula-
tions; *Electric Blankets* by Margaret Dana; photographs.
Federal Trade Commission, Consumer Product Safety Commission, Wash-
ington, D.C. 20207. *Federal Register; Consumer Product Safety*, Vol.
39, No. 27, Part 3; Flammable Fabrics Act—Children's Sleepwear.
Innerspace Co., sales brochures.

National Association of Bedding Manufacturers, 1150 17th Street N.W., Washington, D.C. 20036. Lists of Bedding Law Enforcement officials; summary of General Requirements of State Bedding Laws; Bedding Law Analysis Chart; Uniform Law Labels. (Information available for a fee.)
Simmons Co., sales brochures.
U.S. Department of Commerce, Text of Mattress Standard DOC FF 4-72.
Western Furniture Manufacturers Association, 17071 Ventura Blvd., Encino, Calif. 91316. "Spring Design," August 1970.

8

Soft Goods

To most consumers, fabric-covered sofas and chairs, the so-called soft goods of the home-furnishings industry, represent a sort of upholstered iceberg, most of which is hidden from view by 16 yards of eye-catching fabric and a poor understanding of terminology and construction methods.

After you read this chapter, we suggest that you spend some time comparing the various types of construction and deciding which is the most comfortable for you. Discover for yourself the difference between an expensive sofa or chair and a less expensive similar piece. Soft goods should not be purchased impulsively; they are too expensive for what could turn out to be a big mistake.

Homework

What kind of seating do you need—sofas, chairs, love seats?
How much use will the piece receive?
Who will use it—children, adults, guests only?
Where are you going to use it?
Can you get it in the room?
How much space do you have?

Upholstered furniture should be purchased from the inside out. The finish fabric, although very important, cannot compensate for poor inner construction.

Interior

Good construction begins with the frame, which should be made of kiln-dried hardwood. Elm, gum, alder, and poplar are only a few of the woods used, since each manufacturer is governed not only by availability but also by his own personal feelings concerning one wood or another. We know one who uses magnolia whenever he can get it. About the only way you can tell if wood is kiln dried, besides taking the salesman's word for it, is that the frame will be straight and show no signs of warping and/or beads of "sap."

All joints should be glued and double doweled, and all corners should be corner blocked and screwed.

A layer of strong webbing or tightly woven cloth of jute is then attached to the frame.

The springs are held in place by being tied to each other and to the frame in eight places with heavy flax twine. Each spring is tied at right angles in two directions and diagonally, resulting in eight knots on each spring. This is how the phrase "hand tied eight ways" came to denote fine-quality construction. Some manufacturers have cut labor costs by reducing the number of ties to six. These springs should be of high-grade steel placed close enough together to eliminate sagging but not so close that they rub. Coil springs produce a resilient, comfortable seat referred to as a "spring-edge seat."

"Sagless" springs are flat, wavy lines of high-grade steel which look like grillework and are used in making automobile seats and sometimes in moderately priced furniture or light-in-scale contemporary lines. Sagless springs should be used in conjunction with helical springs, as illustrated, to give them greater strength and stability. Sagless springs are attached to the top of the frame, producing a "rigid-edge seat" that is tighter and less resilient than the "spring-edge seat."

The differences between sagless spring units and coil springs are comfort and cash; the extra cost is due to the additional labor and time needed to tie the coils. If properly installed and constructed of tempered steel, both units are durable, and the decision between the firm seat of the sagless construction and the softer, more luxurious tied coil units becomes a matter of personal choice.

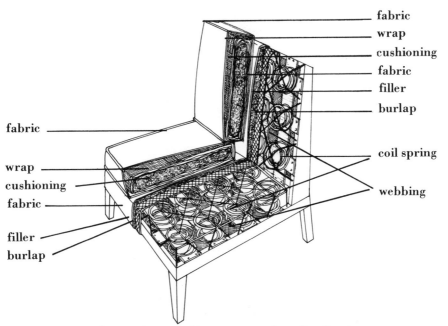

fabric
wrap
cushioning
fabric
filler
burlap

coil spring

webbing

fabric

wrap
cushioning
fabric

filler
burlap

Chair: style, loose back and seat cushions; construction, all coil springs

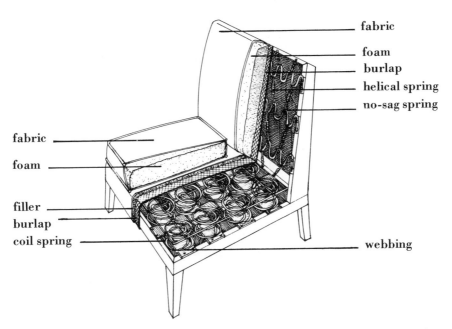

fabric
foam
burlap
helical spring
no-sag spring

fabric

foam

filler
burlap
coil spring

webbing

Chair: style, tight back, loose seat; construction, coil springs on seat, no-sag springs on back

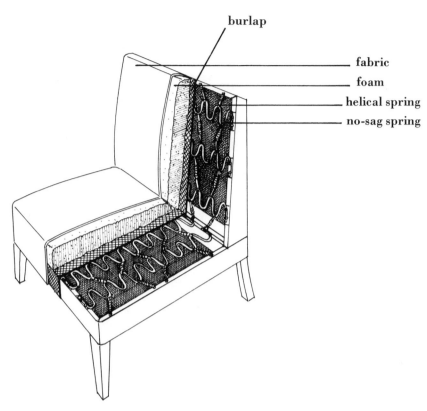

burlap

fabric

foam

helical spring

no-sag spring

Chair: style, tight back, tight seat; construction, no-sag springs

The next step in the construction is covering the springs with burlap which is securely stitched in place. Roll edges (stuffed burlap) are attached to edges of the wood frame to give a "soft edge" to the basic shape and to keep the filling layer from working away from the edges.

A layer of filling material is then laid over the burlap. Satisfactory fillers are kapok, sisal, cotton, and rubberized hair (which is the only odorless hair used). If the chair or sofa has a tight back, tight seat, or both, a layer of one of the fillings normally used in cushions will be placed with the other filler material to take the place of loose cushions.

On certain Scandinavian and lightweight contemporary furniture a layer of foam forms the seat and back and is bonded either to burlap or directly to the webbing which has been attached to a frame of plastic, metal, or wood, thus eliminating all the other steps from frame to cushions. Furniture made completely of foam should be judged on the density of the foam (see chapter 7) to be sure it will hold up under constant use.

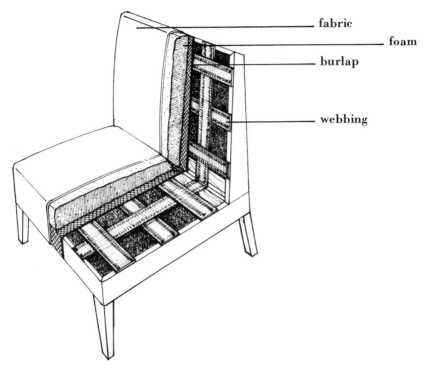

fabric

foam

burlap

webbing

Chair: style, tight back, tight seat; construction, foam bonded directly to webbing

Whatever the filling material and method, this layer is then covered with fabric. Ideally, in better quality traditional furniture the entire unit is first covered with muslin and then with the final decorative fabric. This extra muslin layer is not only a must if you use slipcovers, but it also helps maintain the shape of the piece and reduces the tension on the finish fabric. Because this is equal to double labor, some manufacturers have eliminated the muslin layer. This is one of the acceptable ways to reduce costs, as long as the filler layer is sewn into place to avoid movement and/or lumping and the savings are passed on to the consumer. Compare the cost of a muslin-covered piece with a comparable non-muslin-covered piece to be sure you are getting a true saving.

If muslin is the sixth layer, the seventh and final step becomes the application of the finish fabric and its trim or other decorative touches. This exterior fabric should be firmly attached but not pulled too tightly since stretched fabric will eventually lose its dimensional stability and sag out of shape. It should be used on all exposed parts and on the seat under any loose cushions on medium-priced or expensive furniture. If less expensive fabric is used on this underseat, it should not be exposed, including when people sit down or get up and the cushions move about.

All seams should be straight and inconspicuous. If the exterior fabric has a pattern, it should match where the material is seamed together.

Finer Points of Exterior Construction

Trims come in many forms and should be given careful consideration at the time of purchase. Various types of braids called gimps (or guimpes) are applied with glue and should be firmly and evenly attached. Welts, lengths of covered cording sewn in before the cover is put on the frame, are used to increase the durability of seams and for accent trimming; they should be straight and of uniform size. Nailheads, generally of brass, should be evenly spaced and implanted firmly in the wooden frame.

Skirts, flounces, kickpleats, and so on, are applied by blind tacking (the tacks or staples used for application are hidden beneath the fabric itself) or blind stitching. To hang properly the skirt must be lined with Pellon or its equivalent, not paper.

Tufting, a means whereby threads are pulled through the upholstery materials to provide a depressed decorative surface pattern, is an art and should be done by experts. The tufts should be evenly and artistically spaced and firm but not hard to the touch. Most important, the tufting threads, which are usually held in place by decorative buttons on the face of the fabric, should be tied down through the burlap layer to the webbing underneath, where a small piece of cotton holds the final knot and keeps it from slipping back through the webbing.

Quilting, a type of decorative stitching used to bond a layer of cotton or polyester batting to another fabric, increases the life of the exterior fabric, improving its dimensional stability by taking the strain off the fiber. This is especially effective with cottons, allowing them to be used as permanent upholstery material.

Wooden legs should be free from cracks, firmly attached to a plate on the underside of the upholstered piece, and either finished with paint or stain or covered to blend with the final decorative material. Sofas should have an extra set of legs supporting the center portion to prevent sagging.

Cushions

Cushion filling can be any one or a combination of the following materials:

GOOSE DOWN OR GOOSE DOWN AND FEATHERS

Found as a standard only in very expensive furniture. Other manufacturers may allow you the option of specifying down cushions for an additional charge.

URETHANE FOAM

Resilient, resistant to solvents, and lightweight. It is widely used for both moderate and expensive furniture. A thin layer of synthetic fibers (usually polyester) is sometimes wrapped around the foam to give a softer feel.

RUBBER FOAM

Durable, resilient, and comfortable. It is used in moderate and expensive furniture in states other than California. (See chapters 7 and 12.)

MAN-MADE FILLS

Generally polyesters like Dacron or acrylics such as Acrilan. These are resilient and resistant to solvents and insects. These fillings should be flame treated (see chapter 12), but unless your state has specific laws, the fiber probably will not be.

PREMADE SPRING UNITS

These can also be wrapped with polyester and are the favorites of some manufacturers of moderately priced furniture, while other producers won't use them, claiming inconsistent quality.

Fabrics

The first consideration in fabric selection is the use the upholstered piece is going to receive. Keep your mind on wear and pass by those lovely but too delicate fabrics.

Be sure of dimensional stability by pulling a sample piece of fabric in various directions to see how well it holds its shape. To check tightness of weave and density hold the swatch to the light. Review chapter 1 to reacquaint yourself with the fibers you will be dealing with in upholstery fabrics and the wearing qualities of the weaves and textures.

Cottons are at their best when glazed and/or quilted. When not, cottons are best in low-wear situations, and when easily removable for cleaning. They should be treated to resist soil, fire, and light.

Linens are durable; they serve best when treated for soil resistance and cleaned often. Colors should be fast, and prints may wear off if they do not go all of the way through the fabric. Remember, linens lose some of their durability when flameproofed. Select another fabric for the welts, if possible, to avoid the problem of flax abrasion. Unless they are unbleached, linens are susceptible to sun deterioration. Linen velvets wear well.

Wools wear well and are resistant to perspiration and sunlight. They resist fire and have good resiliency. Wools hide soil and clean well if not stained. They can be scratchy in certain weaves, however, and can trigger allergies. And wool is expensive.

Nylons are durable, soil and perspiration resistant, and resilient. In tight weaves they are very durable but hard to the touch. They must be treated to avoid sun deterioration and static electricity buildup. Nylon high-pile fabrics (velvet and cut velvet) also wear well. If you insist on a white sofa and plan to keep your children, we suggest a nylon twill—and just a little extra care.

Rayons, which are often used in blends lending their excellent color range to more durable fibers, provide the largest selection of fabrics for upholstery. Firm weaves are very important to give rayons more than a moderate resistance to wear. Although rayons should be treated to resist soil, fire, and wrinkling in certain weaves, they are sunlight resistant.

Acrylics do well in low- to moderate-wear areas. They are resistant to most chemicals, sunlight, and perspiration. As they are quite flammable, they should be treated to resist fire.

Modacrylics are found generally in furlike fabrics or in blends to which they contribute their inherent ability to resist fire.

Olefins are durable and resistant to sunlight, abrasion, and perspiration. Once soiled they can be difficult to clean. They have had a limited color range that should be improved now that olefins can be solution dyed, but remember their low melting point (see chapter 1).

Silks are resistant to sunlight and wonderful in low-wear areas. They are the aristocrats of upholstery fabrics. If you select a silk, check chapter 1 to familiarize yourself with its good and bad points.

Vinyls are very durable but not indestructible, as pointed out in chapter 1. The cushion vinyls and the "glove-leather-like" vinyls are the softest, and with minimal care these fabrics will be more than worth their initial cost.

Style

Style is something you are going to have to decide for yourself, but even though this is not a book on decorating, here are a few guidelines.

Sofas and chairs can be tight backed (without pillows), have attached pillow backs, or be designed with loose pillows. They can have a tight seat (no cushions) or loose cushions. The backs and/or seats and/or arms can be tufted.

"Tuxedo" is a sofa style that has arms as high as the back.

Lawson sofas have arms of standard height (21 to 22 inches), which are lower than the back and can be any of several designs (round, square, and Greek key).

A Chesterfield is any large upholstered sofa and is not a style.

A sofa or chair should feel comfortable; sit on it and relax. Does it support your back and do your legs feel comfortable (is the seat too deep or too shallow)? Is the pitch of the back comfortable? The padding should be smooth with no lumps or hard spots. The sides and back should be padded (and no cardboard, please).

These pieces are supposed to be your most comfortable furniture other than your bed, so take time and care when selecting them. After a good refrigerator and a good bed (see chapter 7) we feel the upholstered pieces come next in importance as you allocate your home-furnishing dollars. Because they receive so much constant wear, do not be penny wise and pound foolish in their selection.

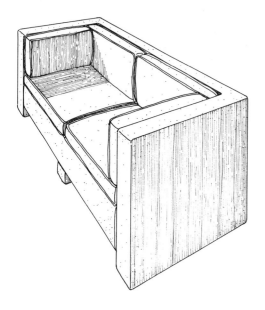

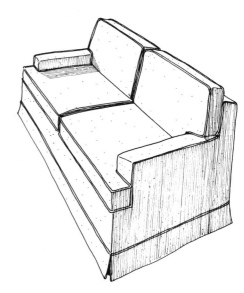

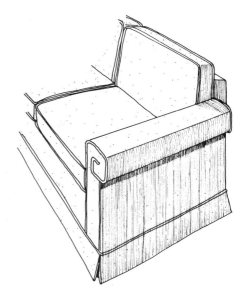

ABOVE LEFT: Tuxedo-style sofa

ABOVE RIGHT: Lawson sofa with square arm

RIGHT: Lawson key arm

Labels and Guarantees

All upholstered furniture should be labeled for its contents and percentages with a label similar to that used on bedding. Care labels should also state the finishes applied to the fabric. See chapter 12 for details about the Kroehler quality guarantee and the Monsanto "Wear-dated" label.

Guarantees should be in writing and clearly stated.

Shopping Hints

1. Take measurements of the room where you plan to put the piece and the route by which it must come into that room from outdoors. This is particularly important if you are buying a large sofa.

2. Sit on the piece; check all the exterior checkpoints already mentioned.

3. Find out what is included in the price—fabric? delivery?

4. Get a firm delivery date, if possible. Be realistic (see chapter 12).

5. Ask to see a cross section of the upholstered area.

6. If you are having the piece upholstered with a custom fabric, get a sample of it to check at home and keep it to recheck when the piece is delivered to be sure it is the correct fabric.

7. Read labels. If there are none, ask questions.

Resources

Department of Consumer Affairs, Bureau of Home Furnishings, State of California, 3401 La Grande Blvd., Sacramento, Calif. 95823. "A Survey of Upholstery Fabrics and Their Flammability Characteristics."

Fabbro, Mario Dal. *Upholstered Furniture: Design and Construction*, 2nd ed. New York: McGraw-Hill, 1957.

Southern Furniture Manufacturers Association, P.O. Box 951, High Point, N.C. 27261. "Buying Upholstered Furniture," North Carolina Agricultural Extension Service, Home Economics, No. 81, February 1972.

9

Case Goods

TECHNICALLY the term *case goods* applies to items of furniture used for storage (such as dressers, cabinets, desks). However, over the years it has become customary to include other nonupholstered home-furnishing articles, such as tables and headboards. In this chapter we have, for the sake of convenience, extended the definition to include types of seating which are not soft goods (dining room chairs and benches, for example). The first case goods were generally the chests used by military officers, priests, and other frequent travelers to transport their personal belongings, a sturdy example of this being the campaign chest, which with its brass-protected corners and inset handles has endured as a respected design style to current times.

Case goods were originally limited to wood construction, except for leather straps, metal hardware, or possibly decorative touches in other materials; but today with the extensive use of plastics, metals, and glass, the term has become generic and covers a broad range of furniture with equally broad function and style. In selecting case goods, however, it is still important to have a working knowledge of woods and of time-honored construction methods, since wood continues to be the most commonly used material. Consider this part of your homework.

Homework

Is the piece of furniture intended to fill specific needs?

Should it be decorative also?

Who is going to use the piece—children, adults, or an entire family?

Measure the area where you wish to place the piece. Don't forget the "human measurements" (see chapter 13).

After you have determined who is using the piece, decide on the finish—tough, delicate, painted, stained, plastic, glass.

Is this a temporary acquisition to see you through a short-term need or is it to be a permanent addition to your home?

If you decide upon antique furniture, read chapter 10.

Woods

Woods are classified by their trees of origin as either soft or hard, and since some so-called hardwoods are actually softer than softwoods, only a limited number of woods lend themselves to the needs of the furniture industry. The bulk of these are hardwoods.

Hardwoods

Hardwood trees have broad, flat leaves that fall off annually. The ones chosen for case-goods construction generally have a natural, distinctive grain, are easily worked, do not split or crack readily, hold screws securely, and are less likely to dent than softwoods. They are used in solid form for both inside and outside construction and as the top layer of veneers.

MAHOGANY

A favorite of fine furniture craftsmen for many years because of its handsome grain, strength, and workability, true mahogany is imported from Central America, the West Indies, South America, and Africa. Not to be confused with genuine mahogany are Philippine mahogany (or lauan) and Primavera, known as white mahogany. Natural mahogany is available in colors from light golden brown to deep reddish brown, the color so often associated with mahogany because of its extensive use. Today the wood is often finished as a light brown or may be bleached to an even lighter tone. Look for a label stating that the wood is solid mahogany or real mahogany. (Note: Solid mahogany is always real mahogany; real mahogany may be either solid or veneer.) Mahogany can be used in combinations of types and/or colors to create veneers and inlays, some of which are intricate and costly, while others are used to reduce production costs. (Veneers are discussed later.)

WALNUT

This hardwood has become synonymous with fine-quality wood, and this is why it has been so widely imitated. The walnut producers, like the mahogany association, promote the use of labels; these distinguish among solid walnut, genuine walnut (which could be a veneer), and walnut finish (which could be anything). Walnut is ideal for furniture because of its natural grain and the number of ways it can be finished. The color and grain vary from species to species, and even the burl, stump, and crotch of walnut trees display beautiful and unusual grains which are used in making expensive furniture or furniture veneers. The wood of the black or American walnut is light to medium brown in tone; the "black" appellation is derived from the dark color of its nutshell. Circassian walnut, which at the height of its furniture usage came from the Balkans and the shores of the Black Sea, is a delicate fawn color with distinguishing dark and irregular streaks marking its grain.

OAK

Since the Middle Ages oak has been easily available and extensively used. Because walnut and other traditional fine-grained hardwoods are becoming more scarce, oak is experiencing a new popularity. Not long ago relegated to such hidden uses as the frames of upholstered furniture, it is now enjoying a renaissance for outer construction, and designers and manufacturers are utilizing its coarse, open grain and natural light to amber tones for the creation of quality furniture. It comes from Asia, North America, Europe, and Africa, and there are about fifty varieties in the United States alone.

MAPLE

A strong, very hard, durable wood which has a close grain that can either be straight, wavy, curly, or have the familiar "bird's-eye" pattern. It is easy to work and does not split easily. Its color ranges from reddish brown to almost white. Maple was a favorite with American colonists and is still associated with furniture from this era, but it is also being made into fine contemporary furniture. It is becoming rare, and therefore more expensive, and is not to be confused with less expensive woods finished in the traditional maple color.

BIRCH

Similar to maple, birch has a very close grain, is durable, and in comparison to the other hardwoods we have mentioned is lower in cost. While its natural color is very light brown, sometimes nearly white, select white birch can be easily stained to resemble other woods and is now being used a great deal for good-quality pieces. In addition, birch is providing structural parts for both fine and "low end" (industry terminology for less expensive) lines and is being used extensively in the manufacture of plywood.

PECAN

A member of the hickory family, pecan is native to the south central United States. It has an open grain, is light brown in color, and can be finished in a variety of colors. It is used to make solid furniture and veneers.

FRUITWOOD

This term refers to the wood of trees that bear fruit; because of their productive nature, the use of the wood for furniture is limited. While cherry is the most familiar, apple and pear are also used. The genuine fruitwoods are not to be confused with the "fruitwood finish" applied to many kinds of wood to simulate the light brown color of French Provincial furniture, which was originally made from real unstained fruitwoods.

TEAK

A medium hardwood that is treasured for its unusual coloring of light or dark brown with fine black streaks running through it, teak is imported from India, Burma, and nearby areas. It is a favorite of furniture designers and craftsmen because of its easy workability. Because of the time required for proper drying and seasoning, good teak is expensive. Less expensive,

possibly unseasoned teaks have been appearing on the market; since there is
no way to determine quality except by checking the straightness of the larger
boards used for tops and sides of furniture, you should get a guarantee
stating that the piece can be returned if it warps.

ROSEWOOD

Hard and durable, imported from India and Brazil, rosewood ranges in its
distinguishing reddish brown color from light to dark, with curving black
streaks much more pronounced than in teak. Used extensively in the
eighteenth century, today it is made into reproductions of pieces of that period as well as contemporary furniture.

GUM

This wood comes from trees that are grown in abundance throughout
North America and south to Guatemala. While it is hard and easy to work, it
is susceptible to splitting, warping, shrinking, and decay. Gum must be sea-
soned properly. Its close grain allows manufacturers to finish it to resemble
many woods, including walnut and mahogany, and it is used extensively for
framework and unexposed parts of furniture.

ASH

A native wood, ash is durable, relatively easy to work, and inexpensive.
Its coarse, open grain is similar to that of oak but sometimes can be "wild,"
an industry term for an overly "active" grain pattern. Ash is used extensively for framework and unexposed parts, and also to make moderately
priced furniture. It varies in color from white to light brown.

POPLAR

A soft, weak, lightweight hardwood, poplar is easy to work and takes stain
or paint well. When used for inexpensive furniture, it is often enameled to
improve its wearing qualities. In veneers it often provides the substratum to
which the finer top layer is attached.

Softwoods

Softwoods come from trees that are evergreens with needles or scalelike leaves. Because they dent and damage easily, their use in the furniture industry is limited.

PINE

Easy to work and close grained, pine is used for certain styles of furniture, especially reproductions of early American rustic pieces and, because it is easily carved, early Georgian. It takes all finishes well and can be painted. Pine is particularly susceptible to atmospheric changes, however; these can cause swelling and contraction and, as a result, warping and problems with seams.

REDWOOD

From the Pacific coast of the United States, redwood is moderately strong in large timbers, but because it is soft and splinters easily its uses are limited to a few California-casual lines and outdoor furniture where its resistance to rot and decay is a plus.

Veneer

Veneers consist of layers of thin wood "slices" and a core of solid lumber or moisture-resistant composition board, all bonded together with adhesives under pressure. If the veneer is to be used for the exposed parts of furniture or walls, the top layer will be a sheet of one of the fine-grained hardwoods. This allows the manufacturer to produce a beautiful-looking product at a far lower cost than the same piece made of solid wood. Besides saving money, this process helps conserve our dwindling fine hardwood forests.

Veneers can provide construction advantages over solid woods. Even on fine furniture, veneers are used on table tops to prevent warping. If solid wood is used, it must be in planks doweled together. These planks are subject to contraction and expansion with changes in the weather (contracting when dry and expanding when moist). This can create actual openings in the seams of the table top. The alternating layers used in veneering eliminate this

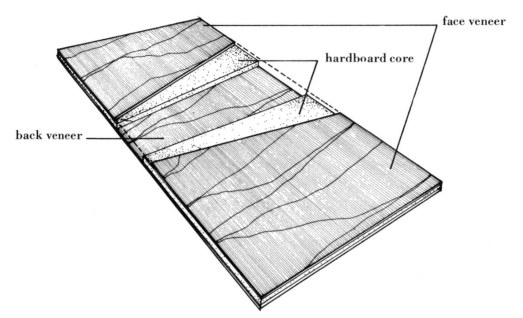

face veneer

hardboard core

back veneer

Basic veneer: wood slices bonded to hardboard core

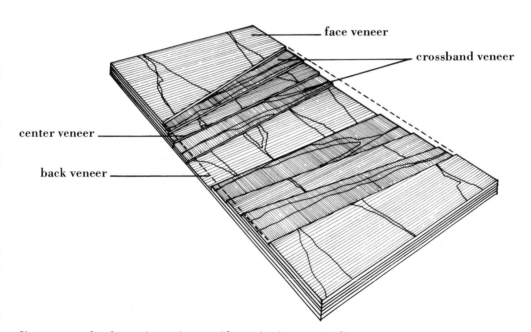

face veneer

crossband veneer

center veneer

back veneer

Veneer core: the alternating grains provide tension in opposite directions

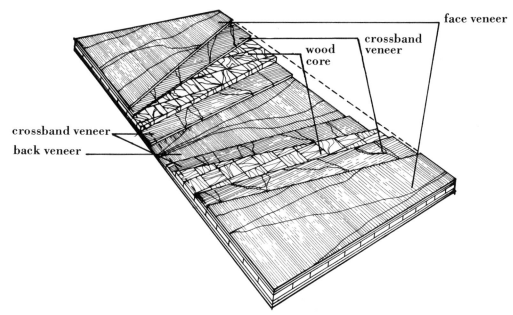

face veneer

crossband
veneer

wood
core

crossband veneer

back veneer

Wood core veneer

problem by providing tension in opposite directions, each counteracting the other.

In addition, veneers allow the manufacturer to create striking designs by cutting and matching the woods to make full use of the distinctive natural patterns within the grain.

When the sheets of veneers are placed all in one direction, the result is called laminated wood, which can be used for curved surfaces where the stress is in one direction.

Because veneers cannot be carved, all sculptured decorative moldings and designs have to be applied onto, and should always blend well with, the veneer surface.

Marquetry, a type of decoration found only on fine veneered furniture or veneered antiques, consists of patterns formed by inlaying various kinds and colors of wood in intricate shapes, sometimes incorporating small pieces of mother-of-pearl and precious metals.

Construction of Wood Furniture

Testing for good construction is not as difficult as most people think it is, and though of course you will want to know about the construction of expensive furniture, even inexpensive furniture does not have to be shabbily made or dangerous.

To assure quality of construction, check these points:

1. The piece of furniture should stay rigid and balanced when you place your hand on the top and try to rock it from side to side. You should sit in chairs to test for steadiness. Rocking chairs should stand firm and not pull over when you place your hand firmly on the arm and pull (as a child might).

2. The finer the furniture, the better the inside and unexposed parts will be finished. If these are not stained, they should be smoothly sanded. Drips and lumps of the finish liquid in crevices and corners, bits of wood or hair caught in the finish, and unfinished backs are all signs of poor-quality workmanship.

3. Check all moving parts. Drawers should slide easily and not move back and forth sideways. A center glide prevents this. Inside there should be small blocks of wood, called reinforcement blocks, for the drawer to rest on, and these should be screwed and glued into place, not stapled. Drawer stops, small pieces of wood or plastic that prevent the drawer from being pulled out too far, are used on good furniture.

At one time dust panels were a sure sign of quality furniture, but this is not an infallible test today. Originally designed to catch the dust created from wood drawers sliding on wood, panels have gradually disappeared from furniture construction as nylon glides and ball-bearing rollers have come into use, thus allowing the manufacturer to market good furniture at a competitive price without sacrificing real quality. If the piece you want passes the other tests for quality, then the presence or absence of dust panels becomes merely a question of aesthetics.

Extension tables need extra support for the leaves. Have the leaves put in and after checking that color and grain match the table, look under the table for supports.

Doors should swing easily and have some type of catch to keep them closed. The hinges should be strong and well enough secured to keep the open door from sagging when you press carefully and firmly down on it.

4. All separate parts should be fitted together securely and firmly. Glue-filled cracks are evidence of very poor workmanship. The front and back and corners should be fitted together by mortise-and-tenon or double-dowel construction. The back should not be just nailed on. All four sides of drawers should be dovetailed. There should be corner blocks to reinforce all major stress joints.

The development of epoxy adhesives has allowed manufacturers to bypass the labor-consuming method of screwing the corner blocks into place. Instead, the blocks are held until the epoxy is dry with a fine staple or pin driven into place by an air gun. This admittedly effective shortcut lacks the fine craftsman's touch of the traditional technique. If screws are used, round-headed screws will require washers; wood screws with tapered heads will not.

Chairs should have corner blocks, particularly where the legs are attached. The legs should be firm, not wobbly; they are sometimes given greater stability by a crosspiece of wood (called a stretcher) used as a brace between the legs.

5. The finish should be smooth, even, and consistent. (If it is glossy, it should be glossy all over.) Run your nail (carefully, of course) along an edge to see if the finish lifts up or flakes off. Either is a sign of a poor finish. Grains should match or blend, and all inlay work should be fitted tightly and feel smooth to the touch.

French polish, a fine and lustrous but time-consuming and complicated method of finishing antiques and some fine furniture, is not often found in today's marketplace. Because it is susceptible to stains from alcohol and moisture and is expensive to produce, most manufacturers have replaced this finish with more durable and quick-drying techniques, some of which give the appearance and luster of true French polish.

6. Hardware should have a smooth finish and be fitted securely into place with washers and screws. Sculptured plastic or wood trims and molding should blend with the wood to which they are attached. Hardware on fine-quality furniture should be cast of good heavyweight metal; less expensive pieces will probably have hardware stamped from lightweight metals.

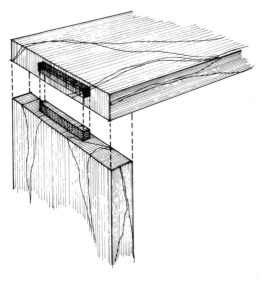

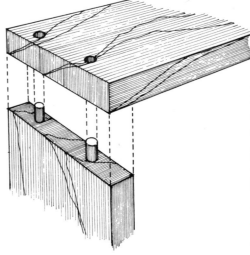

ABOVE LEFT: Mortise-and-tenon joint

ABOVE RIGHT: Double-dowel construction

RIGHT: Dovetail joint

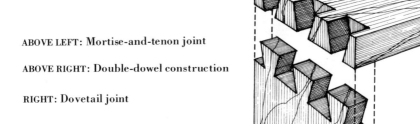

Glass

Glass is used primarily as tops for tables or shelves except for a few unusual and very expensive contemporary pieces.

Glass is priced according to thickness and has become quite expensive. While ¾-inch glass is the most desirable, ½-inch will look well and, if tempered, provide good service for less money. When used as a table top, ½-

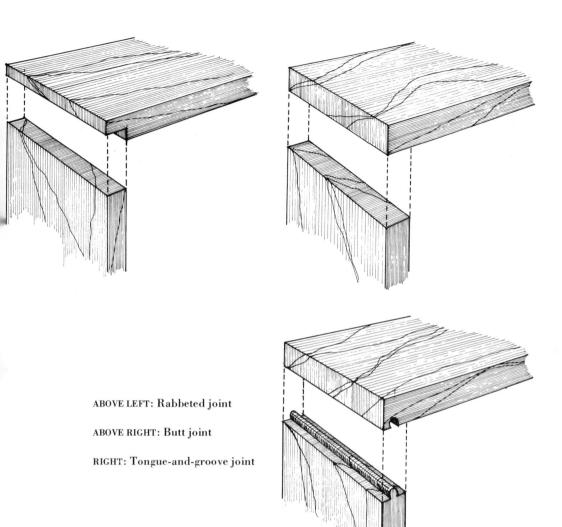

ABOVE LEFT: Rabbeted joint

ABOVE RIGHT: Butt joint

RIGHT: Tongue-and-groove joint

inch glass should always be strengthened by setting it into a supporting frame, which can be part of the furniture design.

Glass of any thickness can present a safety hazard to the visually handi-capped or distracted person when the glass top floats on a pedestal, sits on widely spaced legs, or is placed where householders or guests may not focus on its presence.

Beveled edges (with the glass cut on a slope angled toward the center) act as a prism and definitely do add to the beauty of glass. All glass on fine furniture should be beveled.

If you are buying glass for an existing piece of furniture, have the space measured professionally or measure it very carefully yourself. If you are having the glass beveled, this must be done by an expert glazier who will charge extra for the work.

Plastics

One well-known plastic furniture manufacturer has called plastic furniture the "furniture of chemistry," and we think that fits. Our only quarrel with chemistry in furniture is the same one we stated in connection with fibers in chapter 1: products are brought onto the market without sufficient testing, and advertising extolling their virtues suggests that they have no failings.

Plastics have been called the great pretenders because they have been and are being used in many forms to simulate wood—printed wood finishes, wood-finished vinyl wrap (like skin used over plywood or hardboard), sculptured moldings, and decorative trims. These are all designed to cut the cost of the manufacture of furniture.

On the other hand, the furniture designed specifically to utilize the special qualities of plastic is interesting and at times exciting. As with wood furniture, you get what you pay for. When shopping for "true" plastic furniture, you will need a completely different set of rules for judging good construction.

Because plastic is sold by the pound, a heavier gauge, or thickness, generally indicates better quality. Surfaces should be smooth and without flaws and the color even. As with wood furniture, the high-quality pieces are finished all over (inside and out).

Plastics do require certain kinds of care. A damp cloth and liquid detergent will maintain a piece after an initial application of wax (automobile wax is sometimes suggested because the automobile industry pioneered the finishes used on plastic furniture). Abrasive cleaners and furniture polishes should never be used on plastic furniture.

Although there are a few almost indestructible plastics on the market, they generally are found on a football player's head rather than beside his sofa. Depending upon the force of the impact, certain plastics may be dented beyond repair by a sharp blow. Others, namely acrylics, can be very easily scratched. There are kits available for repair, and a few plastics can be sanded and refinished by professionals.

Plastics are molded, formed into sheets, applied over molds, cut and bent into shapes, or allowed to rise (like dough) and then cut into slabs. All plastics fall into one of two categories, which in oversimplified terms are:

1. Thermoplastics, which can be melted down and reformed. These can be permanently damaged by high heat.

2. Thermoset plastics, which are formed by a chemical reaction when two or more chemicals are put together (similar to epoxy glue). Once they are united, a new material is produced, and the process cannot be reversed.

Plastics are divided into twelve families, as listed in the charts that follow (printed here through the courtesy of Vaungarde, Inc.).

THERMOPLASTICS

ABS Plastic (Acrylonitrile-Butadiene-Styrine, developed in 1948)

Appearance:	Glossy-surfaced, hard, rigid, opaque, in black, white, or colors
Flammability:	Softens and melts but heat must be concentrated and at about 175–212 degrees before damage occurs
Wearability:	Outstanding impact strength; can be dented or scratched under certain conditions; impervious to weather
Maintenance:	Wipe with damp cloth, mild soap, liquid detergent; avoid powdered cleansers; to preserve or heighten shine, polish with automobile wax (or toothpaste)
Uses in furniture:	Chairs, tables, wall systems, interior shells for upholstered pieces, library file drawers
Brand names:	Cycolac

Acrylic (Polymethylmethacrylate, developed in 1936)

Appearance:	Transparent, glasslike; colorless or in colors; light-transmittant (edges will gleam); also opaline, translucent, opaque
Flammability:	Melts and distorts under flame; will not withstand steam sterilizing; loses shape in boiling water
Wearability:	Easily scratched to point where in time it looks cloudy; resistant to sharp blows; strong; can be rigid or resilient
Maintenance:	Wipe with damp cloth; kits are available with materials for buffing and repairing scratches

Uses in furniture: Tables, chairs, étagères, wall units, drawer pulls, substitute for stained glass (in colors) in door panels
Brand names: Plexiglas, Lucite, Acrylite, and Perspex (British)

Polystyrene (developed in 1938)

Appearance: Translucent, becomes opaque with colors or wood tones; smooth, satiny surface or can be textured
Flammability: Can be heated to boiling point of water for short periods; will burn slowly if subjected to direct flame; not harmed by freezing temperatures
Wearability: Rigid, strong, occasionally brittle; most foods and usual household acids have no effect; avoid citrus-rind oil, gasoline, turpentine, nail polish and remover; limited outdoor use
Maintenance: Wipe with damp cloth, mild soap, light detergent, avoid abrasives and cleaning fluids
Uses in furniture: Tables, chairs, legs, drawer and door fronts, headboards, simulated wood carvings, interior shells for upholstered pieces

Nylon (generic name for a family of polyamide resins, developed in 1938)

Appearance: Varies from transparent to opaque, in colors
Flammability: Resistant to extremes of temperature; can be boiled or sterilized
Wearability: Tough with high tensile strength; resilient, resists hard blows; not recommended for continuous outdoor use
Maintenance: Unaffected by all workaday chemicals but easily stained by coffee, tea, colored foods; scouring powders, steel wool to be avoided
Uses in furniture: Drawer guides; glides for chairs

Polyolefins (Polypropylene, developed in 1957; Polypropionate)

Appearance: Semitranslucent, takes color well; rigid in thick sections, flexible in thin
Flammability: Melts under intense heat or flame
Wearability: Fairly scratch resistant
Maintenance: Wipe with damp cloth; use no harsh abrasives
Uses in furniture: School chairs, stadium seats; chairs and tables (Polypropionate)

Polyolefins (Polyethylene, developed in 1942)

Appearance: Waxlike; transparent, translucent, or opaque; in colors; flexible or rigid

Flammability:	Cannot be used over open flame or in hot oven; some types can be sterilized; withstands cold to minus 100 degrees
Wearability:	Resistant to breakage; moistureproof; unaffected by cleaning fluid
Maintenance:	Wipe with damp cloth; use no harsh abrasives
Uses in furniture:	Chairs, tables—especially children's furniture; drawer guides

Vinyl (Polyvinyl Chloride or PVC, developed in 1927)

Appearance:	Clear, translucent, or opaque; in film or sheet form supported or unsupported by a fabric backing; leatherlike surface; colors, textures
Flammability:	Resists heat up to 130 degrees, slow burning; some are self-extinguishing
Wearability:	Generally strong; some can be scratched and lacerated; mostly used indoors, although some can be used outdoors
Maintenance:	Wipe off with damp cloth; cleaning fluids and common chemicals will not affect them; not resistant to nail polish and remover or moth repellents
Uses in furniture:	Upholstery fabrics, inflatable furniture, water-bed "mattresses" and liners
Brand names:	Naugahyde, Boltaflex, Vicritex, Flyhide, Koroseal

THERMOSET PLASTICS

Polyurethane, Rigid (developed in 1954)

Appearance:	Dark brown; can be dyed or spray painted in unlimited colors
Flammability:	Some types are flame resistant
Wearability:	Tough and shock resistant; water-, moisture-, rot-, and verminproof
Maintenance:	Remarkably resistant to a wide variety of common chemicals including solvents and oils
Uses in furniture:	Solid, heavy, tough furniture; also used for drawer and door fronts, interior shells for upholstered pieces
Brand names:	Rubicast, Duromer

Polyurethane, Flexible (developed in 1954)

Appearance:	Cream colored; spongy texture, trapped air cells
Flammability:	Varying degrees of flame retardance
Wearability:	Water and moisture resistant; won't rot
Maintenance:	Remarkably resistant to a wide variety of common chemicals including solvents and oils
Uses in furniture:	Cushioning for upholstery

Polyester (usually reinforced with glass fibers, developed in 1942)

Appearance:	Transparent, translucent; range of bright colors, natural, black, white; crisp and glassy, often with textured look because of glass-fiber reinforcement
Flammability:	Can be fire retardant
Wearability:	Tough, durable, but can be damaged by hard blows; superior surface hardness; good weathering qualities
Maintenance:	Wipe with damp cloth; avoid abrasives; resistant to solvents and acids
Uses in furniture:	Polyester only: frames, rosettes, panels, and simulated carvings for wood furniture; reinforced polyester: interior shells for upholstered pieces; tables, chairs
Brand names:	Fiberglas (a trade name for glass fiber materials) is popularly but erroneously used for the complete compound: fiber-glass-reinforced polyester

Melamine (an amino plastic, developed in 1939)

Appearance:	Translucent or opaque, colors; smooth surface, either glossy or with soft shine
Flammability:	Can stand heat to 210 degrees but should not be used in oven or over open flame—will char or discolor but will not actually burn or soften; unaffected by cold temperatures to minus 70 degrees
Wearability:	Hard and scratch resistant but not unbreakable; should be protected against hard blows; holds colors, lightfast
Maintenance:	Unaffected by detergents, cleaning fluid, nail polish or remover, alcohol, acids, or grease
Uses in furniture:	Laminations to flat surfaces: table, desk, and countertops; sides of cabinets; drawer and door fronts
Brand names:	Formica, Micarta, Parkwood, Pionite, Textolite (laminations); Melmac

Phenolics (developed in 1909)

Appearance:	Opaque with smooth, lustrous surface; black, brown, mottled walnut, and dark colors
Flammability:	Can take temperatures up to 300 degrees; good conductor of heat; can be used in freezer
Wearability:	Strong, hard, resistant to knocks and scratches; tends to yellow on exposure to light
Maintenance:	Wipe with damp cloth; water, alcohol, grease, mild acids, common solvents do not hurt it
Uses in furniture:	Molded drawers, television cabinets
Brand names:	Bakelite

Shopping Hints

1. Check for construction as described in this chapter.

2. Look for quality and content labels.

3. Find out if the price includes delivery from the factory to the store and/or to you.

4. If a piece of furniture comes in a crate, ask if the delivery man will unpack it, take away the crate, and assemble the piece of furniture. Ask how much this costs.

5. If you have to order, get a definite delivery date in writing on the sales slip. Ask the store to call before delivering so you can arrange to be home, but be prepared to deal with one of the home-furnishing consumer's most difficult problems today: delivery. Delivery dates are determined by factory production schedules. Specified amounts of certain pieces are "run" or "cut" at one time. If your selection is not in production or in stock, you may have to wait four to twelve weeks. (Time varies from factory to factory, with custom furniture taking the longest time.) A week before the promised delivery date call your store salesman to be certain that your furniture is on schedule. If there is a delay, determine exactly why. Reputable stores and manufacturers want to deliver your furniture on time, but some delays are unavoidable. Be firm but reasonable.

If you feel the delay is unreasonable or if the furniture is not delivered by the second scheduled date, call the factory yourself. (Customers are entitled to know who the manufacturer is and how to contact the person responsible for expediting deliveries.) If a satisfactory answer cannot be obtained from the manufacturer, contact FICAP (see chapter 12); if all else fails, consult an attorney.

6. If you have to pay in advance, get a signed receipt marked "Paid in full."

7. If you arrange to pick up the item yourself, remember you will probably have no recourse if the piece is damaged.

8. When the furniture is delivered, note any minor damages on the receipt. Get a copy of the delivery receipt. If the piece is not exactly like the one at the store, refuse to accept it and call the store to tell them you are doing this.

9. Before purchasing plastic furniture, review the section on synthetic fibers in chapter 1 and read chapter 12. The charts in this chapter are from a respected company in the plastic furniture business, but let's face it: every manufacturer sees the virtues of his materials in a different light from the one in which he sees their faults. There are many strong, predictable plastics on the market. However, you should remember that acrylics mar easily and really do melt and distort under open-flame tests; that olefins will melt when near open flames or open ovens; that nail polish still stains vinyls; and that polystyrene was one of the materials that made such a poor showing in the California flammability tests quoted in chapter 12. Be selective when bringing plastics into your home.

Resources

Brown, Jan. *Buy It Right.* 1973. Consumer Service Division, Career Institute, 555 East Lange Street, Mundelein, Ill. 60060.

Christian Science Monitor, Home Section, December 24, 1974.

"Growth Market Profile: Plastics in Furniture," reprinted from *Plastics World.*

Kroehler Manufacturing Company, Consumer Education Division, Naperville, Ill. "Let's Talk about Furniture and Construction."

Southern Furniture Manufacturers Association, P.O. Box 951, High Point, N.C. 27261. The Southern Furniture Manufacturers Association (SFMA) is actively working to provide consumers with information on home furnishings and to mediate problems between the consumer and the industry. Send for the fine pamphlets SFMA has produced in cooperation with the North Carolina Cooperative Extension and refer to chapter 12 for more information about the Furniture Industry Consumer Advisory Panel (FICAP).

Vaungarde, Owasso, Mich. "How to Size Up Plastic Furniture."

10

Antiques:
Caveat Emptor

IN the field of law, *Caveat emptor* ("Let the buyer beware") has been a long-established principle, and in no area of consumerism does the phrase have more meaning than in the purchase of art, oriental rugs, and antiques.

Before even beginning to scout the market, you need to understand the term *antique*. The United States government has established for customs purposes that no item can be termed an antique, and therefore be exempt from import duty, unless it is at least one hundred years old. Dealers, the purest of the purists, go one step further and do not consider anything made after 1830. Certain items produced within the past one hundred years satisfy the criteria for a collectible but not for an antique.

Collecting, of antiques and otherwise, should be fun, and your purchases should give you pleasure. Look before you buy, however. Deciding what you are looking for is very important, or, "Let the buyer beware—of himself." Impulse buying is poor judgment in any situation but is particularly precarious with antiques and collectibles. Protect yourself with knowledge. Do your homework and don't forget what you've learned no matter how tempted you are to plunge into a purchase.

Homework

Are you going to buy just a few antiques or collectibles to use as accents, or are you eventually going to replace all your current furniture with "found" items?

Measure the areas where you can use antiques. Put the figures in a notebook and carry it with you to check the size of any "find" you may come upon in your wanderings.

Buy pocket guides on silver, china, glass, or trademarks to carry with you.

Learn about antiques in general by going to museums, local historical societies, lectures, and restored homes and by attending any classes available in your area.

Read periodicals in the field. We'd like to say subscribe, but some of the best are too expensive to invest in until you know where you're going, but worth every penny to the serious collector (see Resources).

Read books—from the local library or, if you are planning to collect, from the beginnings of your own home library.

Sources

One of the better books as a starter for your reference collection is *The Insider's Guide to Antiques, Art and Collectibles,* a compendium of research that is especially helpful for its reference list, which should guide you to other sources of information no novice (or more experienced collector) should be without. Off on a different tack, but definitely worth sending away for, is a series of books called *Discovering Antiques,* incorporating a collection of articles by seventy-five worldwide experts who have written in a direct British manner (see Resources).

The guide to museums mentioned in chapter 11 is a must for antique buffs.

Traveling, which, for better or worse, brings out the acquisitor in all of us, may be a good opportunity to add to one's antique collection, provided that all the caveats are observed. We mention some of the American and Canadian sources (or ways to locate them) under the discussion of folk art (which overlaps the field of antiques and collectibles) in chapter 11. Should your travels take you abroad you are likely to find the markets of Europe, once a good source, as picked over and/or overpriced as those closer to home. However, the emerging nations, especially those formerly associated with the British, French, or Dutch colonial empires, offer many outstanding opportunities for collecting. Some sensitivity must be exercised in this Third World setting, however, for as negative as most governments are today about their colonial past, national pride may oppose the removal of what may with some ambivalence be considered historic treasures. Research the country or countries before beginning your on-the-spot search to check out the latest export regulations, political conditions, and general availability of items of interest.

Research is equally important in the United States. Once you have decided to collect and have studied areas of greatest interest, you should consider getting in touch with a reputable dealer. This is a field where the prospective buyer is very much at the mercy of dealers, and for this reason selecting one ("reputable," "reliable," "respected," "long-established" are appropriate words here) is every bit as important as the selection of the article itself. Even if his services are used (at an established fee) "only" to determine if an object is worth your money or not, it is invaluable for you to be able to trust your dealer. You can write to the Art and Antique Dealers' Association (see Resources) for their directory; a good dealer does not necessarily have to belong to this group but it's a good place to start.

Curators of museums and collections are often good sources of information, but until you develop some expertise, you may not know how to find and approach the ones who specialize in what you need to know.

Sooner or later, you're going to have to trust the integrity of a dealer or dealers who have wider sources than you do and count on him/them to call you when they are on the trail of something they think you would like to own. Your constant homework should help you to learn realistic prices and fine workmanship. And keep looking on your own.

Restoring

Be very wary of pieces described as "easy to restore." Professional restoring is expensive and definitely adds to the value of the piece while adding to its cost. If you intend to do it yourself, you should start with an inexpensive piece and a class in restoration or a good book (check Resources). Many a good piece has been irreparably damaged by amateurs.

Every piece of furniture is like a diary of the people who have used it and the places where it has served. Tables have been eaten off of, chairs sat in, and dresser drawers pulled in and out constantly. Some pieces can be put into good condition and some cannot. You can assume, as a general rule, that the better the condition, the better the antique—and the more valuable.

Shopping Hints

Attend sales at the closings of schools, churches, hotels, and estates. In addition to reputable antique stores, there are antique shows which are advertised in antique publications. Some fine pieces have been found at garage sales and in trash cans, but not many. And you really have to know what you are about to recognize treasures that are hidden so well.

Many antique buffs with a specific common interest band together at what one designer/collector calls "sophisticated swap meets" to share and to bargain in order to expand or balance their individual collections. (This same expert encouraged us to mention that antique collecting should be fun, and to emphasize that the caveats of this long-honored vocation/avocation should not dissuade you from entering into a hobby that could be a pleasant part of your home and life-style forever after.)

Here are a few major points to look for when shopping for antiques:

1. Look for the worn places. Are they in the logical area of wear or is the distressing a bit too much?

2. Very early furniture was not stained with artificial stains and should have a patina from age and soil. If surfaces are glossy, the "old" furniture is a fake or possibly some Victorian covered the original finish with varnish or lacquer, as was the habit in the nineteenth century, even with new furniture.

3. Look under drawers and behind cabinets for unstained wood. Always check with the dealer or curator for permission to inspect thoroughly.

4. If a piece has coil springs, it was made after the mid-1820s because that is when coil springs were invented. The springs may have been added later, however, so do not let that discourage you; just let it be a checkpoint.

5. Know your hardware. *Discovering Antiques*, vol. 1, has a chart that is very handy. It is easy to spot certain designs of specific eras.

6. Look for craftsmen's trademarks. Check your pocket guides. A reputable dealer will welcome your interest.

7. Drawer side construction is a good guide. Dovetailing has become progressively more sophisticated over the years from the 1500s to machine-made furniture.

8. Check for areas where cabinets might be cut and fitted and for sofas that look as though a piece may have been cut right from the center. A lot of old furniture was very large and made for rooms with much higher ceilings than ours. As a result, to make a piece more salable some "clever" people cut pieces down, thereby reducing their value considerably.

Resources

Books

Dorn, Sylvia O'Neill. *The Insider's Guide to Antiques, Art and Collectibles.* Garden City, N.Y.: Doubleday, 1974.

Ratcliff, Rosemary. *Refurbishing Antiques.* New York: Galahad Press, 1971.

Discovering Antiques. New York: Greystone Press, 1971.

Magazines and Newspapers

Antiques, 551 Fifth Avenue, New York, N.Y. 10017.

Christian Science Monitor, October 8, 1974.

Everybody's Money, Summer Canadian edition, 1972.

Organizations

National Art and Antique Dealers' Association, 32 East 57th Street, New York, N.Y. 10022. Membership directory.

Southern Furniture Manufacturers Association, P.O. Box 951, High Point, N.C. 27261. "Periods and Styles," North Carolina Agricultural Extension, Home Economics, No. 79, August 1971.

11

Art as Home Furnishing

DESPITE the rapidly rising cost of living, more and more American consumers are spending a good portion of their discretionary income on art for the home. The reasons for buying art for the home are varied and personal, so the "homework" required before some purchases are made may extend over a number of years, in contrast to the preparation required for purchasing carpets or upholstered pieces. For the latter you match current needs with current options to provide a product that will give easy care and durability along with economy and aesthetic value. Intrinsic and aesthetic values are much more at the heart of the matter with art selections, although certainly your ability to care for your choice is an important consideration.

To make selections that will give long-term value it is necessary to:

Know the difference between original art and reproductions.

Understand various processes and techniques used in different art forms.

Read a variety of reference works about art in general, and about possible specific options.

Visit museums, classes, galleries, craftsmen and artists, reputable dealers.

Learn how to display and care for specific types of art.

Decide upon the art forms that will fit taste, budget, and life-style.

Originals versus Reproductions

Basically, there are two kinds of art—original works and reproductions—
and at this point it is good to remember the advice "Better a good reproduction than a bad original," providing, of course, that you understand what
you are getting. It is also wise to remember that price is not necessarily a
guide to either quality or quantity (size of edition) in dealing with so-called
works of art, and you should be aware of this in order not to fall victim to the
price tag syndrome in judging a possible purchase.

Original art can be divided into two categories: one of a kind (such as a
drawing, oil painting, or sculpture) and one of a series (a print or multiple).
The one of a kind is a single object of art produced by an artist without
intention of exact duplication, although an artist may enjoy a certain art
form so much that he will, at another sitting, or with the encouragement of
an admirer of his first work, produce a nearly identical piece.

With one of a series, in contrast, the artist makes an original (a stone or
plate or cut) for the purpose of having a limited number of copies (ranging
generally from 20 in high-quality small editions to relatively large editions of
150 or 200) produced from it; these are then approved by the artist. It is
therefore important to understand that "original" does not mean unique and
that intent is an important criterion in judging originality. If the artist
creates an image in one medium and it is then copied in another, the result is
not an original, but a reproduction.

When creation of a series of originals involves impressing an image upon
paper or other flat material by one of several processes, the series is called
an "edition," and the units of the series are "prints." "Edition" may also be
applied to a small series of three-dimensional objects, such as sculpture, duplicated under the direction of the artist by means of a bronze-casting technique. Units of a larger series (maybe 100 or 150) having the intent of an
original are known as "multiples"; because of the medium involved (molded
plastic art forms or cast pieces of jewelry, for example) and the size of the
series, these usually involve less personal supervision in production from the
artist who designed the prototype.

Original Graphics

Various processes, each with its own distinguishing qualities, are used to produce original prints: relief, intaglio, planography, and stencil. A fifth process, collagraphy, combines relief and intaglio printing.

Relief Printing

The most common relief printing technique is that using woodcuts or linocuts. The original is made on the cross-grain surface of a piece of wood or on linoleum by cutting with a knife, gouge, burin (a small metal rod with a point sharpened at an oblique angle), or similar sharp tool. The areas cut away remain unprinted (the negative area) and become the white part in the final print. The ink adheres to the raised or uncut parts (the positive area).

In wood engraving the artist uses a block of extremely hard end-grain wood; the harder surface enables him to produce much finer lines. Embossing is done without inking and produces a "white-on-white" design from the pressure of the cut upon the paper.

Intaglio

Intaglio printing began with engraving. The image comes from the gouged-out U- or V-shaped valley produced when the artist rips into the metal with his tool, most often a burin. A linseed oil ink with the consistency of molasses is forced into the crevasses of the design and then wiped from the surface of the plate, which is then placed upon the felt-covered bed of the intaglio press. Paper is placed over the plate and heavy pressure is exerted by a wringer which forces the ink up out of the valleys onto the paper; one inking produces one printing.

In the past most intaglio prints were produced from copper, a soft metal, so some of the crispness of the early prints of an edition might be lost in later impressions. However, it may also be true that the first impression was not inked properly and a third or fourth may be clearer. Alloys used today with copper to produce a harder plate have nearly eliminated this problem in the work of contemporary artists.

In etching a metal plate is coated with an acid resist (literally, a substance that resists acid—will not let it penetrate to the plate) called the ground. The artist then draws his design upon this ground with a sharp needle which removes the ground and exposes the plate surface where the artist has "drawn." When the plate is put into an acid bath, these exposed parts will be etched (eaten away), producing the sunken line which will receive the ink for printing. As in engraving, the ink settles into the sunken or etched areas. After inking, the plate is wiped clean.

The plate in contact with damp paper is passed through the same roller press used for engraved prints, again forcing the paper into the etched areas to receive the ink. In reverse of the relief process, and like the engraving process, etched areas appear in the finished print as black or colored areas, while white areas are those left untouched because of the acid resist. Depth of tone is controlled by depth of etch.

Other variations on the intaglio process are produced through changes in either the etching or the engraving technique. Drypoint, for example, differs from its related forms in that the engraved crevasse is made at an angle to throw up a burr. Printing from the crevasse and the raised burr together is a most delicate process which ends abruptly when the burr breaks off, limiting the number of prints in the edition.

Mezzotint is closely related to drypoint and can be considered a variation on the engraving technique, since no acid is involved. As much as three weeks can be spent in running a rocker device over the plate, kicking up tiny crevasses and burrs which blacken the surface when printed. The ultimate image is produced by selective removal of the burrs. A form favored in the nineteenth century, this technique was employed by the wealthy, who, after their servants had prepared the plates, sat in their gardens picking off burrs to produce the desired mezzotint image.

Aquatints, on the other hand, are primarily etchings, even though the backgrounds are tonal in quality rather than linear. The effect is created by dropping small flecks of rosin on the plate which is heated until the powdered substance melts and produces an acid resist which allows the acid to etch between the melted specks. This creates the tonal background for the etched lines which are drawn over the tint.

Collagraphy

Collagraphs (sometimes incorrectly spelled collographs or colligraphs but actually taken from the same root as the word *collage*) are a combination of relief and intaglio printing, but most examples consist primarily of the former. Some highly creative and artistic effects have resulted from this medium, which involves building up the printing surface (instead of cutting into it to leave a relief) and then, in some instances, incising the resulting surface, thereby introducing the intaglio process. Because a variety of materials have been used to build up the plate or block and because some artists have misused the medium, collagraphy is sometimes misunderstood. One critic has commented that to make a collagraph, "all you need is some Wil-hold glue and some scraps."

Serigraphy or Silk Screening

Quite different from either relief printing or intaglio or any of their variations is the stencil process of serigraphy or silk screening, a technique that is often applied to fabrics as well as to paper. Preparing a tightly stretched screen (which is usually a close-meshed silk but may be nylon or even, as with the ancient Chinese, hair), the artist blocks out the areas not to be printed (the negative space) either by filling the mesh with a varnish or mucilagelike substance or by applying a paper stencil to the screen. What remains is the positive image, through which the printer forces (squeegees) his color to ink the paper or other material placed below. Unlike relief, intaglio, or lithography, the stencil/serigraphy technique is not a reverse process but prints the image as it appears on the screen.

Lithography

A distinct form of the graphic art process is planographic: printing from an even surface rather than from one that is raised (relief), depressed (intaglio), or through which the image passes (stencil). Lithography, which is primarily a chemical process, is the result of the artist's work upon the plane surface (Bavarian limestone in the case of stone lithography) and derives its name from the Greek words for "stone" and "writing."

The original technique involved writing or drawing with a special grease ink on a flat, prepared limestone slab. The ink, or tusche, was sometimes used in the form of pencils or crayons. Water was then sponged onto the surface and a roller holding the printing ink was passed over the stone, the ink adhering to the greasy image portions and being rejected by the moist nonimage portions of the slab.

Because the stones are either thick and cumbersome or thin and fragile, subject to cracking under the extreme pressure of the lithographic press (twelve to eighteen thousand pounds per square inch), many other materials were tried as carriers. Finally a process was developed in which a thin metal sheet is stretched around a cylinder on a rotary press operating at high speed, twenty to thirty thousand times as fast as a hand press; this is present-day offset printing.

Using the hand-printing techniques nearly two centuries old, a printer and a sponger need a whole day to produce fifty high-quality prints; machine fed, an edition of two hundred to five hundred can be printed from the stone in an hour. While many well-known artists working in the lithographic medium eschew large editions or fast production techniques with their diminished quality, some also choose to print by machine, thereby losing the control and quality that is inherent in a fine original.

This process, lacking the hand-rolled ink application before each printing, lacks also the delicacy and luminosity of the more time-consuming method. The latter can often be identified by the four deckle edges of the high-quality paper used. When this paper is fed into a motor-driven press, one edge and one side must be trimmed to provide guides for the feeding operation. Lack of deckling (as in hard-edged or Bauhaus graphics, for example) does not preclude fine hand printing, but the presence of four uncut edges does confirm the nonmechanized process. (Buying an already-framed graphic may not, then, be a convenience but a cover for telltale evidence of production shortcuts.)

A machine-printed print may be exactly what you want, but it is important to know that you are not buying, and should not be paying for, an original. At this point protection for the buyer rests mainly in his/her perceptiveness. Legislation in such states as New York, California, and Illinois requires complete disclosure by sellers of art, and certain artistic groups have sought to set standards. The Print Council of America has established criteria for an original print; in relation to works of art produced as one of a series, the Print Council states:

"An original print is a work of graphic art, the general requirements of which are:

"1. The artist alone has made the image in or upon the plate, stone, wood block or other material, for the purpose of creating a work of graphic art.

"2. The impression is made directly from that original material, by the artist or pursuant to his directions.

"3. The finished print is approved by the artist."

It is important for you, the beginning art collector, as part of your homework, to take pains to learn to differentiate among the various techniques used to create original art, to understand what steps are involved in the various techniques, and to understand the relationship of these steps in producing a print and how much control an artist must exercise over the creation of the image, choice of materials, supervision of the technical aspects, proofing, printing, curating (selection of "good" prints), signing, and numbering in order for the result to be a print of original value.

Although signing a print, usually done in pencil in the lower right-hand corner of the margin, is a comparatively recent development, it has now become necessary in establishing originality. A resolution adopted by the Third International Congress of Plastic Arts in Vienna in 1960 included the following stipulation: "Each print, in order to be considered an original, must bear not only the signature of the artist, but also an indication of the total edition and the serial number of the print."

The number of the print and the size of the edition, usually expressed as a fraction, are also written in pencil but in the lower left-hand corner of the margin. Thus, the fifth print in an edition of twenty-five will be identified by the mark "5/25" on that print, with the artist's signature appearing in the opposite lower corner.

Old and valuable prints by such masters as Rembrandt do not meet these standards, but anyone developing a personal collection should understand them in connection with modern original prints. In this regard we think it worthwhile to quote Hank Baum, owner and director of several art galleries and instructor of graphic arts appreciation classes, who commented in an interview with Nancy Carroll:

"Obviously, a great many of the finest prints ever executed don't conform to these standards. Most Japanese *ukiyo-e* prints, for example, were pulled by God-alone-knows-which-apprentices from blocks cut by skilled but anonymous artisans, as were the woodcuts of most early European masters. Moreover, almost all pre-twentieth-century prints were unsigned and unnumbered, and few, if any, early artists (who, until Dürer's day, were subservient to the printers who employed them) can be said to have exercised any control over the printing of their designs. Consequently, for a collector slavishly to apply a very recent definition of originality to *all* prints would be to deprive himself of the chance to acquire prints for which many a museum curator would gladly barter his eyeteeth. To further confuse the issue, many engravings and woodcuts that originally were conceived as reproductive prints and not works of art in their own right now are recognized to have aesthetic or technical virtues that make any nit-picking definitions irrelevant and that, if they are rare enough, may command far higher prices than many an original print by an inferior and more accessible artist.

"On the other hand, certain abuses have crept into printmaking and print marketing as a direct result of the rising popularity of original prints. A few not overly scrupulous artists have been known, for example, to sign photo-mechanically-made reproductions, thereby certifying them as originals, or to reserve indecently large numbers of 'artist's proofs' and to peddle them to the gullible at inflated prices. There are instances of malpractice, too, among the growing legions of print dealers, the least of which is the gentle insinuation that an artist's proof or a print bearing a low proof number is aesthetically superior (and worth more) than other prints from the same edition that may in fact be equally good or even better. For the beginning collector, the only ways to avoid these and other pitfalls are to educate himself as rapidly as possible, to patronize absolutely reputable dealers, and to seek disinterested expert advice when in doubt."

And where can this expert advice be located? First of all, there is the problem of the reputable dealer. Although it is not necessary to limit oneself to those sellers who are members of the Art Dealers Association of America, it may be reassuring to the babe-in-the-woods art browser to know that while not all dealers of integrity belong to this organization, all dealers who do can be considered of good repute.

And what if you don't have an ADA member in your locality or would like to buy outside that limited circle? Don't depend upon membership in a local dealers' association as a stamp of approval, for many of these organizations are nothing more than highly specialized merchants' clubs: membership does not mean lack of integrity, but it is most certainly not an assurance of good reputation. It would be far better to ask local artists which are the good galleries and use the cumulative opinion of at least five or six artists. Bad news and reports of recurring ripoffs by a dealer travel fast on the artists' underground, and if you have talked to a variety of sincerely-dedicated-to-the-craft artists, you will begin to get a feel for whom you can trust. Ironically, it is not necessarily a good idea to call your local museum curator or university art professor, for many of these live in a very small world indeed and may not really know who is reputable in the commercial sector.

But there are some things you should definitely avoid doing. You should not rely upon so-called collectors' groups for your purchases, nor upon art auctions. Nor should you buy upon impulse: good art is not a souvenir but something purchased with care because you like it and know what your money is buying. If you really must own a $3,000 piece of art for the sake of your ego, at least buy one worth $3,000. It is to the novice, anxious to pick up a bargain but out of his field geographically, artistically, and financially, that many flashy galleries in major cities cater.

While art auctions may be held by thoroughly reliable and long-established firms, they, too, are no place for the beginner. For one thing, this setting offers another opportunity for impulse buying, and too many caveats are involved for the novice who is easily hypnotized by the urge to buy an "autograph" (a print of questionable artistic value or reproductive technique attractive mainly for the artist's signature).

It is also easy to be caught up in the excitement of the occasion, which is similar to that at a horse race with the bidder betting on himself to win—to get the "prize." Most auction rules include a disclaimer as a condition of sale, a statement that absolves the auction house of any responsibility for second thoughts on the part of the purchaser after the thrill has cooled or for the discovery that both the buyer and auctioneer were misinformed as to an item's true worth. (Would you let the seller take back a piece of art if he discovered it was worth ten times more than he had believed before putting it up for auction?) There is a built-in ambivalence about art auctions (or any other kind of auction for that matter): the seller hopes to sell for the highest price possible; the buyer hopes to buy for the lowest price possible. Unless the bidders are all unusually well informed, the seller's expectations are those most likely to be realized amid the heated bidding.

Marry for whatever reason moves you, but buy art for love, not money. It is probably true that in a short while your art purchase will no longer be worth the $50 you paid for it; chances are it will be worth less. Some experts say that 90 percent of all art decreases in value, although some more optimistic souls say the percentage is closer to 80. Whatever the exact figure, it's wise not to buy art as an investment.

Decide what you want and how much you want to spend. Then start studying and start looking. If there is a big blank space staring at you every time you look above your living room sofa, don't let it mesmerize you into impulse buying. Go out immediately and buy the first inexpensive poster or posters ($1 to $5 per) that excite you, or stretch and staple a piece of bold, eye-catching fabric over a rectangular frame (any art supply store can sell you one as a "canvas stretcher" or you can make your own if you're handy). Hang your acquisition in the bare spot and get back to the pleasant task of finding a suitable replacement. Maybe you'll find in the meantime that the poster or art blow-up or framed textile is just right for that spot. If not, the cost is considerably lower than the price, plus framing, that you might have paid for an impetuous purchase that was no more suitable after careful consideration. When the right thing comes along, you can remove your stand-in work of art and donate it to your favorite tax-deductible charity without a twinge of any sort.

Although inexpensive posters are widely used in decoration (more expensive versions are subject to the same caveats as original prints), if their style is not for you, there are other ways to fill that blank space.

If you live in an area blessed enough to boast a good museum, check its rental options. Most museums (and some galleries and libraries) will lease a painting, print, sculpture, or other art object to "try on for size" and often will apply all or part of the rental fee toward the purchase if you find that you want to own the work. Some reputable dealers will even allow you to take a picture (or other potential purchase) home to see how it fits in with your decor.

Museums can provide another service to householders confronted with a gaping hole in their decor, whether it's on the wall or on a table or shelf. When we said, at the beginning of this chapter, "Better a good reproduction than a bad original," we might have used museum replicas as an example. Many of these represent the very best of any given period of art history and, properly chosen, can represent far better workmanship and greater authenticity than the average buyer could obtain anywhere else for any price. The Metropolitan Museum of Art in New York often produces copies by the same techniques used in creating the originals and always employs highly skilled artisans working under the museum staff's direct supervision. Monthly announcements of new reproductions available are issued and represent a wide variety of mediums and origins—oriental porcelain, colonial pewter, limited-edition graphics, Egyptian bronzes, early American glass. Quantities are often limited and purchases can be made only at the museum or by mail. (See Resources for address.)

We have included a very extensive resource section in this chapter. Through the magazines, books, and associations listed you will be able to explore some of the options available and to broaden your knowledge of the art forms that appeal to you: original prints, primitives, watercolors, ethnic or folk crafts, paintings, or whatever. Now what? How does one become an expert or at least expert enough to avoid serious mistakes? Well, we like to recall the off-the-cuff advice of a well-known collector. An expert, he said, says what he thinks, says it first, says it as if he means it, and, when the going gets rough, changes the subject. With that kind of advice, you too are on your way to being an expert in whatever area of art you choose. We will, however, provide a few words of caution.

Begin by avoiding art fads, for a number of reasons. Usually by the time something has become fashionable, the price has been elevated to an unreasonable level. In addition, presuming a certain amount of good taste in the fad (not always true, by any means), the best of the current rage will probably have been picked up by more perceptive collectors who have learned to get in and out of fashion trends, after years of following the art market, by the time you, the beginner, have become sensitive to what's happening.

If, however, you do find yourself riding on the coattails of a fading fad, there may be reasons not to let loose. You may, for example, have found something that nourishes your spirit. And if you have found a particularly good example of the fashion, sooner or later the pendulum will swing it back into popularity. American Indian arts and crafts have been in and out of fashion many times over the past century, and to have disposed of certain blankets, rugs, pottery, or jewelry simply because they were no longer the "in" thing would have meant giving up items that are now appraised in five figures.

A person who has truly learned the art of appreciation will not buy simply because a thing is in vogue—nor sell because it is not. Turquoise inlay and Navajo rugs and San Ildefonso pottery have been giving pleasure to a lot of people for a number of years in which Indian art was not fashionable and will continue to do so for centuries. Neither time nor fashion diminishes the validity of an art form.

Scarcity, however, will affect value. If your study of various mediums brings you into contact with folk or regional crafts or with technical processes or styles no longer being used or produced, and if you enjoy those forms or products or techniques, by all means learn more about them and begin to collect them. In all probability, they will increase in value over the years, but at any rate you will have something unique that expresses your own life-style and personality—a true signature collection.

In your own locality you can become familiar with—and collect—crafts that are associated with the region, either historically or by reason of contemporary artisans and craftsmen. In fact, those deeply interested in preserving the techniques have revived many dying arts and crafts, providing a livelihood in an economically depressed area or renewing ethnic or re-

gional pride. Examples of this have been seen in recent years in such widely
diverse regions and arts as among the Indians of the Dakotas (quilts), the de-
pleted mining areas of Appalachia (earthenware, quilts, pillows), various
reservations throughout the country (especially some of those in the
Southwest listed in the Source Directories suggested in Resources), New England (reproductions of Shaker and colonial furniture and accessories), and,
of course, Alaska and Canada with their Eskimo arts, to name but a few.

Visit local workshops and studios. Chat with the artists and craftsmen. Attend classes at your local Y, art association, continuing education institution
(community adult school, community college, or whatever). Many such continuing education offerings are especially helpful to beginners because they
expose you not alone to one instructor but often to panels of experts or to individual speakers who are established artists in the field and can offer current information about the medium.

If considerable reading in the arts, visiting local galleries, museums, and
studios, or attending classes does not produce an exciting local craft for your
collecting tastes or an unknown but rising star in the graphic arts or another
medium to which you can hitch your wagon, perhaps you can combine travel
with an area of collection that intrigues you. Certainly if contemporary print
making has strong appeal for you, you will sooner or later be thinking in
terms of a trip to areas that support workshops of renown and good repute,
if you do not live in such an area.

You may, then, find yourself planning a vacation trip to New York to visit
the Museum of Modern Art, Ken Tyler, the Universal Limited Editions,
Pratt School of Graphic Arts in Manhattan, or some new workshop that has
caught your fancy in your reading. Or you may head for the west coast by
way of Albuquerque and Tamarind's offshoot at the University of New
Mexico, ending up in Los Angeles for, among other things, UCLA's Grunwald Collection or Gemini Workshop or in San Francisco for the Crownpoint
Workshop, specializing in intaglio. And scattered around the country are
Landfall in Chicago and David Folkman in Houston, for example, if print
making has caught your attention.

If, however, the thought of collecting authentic Native American crafts intrigues you, you can make your way across the country sampling the wares of
various sources listed in the Department of Interior directories mentioned in
Resources. Or you might start out by visiting the shop operated by the department's Indian Arts and Crafts Board in Room 1023 of the main Interior
building in Washington, D.C., between 18th and 19th on C and E Streets,
N.W.

Try to locate the map insert from the December 1972 *National Geographic* to guide you to sites of some of the outstanding Native American crafts. Read *A Guide to America's Indians*, mentioned in the Resource section. In planning your trip, ask your local American Automobile Association office for their map of Indian country, pinpointing reservations, and their Tour Books for the southwestern states. Go with the spirit of the wind, but watch out for those who have set up camp almost next door to some Indian reservations to sell "real" native arts and crafts—machine made in most instances.

Knowledge is always your first and best protection against ill-advised purchases in any area of consumerism, but there are some special safeguards and cautions that apply particularly to Indian arts and crafts. Look, for example, in Resources for *A Consumers Guide to Southwestern Indian Arts and Crafts, Genuine Navajo Rug—Are You Sure?* and other books and periodicals on knowing and buying various types of handmade Indian articles.

Talk to long-established dealers. Look in your Department of Interior directories for authentic Native American sources (most tribes, you will find, now have their own sales outlets). Learn more about the new American Indian Artists and Craftsmen Association being formed with the assistance of the American Indian Management Institute of the Bureau of Indian Affairs—not to be confused with the Indian Arts and Crafts Association (IACA), an independent organization formed among "traders, museums, collectors, individual Indian craftspeople, tribal coops and guilds" whose primary purposes are "the promotion of Indian arts and crafts; development of a world-wide security system to reduce theft of Indian arts and maintenance of high ethical standards." Read about the controversial new law which went into effect in New Mexico in May 1976 to prevent Indian-type articles from being represented as being Indian; called the Indian Arts and Crafts Sales Act, this legislation requires that items be handmade by an Indian in order to bear the label "Indian." Although limited in its scope, it is a landmark since it focuses attention on a whole field of arts and crafts which have been subject to remarkable misrepresentations. Check Resources for our list of reputable sources of Indian crafts and for some more specific information about where to go and what to look for.

You can apply the same kind of traveling-to-the-source planning to any art form or regional craft that catches your interest. Fortified with information from the museum and craft gallery directories mentioned in Resources and other information, you can uncover some of the regional handicrafts in any part of the world in which you have an interest.

Buying art should be the pleasantest part of home furnishing. It gives you an excuse to read about things that interest you, take classes about subjects you've never been able to explore before, travel to some place you've never visited before—or, at least, go to a familiar place with new eyes, new appreciation. If, even after careful study and thoughtful selection, you make a mistake or find that your tastes have changed after a while, the choice is not necessarily irrevocable. The true investment in art, after all, should not be for monetary gain but for growth of your artistic knowledge and an education of your tastes. Perhaps someone else will see your object of art in the same light you once saw it, or the dealer from whom you purchased may help you to sell it in favor of something that appeals more to you. To many dealers that is part of the business side of art, as is returning your money if a sale does not turn out to be everything the dealer promises—which makes art buying from a reputable dealer a lot less hazardous, really, than choosing the fabric for an upholstered piece from which there is no graceful retreat. Even the time-payment plan works to your advantage; most galleries will allow you to pay in installments without the interest rates that raise the final price of other types of home furnishings.

But you'll need proof of purchase, so keep your bill of sale as a verification of purchase—and as a part of your insurance and tax records. (And while we're on the subject of insurance and such, you might find it worth your while, once you discover that you've become a more serious collector than you had at first thought, to send off a dollar to the Appraisers Association of America, Inc., 541 Lexington Avenue, New York, N.Y. 10022, for a directory listing the organization's nationwide membership of over seven hundred appraisers of a wide variety of household items, including art objects.)

Care of Art

Three areas of concern must be considered in protecting your newly selected piece of art from harm and in preserving its value—whether intrinsic or aesthetic or both. In some instances you must establish which value has priority: whether it is more important for the work to be picked up and handled for the tactile pleasure it provides, or to be protected from smudges and possible dropping; whether it is more important to provide a splash of color in your neutral-toned, south-facing living room, or to protect the bright wall hanging or picture from sun and heat damage. Although you should be prepared to make these choices it is not always necessary to do so, for there may be ways of diminishing the potential damage.

Basically, the three damage-producing situations to which your art work will be exposed involve: (1) handling—by you, your family members, your guests, your cleaning person, your mover, even the person or persons to whom you entrust the responsibility of framing or otherwise preparing the article for display and/or storage; (2) the choice of methods and materials for that preparation; and (3) site selection for display or storage.

Extremes of humidity result in one of the greatest threats, and the serious art collector would do well to keep his home within the normal moisture range, about 45 to 60 percent, by using a dehumidifier in moist climates or a humidifier where the weather is drier. Excessive moisture can cause cracking or flaking of paint, corrosion of metal parts or frames, blurring of inks, mildew and mold (through activation of soluble salts in the paper), wrinkling of matting or the art work itself, slackening of canvas, damage to adhesives, sizing, and paper and fabric fiber. At the other extreme, excessive dryness can cause paints, papers, and backings to become brittle, cause separation and buckling of matting, and tightening of the canvas.

Extremes of heat and cold should also be avoided, at the same time that there should be good circulation of air. It is therefore important to have a good air-conditioning system, if at all possible; to avoid storage in closed areas for long periods of time; and to hang or store art work away from cold walls, large expanses of glass, heat registers, fireplaces, air-conditioning outlets and intakes. For similar reasons of extremes of heat, cold, and humidity, valuable art should not be displayed in bathrooms, kitchens, beach and mountain homes, and at poolside. Attics, basements, and storage rooms also present their problems and should be avoided unless there are special storage facilities provided to eliminate damaging excesses.

Contamination is another problem. Closed windows and air conditioners will help to cut down on outside dirt and air pollutants such as sulfur dioxide, which causes bleaching, and hydrogen sulfide, which tarnishes metals and darkens pigments containing lead. Heating dirt may be curtailed by installing an electronic filter on your forced-air heating system. Other contaminants can come from contact with resins and chemicals in certain papers used for matting, dry mountings, folders, backings, hinges. Special museum board, linen pulp papers and tapes, and Japanese hinges should be used; be sure you and your framer exercise great care in the selection of pure, high-quality products that will come in contact with your fine art. Even stretchers of unseasoned wood can cause discoloration or instability of certain paints, and, in reverse, certain wall paints can affect the art work hung upon them: alkyd paints, for example, may damage photographs. What the smoker/collector or his cigarette-, cigar-, and pipe-smoking guests are doing not only to their lungs but to his works of art is a contamination question we will leave to your imagination or further scientific research.

As a positive matter, direct sunlight will kill mold that has begun to develop, but on the negative side, exposure to direct sunlight can also be destructive to color, even penetrating varnished surfaces such as those on oil paintings. Indirect and reflected light, as well as unfiltered fluorescent or ultraviolet light rays, are also damaging to color, and you should make every effort to avoid exposing your art work to light as much as possible, turning off lights, drawing shades, or placing prints and paintings in dark storage when they are not actually on display. Certain mediums, such as prints, watercolors, and pastels, are most easily damaged by strong light, while others, such as the newer acrylics, are less vulnerable.

Matting and framing are so important to the life and beauty of your picture that as much care should be exercised in presenting it as in purchasing it. It is therefore imperative that you spend a great deal of time in considering not only the aesthetics of these steps in the preservation of its value and appearance but the technical aspects as well. Check Resources for a fine forty-eight-page booklet covering all matters of care from handling to restoring; called *How to Care for Works of Art on Paper*, it is published by the Boston Museum of Fine Arts.

In providing proper framing, care should be taken to use raised matting that separates the glass or Plexiglas cover from the art work surface to prevent abrasion and moisture collection. This matting technique will also allow for expansion and contraction caused by outside weather and inside atmospheric changes.

Because nonglare glass must be placed against the art work to avoid a "frosted" look, this protection should never be used on your valuable prints or paintings. However, one decorator says she actually employs raised nonglare surfaces to overlay inexpensive but attractive reproductions and give them a certain antiquity; she cites some Japanese prints in museum reproduction softened by this method. Unauthentic but nice, she feels.

Plexiglas covers are not as susceptible to moisture as glass, but unless properly treated they will collect dust through static buildup. For this reason, Plexiglas should never be used over pastels and similar unstable media, for it may pick up not only static but the entire surface of the drawing, removing the entire "picture" to the back of the framed cover. Antistatic cleaning agents may help to relieve, but not to eliminate, some of the problems of Plexiglas pickup.

Highest-quality museum or rag board (actually made of cellulose fibers rather than rags) should be used for matting, since most mat boards are made of wood pulps whose acids will be absorbed by the art work and cause staining and degeneration. Even coverings of better-quality materials over the wood pulp core will not protect the picture, and this same chemical effect is created by the ill-advised use of wood backing, once a popular method of framing. If you acquire old framed pieces—or not-so-old framed pieces, for that matter—it would be wise to check for damage and/or use of improper materials and to take steps to correct or replace the framing.

Before entrusting your framing to even the well-reputed technician, read your Boston Museum of Fine Arts booklet. Read it, in fact, before even going out to select your work of art (see Resources). If you intend to do your own framing for reasons of thrift or personal gratification, do a lot more reading. Look in the Boston Museum publication for lists of suppliers of quality materials and check out that bibliography for appropriate books on the subject of picture preparation. For some down-to-earth illustrated information you might try to get a copy of *Step by Step Framing*, also listed in Resources.

Pest control is another problem with art objects, especially those involving wood, paper, natural fibers, or paste or glue. Special care should be taken to display or store art objects in places free of such devouring invaders as silverfish, woodworms and beetles, termites, moths, cockroaches, and rats, mice, and other chewing rodents. Fumigation, with care not to contaminate the art pieces, may be necessary if periodic checks show suspicious signs of infestation. Wood and wallpapered surfaces may encourage invasion, so turn your wall hangings around occasionally to look for potential damage.

Cleaning agents may also damage your fine art. Waxes and varnishes will harm certain painted surfaces; these should not be used on frames, either, since they may "bleed" onto the art work itself. Care should also be used in dusting; oil paintings can be scratched or otherwise damaged by feather dusters or cloths. Use a soft brush, such as camel's hair, or possibly even a shaving brush, to prevent chipping or scratching. Acrylic covers or plastic art objects should be washed only with a gentle soap-and-water solution, because many household cleaners will dissolve not only acrylic floor waxes but any product with that same chemical base. Care should be taken in washing the "glass" on any picture to prevent the moisture from running down into the frame and therefore into the matting and picture underneath. This means that even window cleaner should not be sprayed directly onto the surface, but onto a cloth, moistened only enough to remove soil.

Hanging and Lighting

Your art work should be hung at eye level, but just what that means is subject to interpretation. The question becomes whose eye and at what level? Many reputable decorators recommend that seating level provides a much better perspective than does the eye at standing level, but this becomes a matter of personal taste, as does the actual grouping of pictures and should be left to you and your taste or you and your decorator—whichever is the stronger.

But however or wherever you hang your art, take special care in lighting to provide the best viewing. Be sure to avoid glare by using a nonglare glass (if this does not detract from the tones of the art work underneath or harm its surface) or by placing a softening filter or lens on the spotlight focused on it.

Overhead spots, according to some authorities, should be placed on tracks 24 inches from the wall in rooms with 8- to 9-foot ceilings, 30 inches for 9- to 10-foot-high walls, and 36 inches for 10- to 11-foot clearance.

Try to avoid shadows or uneven lighting caused by such things as the upward cast of a light placed at the base of a three-dimensional art object or the frame light often attached at the top of oil paintings. Color is also a consideration in lighting and can be controlled or corrected with various lenses. If a white incandescent light appears too yellow, it can be subdued with a soft blue lens, while various other colors can be used to bring out certain tones or soften others.

A Final Word

Keeping your work of art protected from loss or damage, seeing that it is properly hung or otherwise displayed or stored, are naturally factors that you will have to consider, but they should be only the culmination of the pleasantest part of home furnishing: selecting art. Nothing should wear out (except your patience if you're too tense during the selection period) or spot (if you follow a few simple rules of framing and care) or any of the other traumatic things that can happen to a sofa or other purchased household item. So relax. Find what you like. Buy it. Enjoy it.

General Art Resources

Presuming your access to a library of reasonable size, we suggest that you begin by browsing in the art and reference sections and asking a reference librarian to show you the list of art magazines available in the periodical section. Leaf through some of the art histories and art dictionaries. Glance down the list of offerings under various art headings in *Ulrich's International Periodical Dictionary* and *Subject Guide to Books in Print;* both of these volumes are updated regularly by the publisher, R. R. Bowker Company of New York and London.

If, after general reading, your interest begins to narrow to prints, you might try to pick up a copy of the Print Council of America's *What Is an Original Print?* This informative little booklet used to be dispensed free of charge upon request by the council's New York office, but that has recently been closed for budgetary reasons; the organization itself continues to support the high standards of print making to which it has always been dedicated. If you'd like periodic reports on this area of art, you might subscribe to *The Print Collector's Newsletter,* keeping in mind its narrow focus and the eastern emphasis that its New York place of publication gives. A bimonthly publication, the *Newsletter* may be ordered for $18 a year by writing to 205 East 78th Street, New York, N.Y. 10023.

Read the history of print making from earliest woodblocks to modern American lithography, brought to life in the late fifties and early sixties by the Universal Limited Editions workshop of Tatyana Grosman on Long Island before the beginning of the Tamarind Lithography Workshop in southern California.

Tamarind, operating on grants from the Ford Foundation between 1960 and 1970 under the directorship of June Wayne, reestablished stone lithography as a widespread graphic medium in the United States. From this

highly successful project came the training of master printers and print curators, the encouragement of a number of artists well established in other
mediums to experiment with stone lithography, and the expansion of original
print collections at institutions throughout the country (including the extensive Grunwald Collection at the University of California in Los Angeles and
the collections at the Los Angeles County Museum of Art, the Museum of
Modern Art in New York, and the Chicago Art Institute). Not the least of
Tamarind's accomplishments was the publication of the *Tamarind Book of
Lithography* (Abrams, 1971) by Clinton Adams, former dean of the School
of Fine Arts at the University of Florida and Tamarind's founding assistant
director, and Garo Antreasian, its founding technical director. Both are now
members of the faculty of the University of New Mexico in Albuquerque,
where the Tamarind tradition is carried on.

For books to read from the library, or to own if you get heavily into the
subject of graphics and prints, try the aforementioned Tamarind volume on
lithography; *A Guide to the Collection and Care of Original Prints,* written
by Carl Zigrosser and Christa M. Gaehde with the support of the Print
Council of America and published by Crown in 1965; *How Prints Look* by
William M. Ivins (Boston: Beacon Press, 1958); or *Printmaking* by Gabor
Peterdi, published by Macmillan in a revised edition in 1971. Try also some
by A. Hyatt Mayor (*Popular Prints of America,* published in 1973 by
Crown, or *Prints and People: A Social History of Printed Pictures,* put out
by the Metropolitan Museum of Art in 1971).

Before you begin to select your first prints for your own collection you'll
find it most helpful to read the booklet we have already mentioned in the section on care of art near the end of this chapter, *How to Care for Works of
Art on Paper* written by Francis W. Dolloff and Roy Perkinson and
published by the Boston Museum of Fine Arts. You may order this at $2 per
copy (plus 50 cents for mailing per order of one or two) from the sales desk of
the MFA, 475 Huntington Avenue, Boston, Mass. 02115. Along with this
booklet and the Zigrosser/Gaehde book, you may want to read some books
that deal specifically with framing; you might start with *Step by Step Framing* written by Eamon Toscaro and published in 1971 by Golden Press (New
York). This is also a good time to send $1 to the Appraisers Association of
America, Inc., 541 Lexington Avenue, New York, N.Y. 10022, for their
membership directory; when and if you begin the purchase of art, it will be a
handy little volume to have.

These suggested readings and/or acquisitions will not be enough to keep
you current on what's happening in the art world, however. Your homework

to find the right kind of art for you and your life-style will continue. Go every month or two to the nearest library with an offering of art periodicals and round out your knowledge of the field from such publications as *Art in America* (possibly worth a subscription if your reading of a few issues suggests that), *Art Journal, Arts Magazine, Master Drawings* (a collection of theses), *ARTnews, Artforum* (especially if your taste is for the extreme avant garde), and, for European trends, *Art International,* or for a focus on what's happening in the United Kingdom, the British government's *Craft Monthly.*

If any of these appeal to you strongly enough that you wish to subscribe or if you live at a distance from any library offering them as part of their circulation, here are some addresses and, where possible, the last available subscription rate: *Art in America,* 542 Pacific Avenue, Marion, Ohio 43302 ($17.95 per year); *Art Journal,* published quarterly by the College Art Association of America, Inc., 16 East 52nd Street, New York, N.Y. 10022 (non-members, $8); *Arts Magazine,* 23 East 26th Street, New York, N.Y. 10010 (10 issues per year, $20); *Master Drawings,* published quarterly by Master Drawings Association, Inc., 33 East 36th Street, New York, N.Y. 10016 (membership dues, $20, $18 of which is the subscription rate); *ARTnews,* P.O. Box 969, Farmingdale, N.Y. 11735 ($18 per year); *Artforum,* P.O. Box 980, Farmingdale, N.Y. 11735 ($22.50 per year); *Art International,* via Maraini 17-A 6900, Lugano, Switzerland ($45 a year plus $20, if you want it sent air mail to the United States); *Crafts,* published bimonthly by the Crafts Advisory Committee, 12 Waterloo Place, London SW1Y 4AU, available in the United States at $6.50 per year postpaid from the subscription department, 28 Haymarket, London SW1Y 4YZ.

Send off to some of the leading museums (or check your local museum) for a catalog or listing of publications or art objects available. A dollar, for example, to the Metropolitan Museum of Art, 255 Gracie Station, New York, N.Y. 10028, will bring you advance announcements and catalogs. The Smithsonian Institution has a catalog available from Department 199, Washington, D.C. 20560, and the Boston Museum of Fine Arts' address previously listed (for the book on the care of prints) will bring you a preview of their fine selection, including even reproductions of American furniture.

Ethnic and Regional Arts

American Indian Arts

Perhaps you have begun to be interested in ethnic art or regional folk art and want to read more about it before beginning to collect. To understand the Indian country of the Southwest, home of some of the better-known tribal art—that of the Navajos, the Hopis, the Apaches—you can subscribe to a magazine that is a work of art in itself, *Arizona Highways*, published by the Arizona Department of Transportation at 2039 West Lewis Street, Phoenix, Ariz. 85009 ($6 per year at last writing). Or write to the publication's book department for its definitive *Indian Arts and Crafts*, edited by Clara Lee Tanner from texts prepared by six leading authorities on jewelry, baskets, weaving, pottery, and kachinas; the 176-page hardbound edition with 200 full-color illustrations is available for $17.95 plus $1 for postage and handling.

Other publications which the person beginning to explore Amerind art forms might find worthwhile include *American Indian Art*, published four times per year ($9 for subscribers in the United States) at 7045 Third Avenue, Scottsdale, Ariz. 85251; *A Consumers Guide to Southwestern Indian Arts and Crafts*, written by Mark Bahti, well-known Indian craftsman and dealer and available for $2.75 plus postage from its 1975 publisher, Bahti Indian Arts, 1708 East Speedway, Tucson, Ariz. 85719; *(An Introduction to) Southwestern Indian Arts and Crafts*, written by Mark's father, the late Tom Bahti, another booklet for the beginner, copyrighted in 1966 and in its sixth printing in 1973 for $1 from KC Publications, Box 14883, Las Vegas, Nev. 89114; *Ray Manley's Southwestern Arts & Crafts* (produced by Manley, who has been a photographer for *Arizona Highways* for many years, with Naurice Koonce), published in 1975 by Ray Manley Photography, Inc., 238 South Tucson Boulevard, Tucson, Ariz. 85716; *The Indian Trader*, whose 12 issues a year are available at 75 cents per copy on newsstands and for $10 by mail from the thick tabloid's publication office, Box 867, Gallup, N.M.

The best source of information about Indian ceremonials, reservations, and museums is *A Guide to America's Indians* by Arnold Marquis ($4.95), copyrighted in 1974 by the University of Oklahoma Press, Norman, Okla. 73069. Its wealth of information includes addresses and locations of tribes and reservations, campgrounds on reservations, a calendar of Indian events, and maps for each region of the United States plus appendices of museums, Indian organizations, tribal and Indian-interest publications, and an extensive bibliography which offers a wide range of books about the culture of the Native American but only a few suggestions for volumes on rugs and other arts and crafts. We can't recommend it highly enough as a general travel guide and background to an understanding of the American Indian, however. If you are planning to travel to the Southwest, we also suggest the American Automobile Association's Tour Book for Arizona/New Mexico and the *Visitor's Guide to Arizona's Indian Reservations* by Boye DeMente, published in 1976 and available for $3 plus 40 cents postage from the publishers, Phoenix Books/Publishers, 1641 East McLellan Boulevard, Phoenix, Ariz. 85016. This provides local history, weather conditions, fishing and camping information, all helpful to the first-time visitor to Arizona Indian country.

We'd suggest that you write for back issues of *Arizona Highways*, especially those of early 1974 featuring various Indian art forms—but those became collectors' items almost the moment they hit the newsstands, and even reprints (the first time this magazine has been called upon to publish second runs) were immediately sold out. When we last checked, secondhand copies, when available, were selling at ten to fifteen times the original newsstand price, so it may be difficult for you to find or borrow one just to browse through. But if you do have access, you will enjoy illustrated features on turquoise and the Indian jewelry arts in the January issue, extensive pottery articles in February and May, and an issue on rug and tapestry weaving in July (all 1974 issues).

For additional authentic sources of Native American arts and crafts, from the Eskimos of Alaska to the Seminoles of Florida and from the Penobscots of Maine to the Mojaves of California, write to the U.S. Department of the Interior, Indian Arts and Crafts Board, Washington, D.C. 20240, for free copies of Source Directory 1 (Indian and Eskimo organizations marketing native arts and crafts) and Source Directory 2 (individuals marketing same). Many of these, especially some of the cooperatives or tribal enterprises listed in Directory 1, will send brochures on request, and even those who don't, list the kinds of articles they sell, so that you can get an idea of the products of different tribes in different regions.

You are not always going to be able to deal directly with Indian sources, however, and in those instances be sure that you have done your homework well and that you are dealing with long-established and reputable persons in

Indian trade. Whenever you see the machine-made jewelry side by side or in a case with more expensive silver and turquoise, question whether this is a shop for tourists or for the encouragement of the Indian arts and crafts.

We have a close friend, a long-time collector, who says that Fred Harvey, despite its better-remembered association with travelers and food, is a reputable source of Indian crafts in such locations as Grand Canyon, Death Valley, and even downtown Phoenix. Near Phoenix, in Scottsdale, are two shops that have long-established reputations: Pueblo One—Indian Arts, 3815 North Brown Avenue, Scottsdale, which has among its past credits the appraisal of the famous McCormack Collection; and Tanner's Arts and Crafts shops, which also have locations in San Diego, Calif., and Gallup, N.M.

In developing your own list, read *Arizona Highways* (its March 1975 issue has an excellent article, "A Century of Indian Traders and Trading Posts") and contact the Indian Arts and Crafts Association. Write IACA, P.O. Box 367, Gallup, N.M. 87031, visit them in Suites 6, 7, and 8 at 102 West 66 Avenue, Gallup, or telephone 505-772-9488. Their members are dedicated, according to the organization's by-laws, to the highest standards of ethical practice in the representation of their inventory.

If Indian rugs and blankets excite you, there are some special places you may wish to visit and several books you may wish to read. Russell Foutz at his trading post in Farmington, N.M., has probably the most famous collection in the world; Hubbells, the oldest continuously operated post in the Indian world, at Ganado, Ariz., has long been associated with Navajo rugs and is the place of origin of the famous "Ganado red" used in weaving in that area. If the art of Indian weaving intrigues you that much, it is even possible to enroll in classes (given also during summer sessions) in Navajo rug weaving at Arizona's Navajo Community College, the first college to be established by an Indian tribe on a reservation.

To learn more about the art and how to tell the real from the fake, we suggest reading *Genuine Navajo Rug—Are You Sure?* written by Noel Bennett and available for $1 from the Museum of Navajo Ceremonial Art, P.O. Box 5123 (704 Camino Lejo), Santa Fe, N.M. 87501 (published jointly in 1973 by the Navajo tribe and the museum and printed by the *Navajo Times*, Window Rock, Ariz.); *Navajo Rugs—Past, Present & Future* by Gilbert S. Maxwell in collaboration with Eugene L. Conrotto ($3), published by Best-West Publications, P.O. Box 759, Palm Desert, Calif. (copyrighted 1963, fifteenth printing 1973); *The Story of Navaho Weaving* by Kate Peck Kent, copyrighted by the Heard Museum of Anthropology and Primitive Art, Phoenix,

Ariz., in 1961 (ninth printing, 1974); and *Navajo Rugs (How to Find, Evaluate, Buy and Care for Them)* by Don Dedera, Northland Press, 1975.

When you have read at length about the fascinating history of Navajo weaving and have learned to appreciate the art, you are ready for the adventure of finding your own rug and will want to know about the Crownpoint enterprise. This is an Indian rug cooperative in the northwest quadrant of New Mexico, where at fairly regular intervals (usually about every six weeks) auctions open to both dealers and nonprofessional collectors are held. These sales are always on Friday evenings in the small town of Crownpoint, N.M., northeast of Gallup, and are an outstanding way to support Indian artisans, since they receive a 90 percent return on each purchase, through an exemplary coalition of the Bureau of Indian Affairs, local organizations, and the Navajo weavers to present these auctions. To receive further information and a calendar of which Fridays in which months the sales will be held, write to Crownpoint Rug Weavers' Association, P.O. Box 328, Crownpoint, N.M. 87313.

Eskimo and Other Canadian Arts

If Eskimo crafts (soapstone carvings, ceremonial masks, prints) intrigue you, you may not want to limit yourself to reading about Alaskan sources. Canada's wide range of native arts and crafts includes those of the Eskimos and Indians encouraged in development of their artistic skills by Le Ministre du Nord Canadien et des Ressources Nationales. Once you have developed a certain amount of knowledge, you might, like a friend of ours who is selective and understands quality, deal directly with two cooperatives: Asso. Cooperative de Povungnituk, 55 Avenue Begin, Levis, Quebec; and West-Baffin Eskimo Cooperative, Cape Dorset, N.W.T. The former group has a sales office in the city of Quebec and may be addressed: Povungnituk Cooperative Society, 2841 Le Breton Street, Quebec 10, Que., Canada.

Cooperatives, our friend cautions, exist to encourage all members, from children to the very best master craftsmen, so in order to receive the best when ordering by mail, you'll have to know enough about the art to describe quality, the type of stone you desire, and to *tell* them. She speaks highly of a retail outlet which she has termed "very discriminating": The Quest for Handicrafts, Ltd., Banff, Alberta, Canada. Contact with some such selective resource may be helpful while you're developing your own discriminating tastes.

For information about Canadian resources slanted more to arts than to crafts, you might be interested in the periodical *Artscanada*, 3 Church Street, Toronto, Ontario, with an annual subscription rate of $18 for both Canada and foreign addresses. You might also write to the National Gallery of Canada, Publications Division, 75 Albert Street, Room 330, Ottawa, Ontario, for a list of the gallery's publications.

To learn more not only about native Canadian arts but also about those brought from other parts of the world and made part of the folk culture of the country, read *Crafts Canada: The Useful Arts*, written by Una Abrahamson and published by Clarke, Irwin of Toronto. Distribution in the United States is through Books Canada, Buffalo, New York.

Regional Arts, Museums

The same kinds of folk arts that the colonists and later immigrants brought to Canada exist in the United States. Browse through the shelves of your local library for a sampling of regional crafts that might appeal to your tastes. If your traditional roots go deep, you probably already know about a salty Downeast publication—*Yankee*, Dublin, N.H. 03444; if you don't, you should. For $6 you'll receive twelve issues of this small magazine, which catches the flavor of the region and provides a calendar of local events (fairs, bazaars, exhibitions). There are articles on New England history and culture, past and present, and regional advertisements and shopping columns offering a wide selection of appropriate crafts from tinware sconces to Shaker pantry boxes.

Other regions have similar publications highlighting local history, the provincial arts and crafts, and the regional exhibits and sales where you might find them. *The Ozarks Mountaineer*, less polished than *Yankee*, but well worth the $3.50 per year, is an example. It is published monthly except for January from offices on Star Route 3, Highway 86, Banson, Mo. 65616; subscription mailing address is Star Route 4, Box 10, Forsyth, Mo. 65653.

Before you wander off to sample the arts and crafts that abound throughout North America, go again to your reference library and consult the *Official Museum Directory* (United States and Canada), compiled at regular intervals by the American Association of Museums, 2233 Wisconsin Avenue N.W., Washington, D.C. 20007 (telephone 202-338-5300). A bit expensive to keep on your bedside reading table, the directory is nevertheless an important source of information when you're doing your art homework. If your local library or art association doesn't have it but would like to acquire the latest edition, it is published by National Register Publishing Company, Inc. (a subsidiary of Macmillan, Inc.), 5201 Old Orchard Road, Skokie, Ill. (telephone 312-966-8500).

Armed with all this background on the region you want to visit, you can make your way, for example, through New England, stopping perhaps to view the Garvan Collection at Yale University in New Haven, Conn., for a complete view of American furniture design, before going on to bone up on the rustic arts as displayed at some of the quainter restored villages such as Pittsfield, Sturbridge, Mystic Seaport, Old Salem, or Stockbridge. Your directories, *Festival USA* (an annual published each November by the U.S. Travel Service), and a little homework will help you to uncover some of the regional handicrafts in any part of the country in which you have an interest. The festivals booklet is a nationwide calendar of celebrations, including many ethnic and regional events, throughout the coming year and is available for $1.50 from that revered source of information, the Superintendent of Documents, U.S. Government Printing Office, Washington, D.C. 20402.

Your ancestral roots or your cultural interests might be tied to some other part of the world, but the same kinds of study and travel possibilities exist. You may, in fact, be able to experience beautiful examples of an ethnic craft or art form much closer to home than you might expect. The Afro arts, for example, have been highlighted and encouraged by a striking magazine, *African Arts*, published each quarter ($14 for an annual subscription) by the African Studies Center, University of California, Los Angeles, Calif. 90024, with the aim of acting "as the channel by which gifted and eager artists of Africa may . . . find the visual gallery through which they can address the world." You can read articles on a wide range of art mediums from learned contributors throughout the world and galleries advertised or exhibits calendared to enlarge your own experience with African art.

There's a whole world of art out there. It's waiting for you, and the *Directory of World Museums*, edited by Kenneth Hudson and Ann Nicholls and updated regularly by its publisher, the Columbia University Press (New York), is ready to help you find it. As we have said before, enjoy.

12

Wildfire and Carbide
Blue:
Color the Consumer
Burned Up

O NE evening in late June of 1974 the *Santa Monica Evening Outlook* reported that certain products of a local carpet manufacturer had failed to meet the fire safety standards of the Flammable Fabrics Act, according to the Federal Consumer Product Safety Commission. The commission's action at the time served only to establish an agreement with the offending company that it would make no future violations and to alert those customers who happened to read the announcement of the carpet's failure to meet the criterion for surface flammability of carpets and rugs. Neither the government agency nor the reporting newspaper offered comment on the irony of the color names involved in the violation: Wildfire and Carbide Blue.

Across metropolitan Los Angeles in the City of Commerce on the same June night, flames shot sixty feet into the air and tied up freeway traffic for two miles in each direction when four piles of baled foam rubber caught fire in the storage yard of a cushion company, according to reports in the next morning's *Los Angeles Times*.

And at the same time in the northern part of the state, in Sacramento, researchers in California's Bureau of Home Furnishings of the Department of Consumer Affairs were busily compiling reports on research projects that may well tie the two Los Angeles–area incidents together in more than time and locality. Tests by bureau scientists have shown that dye (ironically again, red is one of the worst offenders) may be the flammable substance in some fabrics. They have also performed dramatic tests showing the pyrotechnic qualities of such household furnishing materials as foam rubber and the kind of plastic covering used on crib bumpers and mattresses.

Fire Tests

You might as well serve or sleep on a keg of dynamite as on some of the articles you may be using in your home right now. Read what happened on January 31, 1974, when the Bureau of Home Furnishings in cooperation with the College of Engineering of the University of California, Berkeley, conducted a number of fire tests in an unfurnished condemned house in South Sacramento, California. Even the researchers were surprised by the wildfire that resulted.

"In these tests two crib systems were tested for flammability characteristics.

"First a wooden crib, with an innerspring mattress filled with flame retardant cotton, a flame retardant cotton filled bumper pad, a fitted cotton sheet, and an acrylic blanket, was tested.

"The wood crib system was ignited when a single paper match was applied to one corner of the acrylic blanket which acted as a fuel source for the system.

"Ignition of this system was characterized by a slowly burning fire, as the acrylic blanket fuel source burned across the surface of the crib mattress, charring the flame retardant cotton mattress and wooden crib. At no time in the burn did either the wooden crib or cotton filled mattress appear to contribute to, or become actively involved in the combustion of the system.

"Within 15 minutes of the start of the ignition all flames had died, and smoldering continued for but a few minutes. The crib system appeared to be still structurally sound."

You may be absolutely unimpressed that the crib was still standing. And the room. And the researchers. And the house. But read on.

"Examination of this crib system following the test confirmed that a surface char of the flame retardant cotton had occurred with unburned, non-smoldering cotton beneath an average ¼″ thick char layer. The wooden crib itself showed little char damage.

"A crib system of this type will pass both cigarette and open flame type tests, and will provide the consumer with considerable added fire protection over systems which only pass smoldering cigarette tests.

"The second crib system tested consisted, with the exception of metal supports and a cotton sheet, entirely of plastic materials. Specifically a polystyrene crib, a polyurethane solid core mattress, a polyurethane filled bumper pad, and an acrylic blanket.

"Application of a single lighted paper match to the acrylic blanket was again the ignition source.

"Combustion with this crib system was characterized by a rapidly spreading, almost explosive, fire, with the production of vast amounts of black, dense smoke.

"In less than *60 seconds* the entire crib system was involved in the fire, and the level of the dense smoke and gases produced was within 4 feet of the floor.

"Within *90 seconds* flames and black smoke were gushing from the windows and doors of the test room, and the fire quickly spread to all other areas of the completely unfurnished house, until the entire building was involved at about *5 minutes* into the burn.

"Highly flammable volatile gases from the burning plastic materials collected throughout the building, resulting in an explosive flashover approximately 4½ minutes after ignition.

"Supervising fire department personnel estimate that, due to the explosive intensity of the fire, the fire was out of control at about 5 minutes into the burn, and that under normal circumstances fire control personnel would not be able to respond quickly enough to a fire of this intensity with any hope of saving the structure."

We trust you are impressed now. We trust, also, that you will be interested in the comments on protective legislation which the report on this incident included:

"The polyurethane mattress in this plastic crib system passes all *existing* mattress flammability regulations. Current federal regulations eliminate mattress materials that can be ignited by a smoldering cigarette, but say nothing about mattress fires from other causes. The serious open flame problem, such as matches, lighters, and candles, accounts for approximately *one-third* of all mattress related fires, according to recent fire report data.

"At the present time there are no flammability regulations of any kind controlling furniture such as the polystyrene crib.

"In recent years plastic furniture has made great advancements. Polystyrene, and other rigid polymeric materials can now be made into furniture that is virtually indistinguishable from wood.

"Industry growth projections indicate that plastics will account for 50 percent of the furniture market by 1980.

"Plastics are also beginning to be used in place of metal exteriors for major home appliances such as washing machines.

"This sort of growth means that we are going to be dealing on a large scale with materials we have little experience with in terms of fire.

"Tests conducted by the Department of Engineering, University of California, Berkeley, show that plastic furniture such [as] baby cribs and chairs burn twice as fast as their wood counterparts.

"In addition, these tests show that you can't make a building safe enough to resist the intensity of heat produced when large pieces of non-flame retardant polystyrene and polyurethane burn."

Because of the results of tests like this, the Department of Consumer Affairs worked closely with other state officials to include upholstered furniture in California's fire laws. A law specifying that all filling materials (primarily the highly flammable untreated polyurethanes) for upholstered furniture must be flame resistant (able to pass state flame tests) was passed and would have gone into effect on April 1, 1975, but the effective date was extended to October 1, 1975, by industry request. A series of injunctions and appeals delayed implementation until March 1, 1977.

Fire Tragedy

Unfortunately, the state's filling law was not in effect in time to save the lives of six people (four of whom were children) in Glendale, California. They died of fumes and flames from a fire traced to the smoldering upholstery of a chair where the lighted end of a cigarette had been dropped much earlier in the evening and had apparently been extinguished. The fire chief interviewed at the scene wondered why the chair had not been put outside.

Similar stories of death and/or destruction of property due to fire are repeatedly heard throughout the United States and the rest of the world more often than we would like to think about.

In August 1970 the main source of fuel and the reason for the rapid spread of a two-million-dollar fire in a gallery of the BOAC passenger terminal at New York's Kennedy International Airport was the polyester and latex foam seat cushions on closely arranged rows of chairs; the PVC covering did not contribute to the speed of the fire but since only light fabric protected the chairs from underneath, flames easily reached the more readily combustible fillings.

After-the-fact tests showed that the foam padding burned strongly once ignited; decomposition of the foam began at a low temperature of less than 150 degrees Centigrade. In the actual fire, gases were released and ignited, and the fire traveled down the 330-foot-long gallery at such speed that people at the opposite end of the building from the fire ran to escape the rapidly advancing flames. Resultant property damage gave the impression that a gas jet had been fiercely burning at ceiling level. It is interesting to note, however, that the 80 percent wool, 20 percent nylon carpeting merely charred, leaving the felt padding intact, even though there was heavy damage to walls, concrete columns, metal items, and floor tiles.

Smoke detectors shut down the mechanical ventilator, but the glazing in the external walls failed, allowing air to flow freely to feed the fire and causing a flashover down the length of the gallery. There were no sprinklers in the passenger area, which was about to be but fortunately had not yet been opened to the public.

This absence of sprinklers in public buildings is the subject of an article in the May 1975 issue of *Consumer Research* magazine. According to the National Fire Protection Association, on the same day in three separate cities (Chicago; Peoria, Illinois; New York City) there were fires in high-rise buildings without sprinkler systems. With human safety as a prime consideration, the NFPA is urging design that would give sprinklers priority over the installation of carpeting when drafting plans for buildings where funds are limited. Although such systems are often considered a luxury, the association points out, their cost is comparable to carpeting, which is seldom placed in that category. We hasten to add that, in our opinion, it is not an either/or decision and that care should be taken in budgeting to allow for both safety devices and fire-retarding interiors.

A more tragic illustration of the dangers of flammable furnishings than was evidenced in the BOAC terminal fire and one that points up the combined need for care in safety regulations and furnishing selection occurred in St. Laurent du Pont, France, later the same year,when 145 young people died.

During the conversion to a nightclub of a single-story stone building with an asbestos cement roof, the owners sprayed the ceiling, walls, partitions, and decorations with a material incorporating foamed polyurethane. Chair cushions were of plastic foam. The fire started in a chair and within two minutes the plastic-lined walls and ceiling were in flames and burning drops of plastic material began to shower down upon the occupants. According to persons outside the building, after five minutes all cries for help from within ceased.

Although blocked and hidden exits were the main cause of the high loss of life, the primary contributing factor to the rapidity and intensity of the fire was the highly combustible plastic furniture and interior.

Incidents such as these demonstrate that it would be a good idea to remove all potential fire hazards from our homes and public buildings; unfortunately in some instances that would probably mean stripping them clean. According to Howard Winslow, chief of the California Bureau of Home Furnishings, anything will burn if a fire becomes hot enough; the bureau is working to prevent fires from starting and to control rapid spread when fires do occur. Most experts agree that achieving this goal means either eliminating the most flammable and toxic materials from our homes or treating them and the less flammable ones so they will resist bursting into flames. It also means designing buildings with the problems of flammability in mind.

The State of California Fire Marshal's Office points out in a bulletin, "Some Practical Aspects of Flameproofing," that flameproofing does not prevent all damage from fire but does slow the spread of fire.

"Many persons have flameproofed rugs with the thought that this would prevent scorch marks from burning cigarettes. As a matter of fact, flameproofing makes rugs more susceptible to scorching than they are normally. This is explained by the fact that one of the primary mechanisms by which flame retardant chemicals function is to cause treated materials to char at lower temperatures so that less flammable components are produced. For this same reason, flameproofing furniture upholstery or mattress ticking will not prevent cigarettes from burning through and eventually igniting the untreated padding material below.

"Flameproofing does not constitute proofing against fire damage of the treated article. Involvement in larger fires of other origin may result in destruction of the treated material and contribution of considerable fuel. As presently developed, flameproofing properly applied will prevent many fires from spreading. Properly treated materials will not flame or support combustion when exposed to small flame sources such as burning cigarettes, candles or waste baskets. This then is the principal value of flameproofing."

Industry Responsibility

Considering the undeniably frightening facts of the rising destruction from fires in our homes and buildings and knowing solutions are or can be available, one would think that all concerned would be making an urgent cooperative effort to reverse this trend, including fire marshals, chemical companies, insurance companies, government agencies, consumer groups, and the furniture industry itself.

Unfortunately, no sooner had the California upholstery filling flammability law become effective than it was challenged by no less than sixty-two furniture manufacturers and eight industry organizations, who filed for an injunction to stop the enforcement of the law. A temporary restraining order was granted, delaying enforcement of the law pending a determination of its legality. Subsequent to language clarification made possible by the Consumer Product Safety Commission Improvement Act of early 1976, the federal district courts determined that the California law was not in conflict with any federal legislation. After the last appeal by the industry group was denied in January 1977, the law finally went into effect the following March 1, nearly two years after it was originally intended to become effective.

When the California law was first passed and before the legal confusion had been resolved, a great hue and cry was heard in the marketplace amid unfounded rumors and misleading information about prices, the fairness of the legislation, and its practicality.

Tragically, designers wrote articles for prestigious publications using erroneous or outdated information to support their position against flammability controls. Many manufacturers made across-the-board price hikes on upholstered goods to cover what is only a small portion of the total expense of soft goods production—the reported 20 percent increase in the cost of fillings—and blamed the new price tagging on the California legislation. Complaints were widespread about having to handle two inventories, one for California and one for the unprotected portions of the country.

There were additional complaints about the high cost of testing imposed by the California standards. This did initially require that a piece of every item in a line be made and sent to the Bureau of Home Furnishings for testing. While this placed a one-time burden on the manufacturer to supply a full range of sample merchandise, the bureau felt that simulation tests could not compare with tests performed on the actual product.

After the initial furor had subsided somewhat, it became apparent that some well-known manufacturers were already conforming to the yet-to-be-enforced law, having discovered that bringing all products up to California standards did not represent any great burden on their profits. We hope that others in the industry will follow these heralds, and that manufacturers whose past accomplishments have included development of a vast array of fine products marketable at affordable prices and pocketable profits will apply their remarkable business acumen and research methods to seek the correct information and to provide a speedy and economically feasible compliance with the law, which was designed not to rob anyone of profit but to save human life.

Possible Solutions

To understand how complex this problem is, one of the first truths with which we must deal is that, except for glass and modacrylics which are inherently flameproof, most fibers will burn, some faster than others. There are several ways to develop flame-resistant fabrics. The fibers can be blended with inherently flameproof ones, the fabrics can be treated with flame retardants, or, best of all, the chemical companies can set their creative genius to the development of flame resistance in the test tube, formulating a synthetic that could from a liquid state be extruded into an acceptable fiber.

Pay little attention to the argument that industry-applied flame treatments wear off in six months, requiring either costly replacement of the item or re-treatment. This, in fact, has not been the case for some time. Treatments now being used have been tested by the California Bureau of Home Furnishings with the aid of an artificial aging process and have been found to have a life expectancy of fifteen years.

True it is that some fibers cannot be flame treated without developing defects, but we see no reason to push the panic button because of this one problem. An article in the *Christian Science Monitor* of July 29, 1975, espouses a negativism we feel is misleading. Not the least of the Doomsday messages contained in the article was the concern that olefin, among other fibers, will be snatched away from the hands of the eager consumer because it cannot at this point be satisfactorily flame treated. But the fact is that olefin's low melting point makes it dangerous. The consumer is being asked not to deal with an inconvenience like the fact that it is difficult to clean once soiled, but to risk danger. We feel consumers should have the opportunity to judge whether olefin's low cost and long wear offset its flammability.

We have heard "new and improved" often enough to have great faith that industry will be able to provide workable answers to these problems, once it settles down to the scientific approach that has helped it protect astronauts from the scorching temperatures of reentry into the earth's atmosphere, to measure and analyze agricultural soil or prospect for oil and minerals from a satellite 570 miles up, or to produce living organisms in a test tube. Until the answer is found, man is more protected on his flights to the moon than he is falling asleep in front of the TV set in his own living room.

We emphasize our point with a series of quotes from *America Burning*, the 1973 report of the National Commission on Fire Prevention and Control:

"During the next hour there is a statistical likelihood that more than 300 destructive fires will rage somewhere in this Nation. When they are extinguished, more than $300,000 worth of property will have been ruined. At least one person will have died. Thirty-four will be injured, some of them crippled or disfigured for life.

"Annually, fire claims nearly 12,000 lives in the United States. Among causes of accidental death, only motor vehicle accidents and falls rank higher. Most of fire's victims die by inhaling smoke or toxic gases well before the flames have reached them.

"The scars and terrifying memories live on with the 300,000 Americans who are injured by fire every year. Of these, nearly 50,000 lie in hospitals for a period ranging from 6 weeks to 2 years. Many of them must return, over and over again, for plastic and reconstructive surgery. Many never resume normal lives.

"The price of destructive fire in the United States amounts, by conservative estimate to at least $11.4 billion a year. . . . Beyond calculation are the losses from businesses that must close and from jobs that are interrupted or destroyed. . . .

"Appallingly, the richest and most technologically advanced nation in the world leads all the major industrialized countries in per capita deaths and property loss from fire. . . . [T]he United States reports a deaths-per-million-population rate nearly twice that of second-ranking Canada (57.1 versus 29.7). . . .

"Americans live side by side, day and night, with ignitable materials, combustible furniture and upholstery, and products and appliances which through wear and misuse may offer dangerous fire potential. . . .

"Building codes do not cover interior furnishings. . . . Moreover, seldom do fire prevention codes apply to private dwellings. . . .

"While furnishings are likely to remain outside of code provisions, the fact that they contribute significantly to combustion hazards means that building codes only partly satisfy the demands of fire safety. . . .

"Except for flammable liquids and the materials that are used in appliances and wiring, few of the materials that go into the home carry labels vouchsafing their fire resistance or warning of their hazards. The unlabeled hazards are found in draperies, rugs, storage cabinets, upholstered chairs, and other furniture. . . .

"Most discussions about fire research focus on particular research problems, rather than on larger questions of what the research can accomplish. . . .

"One need only consider the chief causes of fire losses—carelessness and shortcomings of design—to realize that losses could be significantly reduced through research. . . .

"As important as Federal research is for combating the Nation's fire problems, the responsibility is not solely the Government's.

"Social and legal responsibilities are borne by the private sector as well. . . . [T]he manufacturers of materials that go into the built environment are not responsible for the careless actions that lead to fire accidents. But what happens to those materials as a fire progresses can make the difference between a small loss and a huge one, indeed between life and death. To that extent do manufacturers share in the obligation to make the built environment fire-safe.

"The Government can require that manufacturers make materials fire-safe, as it has done with certain fabrics and as we have recommended that the Consumer Product Safety Commission do for a whole range of materials and products. But industry should accept its responsibilities in the absence of coercion. . . . The task to educate and sensitize Americans to the problems of fire safety, both by government and by private groups, must begin now."

Fire Causes, Hazards

Over and over again, the suggestion has been made that smokers represent the greatest hazard in home fires. "No smoking" is not the easy answer to the problem, for, as we discussed in chapter 7, clearly one-third of mattress fires *alone* are caused by open fires, such as matches and candles. Detailed reports are beginning to be developed which will show what a small portion of home fires even occur in the bedroom. California and Oregon are making annual surveys breaking down rooms of origin, initial ignition sources, and initial material igniting in home fires in each state. In 1974 the Oregon state fire marshal indicated that in 5,477 single-family, apartment, and duplex dwelling fires, only 15 percent were caused by a group that included careless smokers along with candles and matches. Smokers, then, dangerous though they may be, constitute only one of the hazards to home fire safety.

And while *how* the fire starts is important, *what* happens when it has gotten underway is even more important. It is a well-known fact among fire experts that smoke and its toxicity are greater killers than fire itself. Here, again, much misinformation and many misquotes have been seen in print. Claims have been made that the new flammability law is particularly bad because treated filling materials give off smoke that is more toxic than untreated ones.

This is not always true. Although some chemical compounds added to reduce combustibility produce halogens (bromine, chlorine, and fluorine) which are corrosive and toxic, there are many chemicals on the market that produce less toxic smoke than that from untreated material.

In fact, the results of tests conducted in 1975 at the Fire Safety Center Institute of Chemical Biology at the University of San Francisco under a federal grant and presented at a conference on fire safety in early 1976 verify the validity of the new law's flammability standards. In general terms, of several groups of mice used, those exposed to smoke from untreated polyurethane foam and fabrics all died, while those exposed to smoke from treated materials survived as living proof of the importance of flame treatment as a means of *reducing* toxicity.

Results from another group of tests conducted at Harvard University in midsummer of 1975 were reported in the *Christian Science Monitor* under the heading "Fire Testing Reinforces Battle for Home Safety," on August 1, 1975 (only three days after author Jan Brown presented the furniture industry's side of the argument in a bylined article, "Furniture Flammability Debated"). For the Harvard test an inexpensive bedroom set from Sears, Roebuck, gypsum board walls, nylon carpeting, and an untreated polyurethane mattress were set up in a room within a large brick building and, "using an electric igniter to simulate a cigarette," the experimenters started a fire on the mattress. "In a brief 6 minutes, 10 seconds," according to the article, "flames came roaring out the door" with such intensity that scientists, observers from industry, and reporters were driven back by the heat.

This test was the third in a series being conducted annually by Harvard and the Factory Mutual System (FM), a group of four insurance companies which have in the past done research on industrial fire safety and are now applying their experience to home fire problems. The tests are being carried out under a grant from the National Science Foundation.

Consumer Help-Lines

As you can see, it is not paranoid to ask manufacturers to pretest materials and chemicals before marketing them, it is not unreasonable to ask for detailed labels for content, care, and flammability or to expect the merchandise to perform safely, whether or not it is so advertised.

According to the Federal Consumer Product Safety Commission, twenty million consumers are injured in and around the home yearly with thirty thousand resulting deaths. This commission is spending *your* taxes to test materials that could be harmful to the consumer and that *should* have been pretested before they reached the market. As with the case of the carpet company and its flammable merchandise mentioned at the beginning of the chapter, the commission deals more than fairly with business. We feel that a healthy fine to cover the cost of having to test their materials (if the merchandise proves faulty) is in order in addition to banning the sale of the product.

The commission, which is receptive to public complaints, publishes a booklet listing all banned products, and you can get some idea of the problem we face when you see that it is 8 by 10 inches in size and has 101 pages of very small print. Each of these products had to be discovered (by someone who possibly was injured by it), reported, tested, and banned through legal process. Do we have that kind of time and money?

Until that question is answered by some other system (ideally from within the industry and not by government), if you have a complaint, send a letter (it does not have to sound "legal") to the U.S. Consumer Product Safety Commission, or call one of their toll-free numbers (see Resources).

There are other sources of information and places to write for help. The Southern Furniture Manufacturers have sponsored the formation of a group called FICAP (Furniture Industry Consumer Advisory Panel), which hears and processes consumer complaints in the home-furnishings field.

We point out that the SFMA was one of the industry groups which filed suit against the California upholstered filling flammability law. Others who joined in the suit were the Southwestern Furniture Manufacturers Association, the National Association of Furniture Manufacturers, the Upholstery Furniture Action Council, the California Furniture Manufacturers Association, the Retail Association of California, Furniture Manufacturers of Grand Rapids, and the Furniture Retail Association of California.

FICAP, however, assures us that it maintains a neutral position, and since it is, except for the individual manufacturer, one of the few ways the consumer has to communicate with the industry, we urge you to give the panel an opportunity to fulfill its stated purpose. Write to them, be brief, to the point, and include copies of contracts and/or other pertinent information they may need to understand your problem. See Resources for the address.

The carpet industry also had an agency of last resort after complaints had been unsuccessfully handled by the dealer and the manufacturer; the Carpet and Rug Industry Consumer Action Panel (CRICAP), an offshoot of the Carpet and Rug Institute in Dalton, Georgia, was unfortunately disbanded in 1975. Maridel Lessenger Kumbler, a former member of the panel, is working to reinstate CRICAP or find an alternative method of resolving the problems between the industry and the consumer. (See Resources for where to write Ms. Kumbler.)

Some initial efforts besides the Consumer Action Panels have been made.

SFMA, along with the National Association of Furniture Manufacturers (NAFM) and the National Retail Furniture Association (NRFA), published a report entitled "Specifications, Standards and Test Procedures for Upholstered Furniture Fabrics" in April 1969. This report, in a revised edition issued in December 1974, updated the group's information to include standards for cleanability, shrinkability, and colorfastness. While these tests and standards represent a positive step by the industry toward good labeling procedures, some chemists feel that more thorough testing over a longer period will be necessary to establish a completely accurate set of standards.

Warranties, Guarantees

Although there is a scholarly difference in the meanings of *guarantee* and *warranty*, in recent legislation *warranty* has come to be the general term covering returns, refunds, repairs, or replacements. The law applies to both written and implied warranties, but rather than rely on the hard-to-establish "implied" warranty, do as we have said many times before: get it in writing.

If there is a written warranty, the Federal Consumer Product Warranty Act specifies that the responsibility of the manufacturer must be printed in clear, nontechnical language on a well-displayed tag. On products costing ten dollars or more, the warranty must state whether it is limited or full. If it is a full warranty, it will cover all charges. If the repairs are not satisfactory, you are entitled to a replacement or refund. On products sold for five dollars or more, a limited warranty must spell out the exact length and extent of the coverage. The address of the warrantor and how to file a claim should also appear on the tag.

To report violations or for more details, contact the Bureau of Consumer Affairs, Federal Trade Commission, Washington, D.C. 20580. Failing satisfaction from one of the bureau's arbitration panels, the consumer's remaining recourse is to file an individual or class-action suit.

Your real guarantee of a good product is to shop knowledgeably. Consumer complaint research is revealing that a large portion of complaints result from misleading or vague information at the time of sale. Read labels and ask questions.

Simmons Promise

On the positive side Simmons has a long record of standing behind their products. This company has had a generous warranty for many years, and its current one, backed up by sixty-seven centers nationwide, not only complies with California legislation (the most stringent because of the Song-Beverly law and its revisions) but is good throughout the United States.

For its 1976 line, Simmons, a well-respected and long-established company, has set forth a durability code, based, according to the "Simmons Promise" affixed to each Hide-A-Bed, on tests administered by the previously mentioned organizations and expanded from the 1974 list to include breaking and tearing; resistance to yarn slippage; resistance to changes in appearance, hand, and character; fabric shrinkage; crocking and staining; and colorfastness to light, water, and gas fumes. A cleaning code, which specifies whether a fabric can be cleaned with water only, solvent only, with both, or not at all, is included with the promise.

We commend this well-presented initial attempt at fabric coding, but it needs much more attention to clear up some of its ambiguities. On the cleaning code alone, several questions remained unanswered when we approached department store salespersons. If, for example, the cleaning code is "S" ("Clean this fabric with pure solvents"), what does one do about the appended warning: "[Use] only suds of foam. Most upholstery fabrics must have some type of backing; cleaning fluids have a tendency to destroy the backing, causing the yarns to shrink when wet." Certainly the easiest of the cleanability codes to understand (and probably the most honest) is the "X"-rated one which allows only for cleaning by "vacuuming or light brushing to prevent accumulation of dust or grime."

More important considerations for the consumer than the "how" of cleaning are the fabric's resistance to soil in the first place and its ability to be restored to its original condition by cleaning, whatever the method. Therefore, it does little good to know that white Haitian or Indian cotton is "W" (to be washed with water-based foams or cleaning agents) without considering how fast it attracts soil and whether or not that soil can be removed by that method or any other.

Additional questions arise about the testing methods used to establish the four durability categories: heavy duty (hhh), medium duty (mmm), light duty (lll), and delicate (ddd). For example, fabrics with the heavy-duty rating are "suitable for an active family with children," but some of the lightweight 100 percent cottons labeled under this category were certainly not meant to withstand the same treatment as the vinyls with which they shared an "hhh" label. The established categories, based upon the criteria set by the SFMA, the NAFM, and the NRFA mentioned earlier, do not emphasize the fact that durability and soil resistance/cleanability are inseparable parts of the whole. What we need is a clearer definition of durability or, as customers, a better understanding of the limitations of such arbitrary labeling, however well meaning.

Since Simmons has worked hard to present a breakthrough in industry coding of upholstery fabrics, you as a consumer must encourage further improvement by carefully reading the labels, by intelligent questioning, and by realistic awareness of what your chosen fabric can and cannot do (see chapter 1).

Kroehler, Monsanto, and Others

Two other bright spots in the home-furnishings industry are the Kroehler Quality Commitment and the Monsanto "Wear-Dated" label. The Kroehler warranty is for five years on all parts and for one year on mattresses and fabric, applied to all of the Kroehler products when they are sold new. This includes the cost of getting the defective merchandise from your dealer to the Kroehler factory. There are a few very fair stipulations to this warranty, so contact your Kroehler dealer to see if your Kroehler furniture is covered (see Resources).

The Monsanto "Wear-Dated" label is a guarantee of from one to five years on their fabrics and other items. If a product does not wear as it should when used properly, Monsanto will return your money. In Monsanto's testing laboratories every manufacturer's merchandise must comply with certain standards before Monsanto will put its "Wear-Dated" label on a product. Started in 1962, this guarantee system has been used extensively in the clothing business and can now be found on many items in the home-furnishings field. We found no mention of who picks up the tab for freight to the factory, so check that before you ship your sofa to Monsanto even if you have cause to do so. Your dealer should willingly work with you on any problems as this label and its guarantee have real meaning.

There are also some smaller companies offering excellent warranties and guarantees. For example, Tomlinson, manufacturers of custom furniture since 1900, has in the past backed up the quality of its furniture with a willingness to repair defects long after any reasonable warranty would have expired. Many family-owned makers of furniture have built their reputations on such responsibility to their customers, and some open their factories periodically in order to share with the public the intricacies and professional quality of their workmanship. Check with your manufacturer's public relations department to see what services are offered.

Consumer Options and Resources

Consumers have a right to protection from highly flammable, dangerous, or defective materials and from the manufacturers who make them and the dealers who sell them. Steps are being taken to curb those offenders.

Ultimately, the answer lies with the consumer's desire for true change. We must be constantly alert and open-minded at the same time, for witch hunting will only push consumers and industry farther apart. Valid complaints backed up with records and perseverance should get the attention of businessmen of integrity, and eventually the unscrupulous people in business will have to comply or get out. Admittedly, reassessing products, retooling, and so on, cost time and money and there will be some valid expense involved while removing these safety threats from our homes. On the other hand, we have pointed out several manufacturers who are making and keeping their pledge of integrity to the consumer and they have not priced themselves out of the competitive marketplace.

Consumers must work continually together. Grassroots groups, such as the Virginia Citizens Consumer Council, Inc. (VCCC), have achieved special legislation through their lobbying efforts in Washington. The Oregon Consumer League has also been active in the field of legislation. For the address of a group in your area, write the U.S. Department of Health, Education and Welfare, Office of Consumer Affairs (see Resources).

Attend seminars and read materials supplied by your consumer groups. Find your own sources of information by consulting various consumer bibliographies listed in Resources or write letters to make your concerns known with the aid of two "Consumer's Complaint Directory" publications, one by Macmillan and one from *Everyman's Money* (again, see Resources). Look at the end of this chapter for information on ordering *Buy It Right*, a small paperback providing consumer tips on furniture buying, but keep in mind that its author, Jan Brown, brings a strong bias toward industry to her suggestions, carefully avoiding negative features of home-furnishing products. She is the same Jan Brown who offered without question the furniture manufacturers' view of flammability legislation in the July 29, 1975, *Christian Science Monitor* article, mentioned earlier in this chapter.

If your state does not have adequate fire protection laws, and if you or your consumer group is interested in obtaining copies of California's fire laws for bedding and upholstered furniture, consult the Resources section for the address of the Bureau of Home Furnishings. You will also be able to obtain an excellent booklet listing all of the flame-retardant fabrics, materials, and chemicals approved by the California State Fire Marshal's Office or a series of pamphlets on fire protection in your home from the National Fire Protection Association. Absolutely required reading is the aforementioned paperback, *America Burning*, the lengthy report made in 1973 by the National Commission on Fire Prevention and Control after a two-year study on possible measures to reduce fire, many of the recommendations so highly controversial that a minority report was of necessity appended. We, however, support much of what the majority of the commission has to say about the responsibility of consumer and industry alike.

Change is going to be necessary, and both the consumer and the producer will need to participate in that change. As the world grows smaller and buildings taller, what happens to our neighbor happens to us. When an entire floor of a high-rise building in New York City can be gutted from a fire that started in a baby bed or an entire block of apartments can become involved in flame from a building under construction in Santa Monica, California, we have no choice but to become our brothers' keepers.

Resources

Books and Reference Works

Darden, Lloyd. *The Earth in the Looking Glass.* Garden City, N.Y.: Anchor Press/Doubleday, 1974.

Rosenbloom, Joseph. *Consumer Complaint Guide 1975.* New York: Macmillan Information (a division of Macmillan), 1975.

Consumer Education Bibliography. Prepared by the Office of Consumer Affairs, Department of Health, Education and Welfare, Washington, D.C. 20201. $1.60.

Consumer Information. A quarterly catalog of selected federal publications of consumer interest. Free upon request from the Consumer Information Center, Pueblo, Colo. 81009.

Directory, Federal, State, County and City Government Consumer Offices. Department of Health, Education and Welfare Publication No. 76–104, prepared by the Office of Consumer Affairs, Department of Health, Education and Welfare, Washington, D.C. 20201. $.90.

Magazines and Newspapers

Christian Science Monitor, October 8, 1974; January 8, 1975; July 29, 1975; and August 1, 1975.

Consumer News. Twice-monthly newsletter on federal consumer actions, etc. Annual subscription $4.00. Available from Consumer Information Center, Pueblo, Colo. 81009.

Consumer Research, published monthly by Consumer Research, Inc., Washington, N.J. 07882. See especially the article "Fires in High Rise Buildings," May 1975, p. 6; and "Get the Answers Before Buying a Carpet," April 1976, p. 12, and Maridel Lessenger Kumbler's address taken from that article (Carpets and Rugs, Box 1381, Marshalltown, Iowa 50158).

Everybody's Money. Autumn 1974 issue—reprints from selected articles.

House Beautiful, August 1974.

Los Angeles Times. June 26, 1974; July 1, 1974; July 26, 1974; October 25, 1974; November 3, 1974; and February 18, 1975.

Santa Monica Evening Outlook, March 12, 1974; June 26, 1974; and November 11, 1974.

Organizations

Bureau of Consumer Affairs, Box 310, Sacramento, Calif. 95802. Articles and booklets.

Consumer Federation of America, 1012 14th Street N.W., Washington, D.C. 20005.

Consumer Product Safety Commission. Address complaints or requests for booklets such as "Banned Products" to William White, Bureau of Information and Education, CPSC, 5401 Westbard Avenue, Bethesda, Md. 20207. Toll-free numbers for complaints: 800-638-2666 or (in Maryland only) 800-492-2937.

Department of Consumer Affairs, Bureau of Home Furnishings, State of California, 3401 La Grande Blvd., Sacramento, Calif. 95823. Howard Winslow, Chief. Test and result reports; script of movie *Unfurnishing Your Home.*

Department of Justice, State of California, 217 West First Street, Los Angeles, Calif. 90012. "On Guard."

EM, P.O. Box 431, Madison, Wis. 53701. "Consumer Complaint Directory" and "Bibliography for Consumers." $1.00 each.

Experimental Building Station, Department of Housing and Construction, P.O. Box 30, Chatswood N.S.W. 2067, Australia. Notes on the Science of Building, "Fire Hazards of Furniture and Furnishings."

FICAP (Furniture Industry Consumer Advisory Panel), P.O. Box 951, High Point, N.C. 27261.

Fire Marshal's Office, State of California. "Flame Retardant Fabrics, Materials and Applications."

International Conference on Fire Safety at the University of San Francisco, San Francisco, Calif., January 12–16, 1976. Manuscript presented by Carlos J. Hilado.

Kroehler, Consumer Education Division, 222 East Fifth Avenue, Naperville, Ill. 60540. Booklets.

Monsanto Textiles Company, 1114 Avenue of the Americas, New York, N.Y. 10036. Booklets.

National Commission on Fire Prevention and Control, 1730 K Street N.W., Washington, D.C. 20006. *America Burning.* $3.10.

National Fire Prevention Association, 60 Batterymarch Street, Boston, Mass. 02110. Booklets.

State of Illinois, Attorney General's Office. Booklets.

Simmons Company, 280 Park Avenue, New York, N.Y. 10017. The Simmons Promise label.

Tomlinson Furniture, 305 High Avenue West, High Point, N.C. 27261.

13

Putting It
All Together

THE whole point of this book is to establish a look-before-you-leap approach to selecting home furnishings, and so this final chapter is of great importance. We urge you to make plans and follow them. We encourage you to sit down with the persons who share your living quarters, from breadwinner(s) through the smallest Little Leaguer and friend Airedale in order to determine each life-style and its furnishing needs. (A fringe benefit of polling the whole team is that that Little Leaguer will someday be a better consumer in his or her own right by understanding now the planning necessary to good buying.)

Having established family needs, take one room at a time and analyze its anticipated uses and how, through wise furnishing, to expand those uses to get ultimate function from the space. The key to good planning is measuring: the areas to be filled, the people who use them, and then the furniture being considered.

Become familiar with certain "living measurements" that were originally for the use of professionals only. These are based on a statement by Pythagoras which translates "Man is the measure of all things" and which Euclid restated in a mathematical formula that was later used by Leonardo da Vinci to illustrate his concepts of human proportion.

You do not have to go into higher mathematics to understand that there are on the market many uneasy chairs, tables that do not function, and light fixtures that provide no useful light. Quite often man has been forgotten in the design of items for his world. Sometimes designers appear to be designing for design's sake alone without regard for comfort, care, or cost to the consumer. The only way for the consumer to get the attention of the manu-facturers of home furnishings is to know what he or she needs and to refuse to buy anything less.

We would like to recommend a delightful and very informative book, used by designers since its first publication in 1948; *Anatomy for Interior Designers*, by Julius Panero, makes what can be a dull but necessary subject light and easy reading. Another book that contains valuable data about spatial requirements is *Nomadic Furniture* by James Hennessey and Victor Papanek. Papanek has been a leader in teaching young designers the idea of fitting designs to people instead of people to designs and in this book translates that research of human measurement (both here and in other parts of the world) into furnishings that give both comfort and mobility to a world of modern nomads.

We also advocate long-term planning for furniture needs. Take each room of the house or apartment and plan the furniture needed even if it cannot all be purchased at once. In this way you can get a complete view of your future spending requirements and will be saved from buying a sofa that doesn't quite fit or doesn't look right or doesn't wear well in that setting or, equally bad, a breakfront when the sofa had greater priority. This also enables you to take advantage of sales with full knowledge of what you need and want (since you do not have the privilege of returning sale items). These room-planning lists, put into a notebook along with other furnishing information in pocketed folders, might look something like this:

FAMILY ROOM

Item needed	Size requirements	Finish or color	Fabric (wear required)	General color	Cost estimate

To facilitate this kind of planning, measure with a metal tape or folding ruler the room where you intend to place or replace furniture. (This plan-ning is good for moving day, too; the movers will bless you for knowing where each piece is supposed to go.)

If you have a blueprint, double-check the measurements, since few build-ings follow the original plans exactly. (More than one apartment dweller has been stuck with a refrigerator that simply did not fit the space for which it was ordered, based on measurements from the rental brochure.)

Draw the projected room layout on graph paper (¼ inch to 1 foot is a good scale, used by a majority of professional designers) to your exact room measurements. Then mark in doors, windows, and electrical outlets. (You can do this any way that you will clearly understand, but there are standard symbols used by the building trade and interior designers. You can pick these up quickly by checking out a book on home building from the library.)

Measure your existing furniture and any pieces you are considering buying. You can invest in a designer's set of templates, but there is no one simple template that covers all furniture sizes and shapes. We suggest you draw the sizes on heavy paper or lightweight cardboard and cut them out. There are a number of furniture "decorating" kits on the market; however, no one or even a combination will provide all the sizes and shapes you need. Besides, they're expensive. Your homemade cutouts will do the job nicely unless you have to turn this in as a term project in your Home Decorating for the Homemaker class.

Move the cutouts about on the graph paper to get a feel for their placement before drawing them into the plan. Remember to leave room to pull out drawers without being pinned against the opposite wall (about 36 inches) and for doors to be opened and shut (an arc the exact width of the door). Place lights near plugs or where the cord can be run along the wall to a plug (never across a room to be tripped over or under a rug to provide a fire hazard).

When measuring rooms, the height is important for certain calculations, such as wallpaper and draperies. The furniture measurements should include not only the length and width (depth) but the height as well; chairs and sofas should include the height at the back and at the arm. Height is important in buying or placing tables near sofas and chairs, in matching dining tables or desks to seating, in providing functional lighting.

Develop traffic patterns—the way people move in and through a room. If, after placement, you discover that you have guessed wrong, rearrange the furniture to "give in" to the natural flow of a room and its inhabitants.

Create "working" groups of furniture—conversation areas, study areas, work areas. A good example of the importance of space planning can be seen in the food serving areas of a home. Since eating is both a necessity and a social experience, a great deal of time is spent in thinking about, preparing, and enjoying our daily meals. As much time and effort should be put into the selection of furniture and materials used in the dining area.

Human proportion space planners say a dining table should allow each person—adult and child (they do grow up rapidly)—at least 24 inches of elbow room and 32 inches from the edge of the table to push back one's chair and rise with something approaching grace and dignity. Even serving requires special consideration: to edge past persons seated at a table one must allow a minimum of 36 to 44 inches between the table and a wall or door. And the host needs at least an additional 19 inches to serve from the head of the table to the first guest on either side.

Even though the items needed to finish a meal from "outside to in" take up a space of 24 by 15 inches, the place mats available generally all measure 18 inches wide. We do not know why this perversity exists but our guess is that it has something to do with getting the most out of a certain width of material. It is good for production costs but hard on the consumer.

Measure halls and entries for moving purposes. We know a person in the home-furnishings field whose wife is considering chopping up a perfectly good, hardly worn, solid, curved sofa which measures 15 feet from arm to arm because it cannot be moved from the apartment (it was moved in before the building was closed up). In order to change her decor she will probably have the options of taking a course in upholstering or having an upholsterer take up residence for a while.

Avoiding gross errors in judgment takes a little planning—or a lot, depending upon the problem involved. All problems, however, lend themselves to systematic analysis and solution. We see no reason why the strategy that has been used by engineers to build the Minuteman missile, by business executives to run large corporate bodies, or by career counselors to establish job objectives cannot also be applied to choices in wallpaper, carpeting, or upholstered furniture. System Engineer Methodology (SEM), management flow chart, career decision strategy, or whatever it may be called, the procedure is basically the same and the essential elements are:

1. Identify and state your objective.
2. Identify the means (the method), gather data, establish the alternatives.
3. Develop special requirements, logistics of project.
4. Implement program, undertake constructive action.
5. Operate, function at objective level.
6. Develop "direct access change loop," design "feedback linkage system."

The clue to success in this methodology is step 6, which in reality is an integral part of each of the other steps in the program. By being prepared at any stage of decision making to accept the fact that what you have done up to that point in planning is not going to continue to work, you have faced a reality that will save you time, money, and/or energy, not to mention an ineffective decision.

In other words, you have established alternatives and are ready to put them into action. This can, we repeat, take place at any phase of the system. You could, for example, discover at step 1 that your objective is not what you thought it was, at step 2 that the product you want is not available on the market—or, at step 5, that the purchased item no longer meets your needs or must be replaced for some functional reason (care problems, obsolescence, deterioration). You will then return to the step/phase which will make possible the choice of an alternative. The better you have prepared yourself during your initial use of the system, the less distance you will have to go back to "plug in" to the decision-making project required for your new choice. Additionally, step 6 should be so designed that all other phases (steps) have been kept current and you have had constant feedback that has kept you aware of such changes as family needs, industry product innovation, and so on.

Here is how SEM applies to home-furnishings selection:

1. *Identifying the objective.* What do you really need or desire? (There is a difference.) What should it do? What are your priorities?
2. *Identifying the methods.* Do your homework. Read. Which material will do the job best for you? How much should you pay? What are the options, the viable alternatives?
3. *Developing the requirements.* Where do you look? Will you need expert advice or help? How long can you wait for delivery of the item? What tools will you need or persons must you contact in advance?
4. *Implementing the program.* Do your shopping. Buy. Place orders. Call workmen/installers. Arrange delivery. This becomes the most critical step and the one that most often requires the "direct access change loop" activation. How far *back* you have to go depends upon how thoroughly you have prepared yourself in steps 1, 2, and 3.
5. *Functioning at operational level.* Receive delivery. Oversee installation. Use the product. Enjoy.
6. *Receiving and using feedback.* This constant reevaluation of input to the system goes on at every step so that if what you have done before is not working or needs updating, you are ready to swing into action. The next time through the loop will be a lot less scary—and it may take minutes instead of days or weeks.

To wrap it all up, we would like you to close this book and begin to look at your needs in a new way, be able to define them on paper, and as a result be able to shop wisely, efficiently, and with greater confidence and ease. You do not need a degree in interior design to create a gracious home; trust your own good taste and develop it with classes and reading.

If you decide you need or would like the services of a professional decorator, do your homework first and do it well. This will enable you to ask carefully thought-out questions and communicate your needs and priorities.

Then listen carefully and be prepared to pay for the services. A true professional will respect your taste and your pocketbook. Decorating help can be found through the American Society of Interior Designers, the National Home Fashions League (NHFL) (see Resources), and/or by asking for referrals from sales people at model complexes you particularly like and by consulting friends who have tastes and budgets similar to yours and have used decorators.

The home-furnishings industry is of great importance both to our economy and as a source of personal emotional satisfaction or aggravation to its consumers. It behooves the buying public to be constructively involved in the continued simplification and upgrading of this all-important industry. The many voluntary efforts now being made by the industry to develop standards and self-regulating methods can best be encouraged by consumers who understand the options available, the manufacturing changes necessary to provide these options, and whether it is necessary or proper to pay extra for natural progressive developments in any area of the industry. Everyone, from designer through manufacturer, wholesaler, retail salesman, and delivery man to the consumer, must function together to establish an economy of time, material, and design that works to the benefit of all.

Resources

Books

Hennessey, James, and Papanek, Victor. *Nomadic Furniture*. New York: Pantheon, 1973. (Note: *Nomadic Furniture II* is now available.)

Panero, Julius. *Anatomy for Interior Designers*, 3rd ed. Illustrated by Nino Repetto. New York: Whitney Library of Design (18 East 50th Street, New York, N.Y. 10022), 1969.

Organizations

American Society of Interior Designers (formerly AID/NSID), 730 Fifth Avenue, New York, N.Y. 10019.

National Home Fashions League (NHFL), 107 World Trade Center, Dallas, Tex. 75207.

APPENDICES

GLOSSARY
FIBER TRADEMARKS

GLOSSARY

Coming to Terms with Fibers and Fabrics

Abrasion. Wearing away of the surface of a material by friction.

Abrasion resistance. Degree of resistance to surface wear by rubbing.

Absorbency. Extent to which a fiber or other product takes in and retains moisture.

Antique satin. Satin weave with a "silklike" look; comes in different weights for draperies and upholstery.

Atmospheric fading. Tendency of certain colors in acetate fabrics to change or fade due to smoke, soot, or acidic fumes in the air.

Bark cloth. Firm, plain weave with an irregular texture due to yarns of uneven widths.

Batiste. Fine, thin, plain weave made from cotton, linen, or synthetics. Dainty in appearance.

Bleeding. Excess dye tends to "bleed" or run when fabrics are washed.

Blending. The combing together of two or more fibers before the spinning process.

Bobbinet. Machine-made reproduction of bobbin lace.

Bonded fabrics. 1. Webs of fibers adhesively bonded to one another with a bonding material or by the action of thermoplastic fibers. 2. Layered fabric structure wherein a face fabric is joined with an adhesive to a backing fabric which does not significantly add to the thickness of the combined fabrics (example: tricot backing).

Bouclé. Irregular-surfaced fabric made from special twisted bouclé yarns. Takes its name from the French word for *buckle* or *ringlet*, describing the small loops on the surface of the fabric.

209

Broadcloth. Plain or twill weave, generally made from cotton and/or cotton and polyester blends.

Brocade. Fabric woven on a jacquard loom, with multicolored floral or other stylized patterns woven into a background to give a heavily embroidered, raised, or embossed look. The face is easily distinguished from the back.

Brocatelle. Fabric similar to brocade, but having multicolored designs in high relief worked in one weave and the ground in another, such as a satin figure on a plain-weave ground.

Buckram. *See* Crinoline.

Bulk yarns. Yarns that have been increased in mass, bulk, or size without increasing their weight or length.

Burlap. Loose, heavy, plain weave and coarse basketweave.

Candle. Term used in speaking of casements: the way a fabric appears when held up to the light or how the light comes through when the casement is actually hung.

Canvas. Heavy, coarse, durable cloth in a plain weave, generally of cotton, linen, or hemp.

Carding. Process of separating fibers from each other, laying them parallel in a thin web.

Casement cloth. Term for a number of curtain materials in a variety of weaves and fibers. They can be tightly woven or in very open weaves.

Cellulose. Fibrous substance found in the cell walls of plants.

Challis. Fabric made from wool, cotton, or rayon in a soft, tight, plain weave. Has give and stretchability.

Chambray. Originally a variety of plain-weave gingham with white filling threads over a colored warp.

Chenille. A yarn that has a pile protruding all around at right angles (from the French for "caterpillar"). After weaving, the fabric is cut between the bunches of warps and twisted, forming the chenille effect. Can be tight and low or "furry."

China silk. Fabric in a semisheer plain weave that is soft with a slight sheen. Has body without bulk.

Chintz. Fine printed cotton in a close, plain weave. The patterns are either floral, birds, or scenes, in bright colors. Can be finished with a sheen that is nonpermanent unless the "glaze" is baked in. "Glazed chintz" should be dry cleaned. Quilting improves the wear and accents the beauty of the design.

Colorfastness. How well a color remains in a fabric when submitted to a number of standard tests simulating conditions such as sunlight and washing which affect fading.

Combination. Individual yarns composed of one fiber combined during weaving of a fabric with yarns composed entirely of another fiber: i.e., a fabric of a rayon warp and cotton filling yarns. Plied yarn composed of two or more strands, each made of a different fiber.

Combing. Process that produces even, compact, fine, and smooth yarns by eliminating short fibers.

Corduroy. Fabric made originally from cotton, but now from certain synthetics. Has a pile weave in a raised stripelike pattern of various widths. Durable, with some high-pile soil problems.

Cotton. Fibers from the boll (seed pod) of the cotton plant. Long staple—the best quality is Sea Island; next, Egyptian Pima type. Supima, developed in the United States, is a very high-grade cotton. Medium or ordinary staple—not as fine or as soft as the long staple, but much more plentiful and less expensive. These comprise 50 percent of the cottons used. Short or very short staple— coarse and harsher, generally from India and other Asiatic countries. Used for cheap fabrics and where softness is not required.

Count (of cloth). Number of yarns or threads per square inch of fabric.

Crease retention. Ability to hold a pressed-in crease.

Cretonne. Similar to chintz but never glazed. A cotton in a compact, plain, or twill weave with a medium texture. The designs are bolder than those of chintz.

Crinoline (or buckram). Very inexpensive, tightly textured cotton cloth, heavily sized, in a plain weave. Sturdy in feel, stiff and boardy.

Crocking. Transfer of color from the surface of a fabric to another surface by rubbing. Not colorfast. Generally caused by poor dye or incorrect dye for the fabric.

Cut pile. Fabric woven with an extra set of either warp or filling threads that form a pile, which is later cut; in designs or stripes, corduroy, velvet. If the pile is not cut, it is known as looped, or uncut, pile.

Damask. Firm, lustrous fabric, similar to brocade, woven on a jacquard loom. The patterns are woven so that the designs are reversible, one side with a satin look and the other duller, but the design is not raised as in brocade.

Denier. Term taken from the name of the old French coin once used to measure silk, now the international unit of measure to establish the weight of silk and synthetic staple fibers other than glass. In this system low numbers represent the finer weight, the higher, the heavier, stronger yarns. Lightness for sleeping bags and comforters, fineness for hosiery, can be obtained with low denier; strength and durability in rope or heavy-duty fabrics such as canvas have a higher denier. Technically, denier represents the number of grams for each 9,000 meters of fabric.

Denim. Heavy, compact twill weave of cotton. From *Serge de Nîmes*, the durable cloth from Nîmes, France, used by Levi Strauss for his now famous Levis.

Dimensional stability. Tendency of a fabric or garment to retain its shape and size after being subjected to wear, washing, or dry cleaning.

Dimity. Sheer, corded cotton in a twill weave.

Drapability. Fabric's ability to fall into graceful folds when hung. Fabrics that are soft and pliable are often said to have good drapability.

Drill. Firm, heavy, very durable cotton in a twill weave.

Duck. Cotton woven in close, plain, or ribbed weaves, similar to lightweight canvas. Very durable. Some has a special finish that makes it resistant to fire, water, and mildew and so can be used for awnings.

Dyeability. Fabric's ability to take dyes easily and well.

Easy care (minimum care). Term applied to fabrics, garments, and household textile articles that can be washed satisfactorily by common home-laundering methods and used after light ironing. By "light ironing" is meant no starching, no dampening, and relatively little physical effort. Compare with Wash and wear.

Elasticity. Ability of a material to return quickly to substantially the original dimensions after being stretched.

Embossing. Process of pressing a raised design into a fabric by passing the fabric between hot engraved rollers.

Fabric. Refers (as it has developed through use) to cloth. This can be woven, knitted, felted, laced, or laminated, as in the case of some plastics.

Face. Side of a fabric that is intended to be shown and, by reason of weave or finish, presents the better appearance.

Faille. Silk or rayon fabric in a plain weave with a crosswise ribbed effect. Soft to crisp in feel. Belongs to the grosgrain family of fabrics.

Felt. Nonwoven fabric of wool, rayon, synthetic, or blends. Cannot be washed but is resistant to soil.

Felting. Undesirable condition which develops when fibers mat down under heat, abrasion, and moisture.

Fiberfill. Virgin synthetic fibers specially engineered as to fineness, cut length, and crimp for use as filling materials.

Fiber glass. Fibers of glass in a variety of weaves and weights from very sheer open weaves to heavy draperies, translucent or opaque.

Fillet. Net or lace with a simple pattern on a square mesh background.

Filling yarn. The crosswise yarn in a woven fabric (English term—weft) at right angles to the warp yarn.

Finish. Any treatment of a fabric to give a specific effect, to give luster, softness, waterproofing, etc.

Flameproof. Quality of a fabric that will not burn when exposed to open flames but could melt under intense heat.

Flame or fire resistant. Quality of a fabric that does not burn readily when subjected to the open flame test.

Flame or fire retardant. Having the property of being self-extinguishing when submitted to direct flame.

(Inherently) flame- or fireproof, -resistant, or -retardant. Having that property "built in" to the fiber, either as a natural characteristic or through the normal chemical makeup (in the case of a synthetic fiber). Needing no added chemical treatment to provide its negative response to fire.

Flashover. Point of heat at which flammable gases released in earlier stages of a fire
ignite simultaneously causing widespread fire, sometimes enveloping an entire
house at one time.

Frieze, Frizé. Heavy pile weave with loops cut and uncut to form patterns.

Generic. Applying to a general kind, class, or group, as of fiber. Not specific, not
trademarked.

Grain. Together, the warp (lengthwise) and the filling (crosswise) yarns make up the
grain of a woven fabric.

Gray goods. Fabrics that have been woven without being first solution dyed. They
must be dyed, printed, and/or finished before being sold. Some companies deal
only with gray goods, leaving the later steps to other processors.

Ground. Basic part of the fabric surrounding the design; the background.

Hand. Term used to describe a composite of textile properties such as flexibility, resiliency, softness or stiffness, texture, and warmth. The "feel" of the fabric.

Heat sensitivity. Property of a material which causes softening, shrinking, melting,
or discoloration when heat is applied.

Heat set. Use of heat on synthetic fabrics to stabilize size or shape, or to make pleats
and creases durable to repeated laundering or dry cleaning.

Homespun. Rough and irregular textured fabric woven in a loose, plain weave of irregular yarns. Very durable.

Hopsacking. Another loose, plain weave that is coarse and heavy. Inexpensive and
durable.

Indian Head. Trade name that has come into general use. Cotton in plain weaves,
compact and smooth. Vat dyed, permanent finished, colorfast, shrink resistant,
durable.

India print. Cotton cloth from India or Persia printed with intricate designs in clear
or dull colors that tend to fade.

Insulation. One of two processes applied to a fabric (usually to drapery material) to
alter its thermal properties. In one, metal coats one side of fabric to reflect heat;
for the other, a plastic foam is bonded to the fabric to trap and retain heat.

Jacquard loom. Celebrated method invented by Joseph Marie Jacquard of Lyons,
France, at the beginning of the nineteenth century. This loom revolutionized the
fabric industry because it enabled various complicated designs to be made by
machine rather than by hand. The loom is a mechanism by which large numbers
of ends may be controlled independently and complicated patterns produced.
Jacquard patterns include brocade, brocatelle, matelassé, and damask.

Lamination. Process of joining two or more layers of material together by flame
bonding, resins, or adhesives. See Bonded.

Lightfast (sunfast). Colors that will not fade with normal exposure to sunlight. No
color is entirely fast to light, but some are more resistant than others. Colorfast
dyes are also lightfast, but there are additional standards involved. See
Colorfast.

Linen. Plain, firm, smooth weave that is cool to the touch.

Lofted yarns. Yarns with increased bulk and thickness but without an increase in weight. When pressure is applied to and then removed from a lofted yarn fabric, it will spring back to its original thickness and bulk.

Loom. Machine by which thread or yarn is woven into cloth.

Macramé lace. One of the oldest types of lace, distinguished by knotting.

Marquisette. Made from many fibers, a sheer and netlike fabric that can range from soft to crisp and from fine to coarse.

Mat. Lusterless and dull surface (example: mat jersey).

Matelassé. Made on a jacquard loom; a double-woven fabric with a quilted or "pouch" effect, produced by interweaving when the pattern is being formed.

Mercerizing. Treatment applied to cotton and some rayon to add strength, luster, absorbency, and an increased affinity for dyes. (See finishes section of chapter 1.)

Mohair. Hair of the Angora goat, also a mixture of cotton and wool. Can be woven in plain, twill, or pile weaves. The hair weaves are resilient and durable; the fiber weaves are more delicate but also resilient.

Moiré. Ribbed, plain weave with a watermarked finish created by the process of calendering. This finish generally washes out. There is also "printed" moiré.

Muslin. Any of a variety of fine, durable, plain-woven cotton cloths from light to heavy weight.

Nap. Soft, downy surface of some fabrics, may come off with wear or with static electricity. Can be raised with brushing.

Needlepoint. Originally embroidery of varying fineness worked with woolen threads upon a canvas and used for upholstery. Now imitated on the jacquard loom.

Organdy. Sheer, crisp cotton in a plain, compact weave. The crispness is a finish and will wash out unless labeled as permanent.

Oxford cloth. Available in light to medium weights in plain or basketweave. Generally made of cotton or blends. Durable.

Pellon. Trade name used generically in the industry for nonwoven inner facings and inner linings.

Piece goods. Any fabric that has been made up for sale, usually used in reference to that sold by the yard in retail stores.

Pilling. Formation of pills (bunches or balls of tangled fibers) on the fabric surface, usually from abrasion.

Plush. Exaggerated form of velvet with a much higher pile.

Ply. Ply yarns are formed by twisting together two or more single strands.

Preshrunk. Term used to describe fabrics that have been subjected to the shrinking process before being put on the market. The percentage of residual shrinkage (possibility of further shrinking) must be declared.

Rayon. First man-made fiber, produced from regenerated cellulose. There are several types of rayon used today, most made by the viscose process. Other processes: High wet modulus—a rayon that shows greater dimensional stability in washing than viscose rayon. Cuprammonium rayon—a very fine filament rayon used for curtains. Saponified rayon—an exceptionally high tenacity rayon. Long wearing, stable, and fine, used widely for home furnishings.

Repeat. An entire pattern for design or texture that is repeated periodically; length and size can vary greatly.

Resiliency. Property of fibers or fabrics that causes them to spring back when crushed or wrinkled.

Sateen. Finely woven cotton in a satin weave. Its shiny finish is often from mercerization. It is inexpensive and durable.

Satin. Woven in a satin weave. Smooth and flat, with a glossy finish.

Seconds. Classification for usable imperfect goods.

Sheeting. Made of cotton or blends in a smooth, plain weave.

Shuttle. In weaving, instrument used to carry the filling thread back and forth between the warp threads.

Shuttleless loom. Can be either air-jet or water-jet. With the air-jet loom the filling yarn is propelled by a jet of air rather than a shuttle. With the water-jet the yarn is, obviously, propelled by a jet of water. The shuttleless looms are considered faster than conventional looms.

Silk. Cocoon—the case spun by the silkworm, serving as a covering, source of the silk filament. Doupione or Duppioni—silk from two silkworms which spin their cocoons together. The resulting yarn is irregular, uneven, and large in diameter. Reeled—long, continuous filament. Spun—waste silk and silk from pierced cocoons, recycled by commercial spinning. Wild or tussah—from the wild, uncultivated silkworm. Fibers are shorter than reeled silk; color, darker.

Slub yarns. Yarn of any type that is irregular in diameter, which may be caused by error, nature, or purposefully made with slubs to bring out some desired effect.

Soil repellency. Capacity of a fabric to resist absorption of soils or stains. Water repellents resist waterborne stains, and oil repellents resist greasy or oily stains.

Spinneret. In the process of "spinning" synthetic fibers, the device through which the liquid materials are extruded.

Spun yarn. Yarn composed of short length or staple fibers twisted together into continuous lengths.

Staple. Length of the raw fiber, both natural and man-made. Term for short fibers, as opposed to continuous filament.

Static electricity. Electricity generated by friction of a fabric against itself or other objects. Can be caused by walking across certain types of carpets.

Sunlight resistance. Resistance to fading and deterioration when exposed to the ultraviolet rays of sunlight.

Taffeta. Smooth, plain weave which has a slightly iridescent sheen and crisp finish.

Tapestry. Ornamental fabric woven on a jacquard loom; the design is usually a picture and sometimes illustrates a story.

Tensile strength. Breaking strength of yarns or fabrics. High tensile strength means strong yarns or fabrics.

Textile. Refers to woven fabrics only.

Thermoplastic. Having the property of becoming soft under application of heat. Will harden when heat source is removed.

Ticking. Strong, durable, closely woven fabric in a twill, plain, or satin weave. Used originally for mattress covers, its name comes from being used to make these "bed ticks."

Toile. French term used to describe plain or twill linen fabrics.

Toile de Jouy. White or beige linen or cotton printed with florals or gay country scenes in one color. Jouy is the name of the town where this type of material was first developed at the request of Marie Antoinette.

Trade names (trademarks, brand names). Names that identify the products of a particular manufacturer and are registered with the United States Patent Office.

Tweed. Fabric originally made from wool with a rough surface in a plain, twill, or herringbone twill weave of two or more colors.

Twill. Fabric woven in such a way that a raised welt is formed diagonally on the face of the material.

Velour. Low, very dense, and stiff cut-pile fabric with a subtle luster. Durable but not as luxurious as velvet. Used for upholstery.

Velvet. Fabric with a short (up to ⅛ inch), thick warp pile surface and a plain back.

Velveteen. Not as closely woven as velvet, with a slightly higher pile; made only of cotton.

Warp. Lengthwise yarns in woven fabrics (English term—*woof*).

Wash and wear. Term applied to garments that satisfactorily retain their original appearance after repeated wear and suitable for home laundering with little or no pressing or ironing. Compare with Easy care.

Water resistance. Resistance to wetting and the penetration of water.

Wicking. Characteristic that allows water to travel rapidly along fibers and through the fabric, as opposed to absorbency, which means that the moisture is retained within the fibers of the fabric.

Wool. Made from the fleece of sheep or lambs or from the hair of the camel, Angora goat, Cashmere goat, alpaca, llama, or vicuña. Terms used by the industry, some of which were established by the Wool Products Labeling Act of 1939: Wool—on a label refers to fleece wool being used for the first time in the *complete* manufacture of a wool product. May also include any new fleece processed up to but not including weaving or felting and any clips of knitted fabric made of new wool and not used or worn in any way. "Wool" may therefore contain certain wastes, resulting from carding, combing, and spinning, but recovered and reprocessed before use. Virgin wool—wool that has never been made into cloth or used for any other purpose, without waste materials. Reprocessed wool—wool obtained from scraps and clips of new woven or felted fabrics made from previously unused wool. In other words, new wool that has actually been involved in the construction process: the trimmings on the cutting room floor. Reused wool—obtained from used rags and old clothing that has been worn and then reprocessed. With continued great demand for wool products, dwindling supplies, and emphasis on recycling of natural products, "reprocessed" and "reused" will both be seen more on the labels of rough finished goods where short staples will not detract from the final effect: a serviceable but coarse finish, like a homespun or a felt. Woolen—fabric with soft, fuzzy surfaces, made from carded short wool fibers spun with medium twist into soft, bulky yarns. Worsted—smooth-surfaced wool fabric made from smooth, light yarns spun with a high twist from carded and combed long fibers.

Wrinkle resistance. That natural property of a fabric which enables it to resist the formation of wrinkles; preferred term to the sometimes used *crease resistance*.

Yarn. Product of fibers twisted into a continuous strand or strands to be used in weaving and knitting fabrics.

Coming to Terms with Windows

Apron. The lower portion of a window casing that is located under the sill.

Austrian shade. A vertically shirred curtain, with pull cords for raising or lowering, that can be used in place of a shade for a softer, decorative effect.

Barrel pleating. Decorative tubular pleats spaced evenly across a drapery heading; often called cartridge pleats.

Baton. A rod with a handle that is used for opening and closing draperies manually.

Bottom-up shade. A spring-roller shade mounted at the bottom of a window and pulled upward to close.

Box pleating. Decorative pleats spaced evenly across a drapery heading; they are sewn in and pressed flat.

Brackets. Devices attached to the wall or window casing to support window hardware and accessories such as curtain rods, cornices, and valances.

Buckram. A plain-weave jute cloth sized and stiffened with glue, used for interlining draperies, drapery headings, and valances to give them more weight.

Café curtains. Short curtains hung on rods. They usually are tiered, hanging from several levels.

Canopy. A fabric-covered awning over a window, used decoratively both indoors and outdoors.

Carriers. Metal or plastic eyelets in a traverse track. They hold hooks in the drapery heading and move the drapery along the track.

Cascade. A decorative fall of material that is gathered at the outer corners of the drapery heading and hangs in folds of graduating lengths at the sides of the window.

Casement window. A window that swings in or out by means of hinges at either the top or the side.

Cathedral window. A window that meets the roofline in a room with a ceiling higher than one story (called a cathedral ceiling). The window is slanted at the top to follow the roofline.

Clerestory window. A narrow, usually shallow window located near the ceiling.

Dormer window. A window built out from a sloping roof, giving light and air to a top-floor room or attic.

Double-hung window. The most common window type, opened by pushing the lower half up or the upper half down.

Facing. A lining at the edges of draperies that gives them more body.

Fanlight. A semicircular window over a door or window, with radiating sash bars resembling the ribs of a fan.

Festoon. A decorative chain or strip of fabric that loops over a valance pole or rod; silken ropes and garlands are some typical examples.

Finial. A decorative wooden or metal endpiece for a curtain rod or for the top of a cornice.

French door. A door with rectangular glass panels from top to bottom. French doors usually are used in pairs and often are covered with sheer stretch curtains.

French pleating. Decorative pleats for the heading of draperies. The fabric is gathered and stitched in small folds at regular intervals.

Hardware. The necessary accessories for the operation of windows such as pulls, locks, and weights. Also the fixtures for the operation and installation of window treatments such as rods, brackets, pulley weights, holdbacks, hooks, rings, carriers, finials, clips.

Horizontal shade. A window shade that moves horizontally with pulleys and cords over a horizontally placed window, such as a skylight.

Jabot. A pleated piece of fabric that hangs decoratively over or under the swags or sides of a valance.

Jalousie. A shutter-type window with adjustable, horizontal louvers of glass, wood, or metal that are cranked open and angled to control ventilation and light.

Lambrequin. A decorative drapery or frame over the top and sides of a window. The frame usually is made of plywood, covered and trimmed.

Lunette. A window in the shape of a half moon that is above a door or other windows.

Opaque. Impenetrable by light; lined draperies often are opaque.

Overdraperies. The outermost and most decorative draperies at a window.

Pavilion. A decorative window treatment that features draperies tied back like the flap of a tent.

Pelmet. A shaped cornice or valance that conceals the drapery rod. It usually is made on a wire frame.

Pinch pleating. Decorative pleats evenly spaced across a drapery heading. Folds of fabric are pinched or squeezed together and "tacked" (sewn) at the pinched point.

Pleating tape. A special tape attached to the back of the drapery heading that pulls the drapery into pleats. Special hooks fit into the tape for hanging.

Pouf curtains. Curtains gathered horizontally in several places to create a series of puffs of fabric. The puffs are held in place by tiebacks, cords, or stitching, giving the effect of tiers.

Priscilla curtains. Ruffled, crisscrossed tiebacks, usually of sheer or of medium-weight fabric.

Return. The section of drapery that covers the brackets that support the rod as well as the space between the rod and the wall.

Roman shade. A decorative shade, made of a horizontally pleated panel of fabric, that is raised and lowered with cords. It is a more tailored treatment of an Austrian shade.

Sash curtain. A sheer curtain close to the windowpanes; same as glass curtain and undercurtain.

Sheer. Thin, fine, and transparent; also a term for lightweight, transparent curtains, as in "a pair of sheers."

Shirring. A decorative gathering of cloth into three or more parallel rows. Shirring can be used for a decorative drapery heading.

Stretch curtain. A curtain gathered on rods top and bottom to stretch tautly over a window or "rod top and bottom."

Swag. Fabric draped decoratively at the top of a window over drapery headings and caught up at the ends.

Tier. One of a series of rows placed one above another; café curtains may be in tiers.

Track. A drapery rod in which carriers are installed to move draperies that are suspended from the carriers by hooks. An electric track is an electromagnetically powered traverse rod.

Traverse. Used to describe the type of rod or cord by which draperies can be opened or closed.

FIBER TRADEMARKS*

Fiber Trademarks of Member Companies, Man-Made Fiber Producers

In the lists of trademarks of Members of Man-Made Fiber Producers Association, Inc., on the following pages, the term *fiber trademarks* is used as defined by the Federal Trade Commission in Paragraph (r) of Rule 1 of its Rules and Regulations issued under the Textile Products Identification Act: *"(r) The term 'fiber trademark' means a word or words used by a person to identify a particular fiber produced or sold by him and to distinguish it from fibers of the same generic class produced or sold by others. Such term shall not include any trademark, product mark, house mark, trade name or other name which does not identify a particular fiber."*

Trademark	Generic name	Member company
ACELE	acetate	E. I. du Pont de Nemours & Company, Inc.
ACRILAN	acrylic, modacrylic	Monsanto Textiles Company
ANSO	nylon	Allied Chemical Corporation, Fibers Division
ANTRON	nylon	E. I. du Pont de Nemours & Company, Inc.
ARILOFT	acetate	Eastman Kodak Company, Tennessee Eastman Company Division
ARNEL	triacetate	Celanese Fibers Marketing Co., Celanese Corp.
AVICOLOR	acetate, rayon	Avtex Fibers Inc.

*From *Man-Made Fiber Fact Book*. Used with permission.

Trademark	*Generic name*	*Member company*
AVLIN	polyester	Avtex Fibers Inc.
AVRIL	rayon (high wet modulus)	Avtex Fibers Inc.
BEAU-GRIP	rayon	Beaunit Corporation
BEAUNIT NYLON	nylon	Beaunit Corporation
BI-LOFT	acrylic	Monsanto Textiles Company
BLUE "C"	nylon, polyester	Monsanto Textiles Company
BRIGLO	rayon	American Enka Company
CADON	nylon	Monsanto Textiles Company
CANTRECE	nylon	E. I. du Pont de Nemours & Company, Inc.
CAPROLAN	nylon, polyester	Allied Chemical Corporation
CELACLOUD	acetate fiberfill	Celanese Fibers Marketing Co., Celanese Corp.
CELANESE	nylon	Fiber Industries Inc., Marketed by Celanese Fibers Marketing Co., a Division of Celanese Corp.
CHROMSPUN	acetate	Eastman Kodak Company, Tennessee Eastman Company Division
COLORAY	rayon	Courtaulds North America Inc.
CORDURA	nylon	E. I. du Pont de Nemours & Company, Inc.
COURTAULDS NYLON	nylon	Courtaulds North America Inc.
CREPESET	nylon	American Enka Company
CRESLAN	acrylic	American Cyanamid Company
CUMULOFT	nylon	Monsanto Textiles Company
DACRON	polyester	E. I. du Pont de Nemours & Company, Inc.
DOWN-TO-EARTH TONES	nylon, polyester	Rohm and Haas Company, Fibers Division
ELURA	modacrylic	Monsanto Textiles Company
ENCEL	rayon	American Enka Company
ENCRON	polyester	American Enka Company
ENGLO	rayon	American Enka Company
ENKA	rayon, nylon, polyester	American Enka Company
ENKALOFT	nylon	American Enka Company
ENKALURE	nylon	American Enka Company
ENKASHEER	nylon	American Enka Company
ENKROME	rayon	American Enka Company
ESTRON	acetate	Eastman Kodak Company, Tennessee Eastman Company Division

Trademark	*Generic name*	*Member company*
FIBER 700	rayon (high wet modulus)	American Enka Company
FIBRO	rayon	Courtaulds North America Inc.
FORTREL	polyester	Fiber Industries Inc., Marketed by Celanese Fibers Marketing Co., a Division of Celanese Corp.
HERCULON	olefin	Hercules Incorporated, Fibers Division
HYSTRON	polyester	Hoechst Fibers Industries
I.T.	rayon	American Enka Company
JETSPUN	rayon	American Enka Company
KEVLAR	aramid	E. I. du Pont de Nemours & Company, Inc.
KODEL	polyester	Eastman Kodak Company, Tennessee Eastman Company Division
KOLORBON	rayon	American Enka Company
LOFTURA	acetate	Eastman Kodak Company, Tennessee Eastman Company Division
LUREX	metallic	Dow Badische Company
LYCRA	spandex	E. I. du Pont de Nemours & Company, Inc.
MARVESS	olefin	Phillips Fibers Corporation, Subsidiary of Phillips Petroleum Company
MONVELLE	biconstituent nylon/spandex	Monsanto Textiles Company
MULTISHEER	nylon	American Enka Company
NOMEX	aramid	E. I. du Pont de Nemours & Company, Inc.
ORLON	acrylic	E. I. du Pont de Nemours & Company, Inc.
POLYLOOM	olefin	Chevron Chemical Company, Fibers Division
QIANA	nylon	E. I. du Pont de Nemours & Company, Inc.
QUINTESS	polyester	Phillips Fibers Corporation, Subsidiary of Phillips Petroleum Company

Trademark	*Generic name*	*Member company*
RANDOM-SET	nylon	Rohm and Haas Company, Fibers Division
RANDOM-TONE	nylon	Rohm and Haas Company, Fibers Division
SAYFR	FR acetate	Avtex Fibers Inc.
SEF	modacrylic	Monsanto Textiles Company
SHANTURA	polyester	Rohm and Haas Company
SHAREEN	nylon	Courtaulds North America Inc.
SKYLOFT	rayon	American Enka Company
SOFTGLO	rayon	American Enka Company
SPECTRAN	polyester	Monsanto Textiles Company
STRIA	nylon	American Enka Company
SUPER BULK	nylon	American Enka Company
SUPER WHITE	rayon	American Enka Company
SUPRENKA	rayon	American Enka Company
TEFLON	fluorocarbon	E. I. du Pont de Nemours & Company, Inc.
TEXTURA	polyester	Rohm and Haas Company, Fibers Division
TREVIRA	polyester	Hoechst Fibers Industries
TWISLOC	polyester	Monsanto Textiles Company
TWIX	nylon	American Enka Company
ULSTRON	nylon	Monsanto Textiles Company
ULTRON	nylon	Monsanto Textiles Company
VARILINE	nylon	American Enka Company
VECANA	nylon	Chevron Chemical Company
VECTRA	olefin	Vectra Corporation, subsidiary of Chevron Chemical Company
VEREL	modacrylic	Eastman Kodak Company, Tennessee Eastman Company Division
VYCRON	polyester	Beaunit Corporation
XENA	rayon (high wet modulus)	Beaunit Corporation
X-STATIC	nylon, metallic	Rohm and Haas Company, Fibers Division
ZANTREL	rayon (high wet modulus)	American Enka Company
ZEFRAN	acrylic, nylon, polyester	Dow Badische Company
ZEFSTAT	acrylic, nylon	Dow Badische Company

Fiber Trademarks Listed by Generic Fiber Name

Acetate	Acele	filament yarn	E. I. du Pont de Nemours & Co., Inc.
	Ariloft	filament yarn	Eastman Kodak Co., Tennessee Eastman Co. Div.
	Avicolor	solution-dyed filament	Avtex Fibers Inc.
	Celacloud	crimped staple fiberfill	Celanese Fibers Marketing Co., Celanese Corp.
	Chromspun	solution-dyed filament yarn	Eastman Kodak Co., Tennessee Eastman Co. Div.
	Estron	filament yarn and cigarette filter tow	Eastman Kodak Co., Tennessee Eastman Co. Div.
	Loftura	slub voluminized filament yarn	Eastman Kodak Co., Tennessee Eastman Co. Div.
	SayFR	fire-resistant filament acetate	Avtex Fibers Inc.
Acrylic	Acrilan	staple and tow	Monsanto Textiles Co.
	Bi-Loft	fibers, filaments	Monsanto Textiles Co.
	Creslan	staple and tow	American Cyanamid Co.
	Orlon	staple and tow	E. I. du Pont de Nemours & Co., Inc.
	Zefran	acrylic, dyeable and producer colored	Dow Badische Co.
	Zefstat	acrylic	Dow Badische Co.
Aramid	Kevlar	filament	E. I. du Pont de Nemours & Co., Inc.
	Nomex	filament and staple	E. I. du Pont de Nemours & Co., Inc.
Biconstituent	Monvelle	biconstituent nylon-spandex fiber	Monsanto Textiles Co.
Fluorocarbon	Teflon	fluorocarbon	E. I. du Pont de Nemours & Co., Inc.
Metallic	Lurex	yarn of slit film	Dow Badische Co.
	X-Static	metallic	Rohm and Haas Co.
Modacrylic	Acrilan	staple and tow	Monsanto Textiles Co.
	Elura	modacrylic	Monsanto Textiles Co.

	SEF	modacrylic	Monsanto Textiles Co.
	Verel	modacrylic	Eastman Kodak Co., Tennessee Eastman Co. Div.
Nylon	Anso	nylon filament and staple soil-resistant carpet yarn	Allied Chemical Corp., Fibers Division
	Antron	nylon	E. I. du Pont de Nemours & Co., Inc.
	Beaunit Nylon	nylon filament, staple and tow, plied and heat set 2,500 denier and white and space dyed	Beaunit Corp.
	Blue "C"	nylon	Monsanto Textiles Co.
	Cadon	filament yarn and multilobal monofilament	Monsanto Textiles Co.
	Cantrece	nylon	E. I. du Pont de Nemours & Co., Inc.
	Caprolan	yarns, monofila-ments and tex-tured yarns	Allied Chemical Corp., Fibers Division
	Celanese	nylon	Fiber Industries, Inc., Marketed by Celanese Fibers Marketing Co., Celanese Corp.
	Cordura	nylon	E. I. du Pont de Nemours & Co., Inc.
	Courtaulds Nylon	nylon producer crimped fila-ment yarn	Courtaulds North America Inc.
	Crepeset	patented continuous mo-nofilament that develops a regular crimp, also available in anti-cling yarn	American Enka Co.
	Cumuloft	textured filament carpet yarn	Monsanto Textiles Co.

Down-to-Earth Tones	nylon	Rohm and Haas Co.
Enka	nylon filament, staple	American Enka Co.
Enkaloft	textured multilobal continuous filament carpet yarn and staple	American Enka Co.
Enkalure	multilobal continuous filament apparel yarn and textured delayed soiling carpet yarn	American Enka Co.
Enkasheer	continuous monofilament torque yarn for ladies' stretch hosiery (patented process)	American Enka Co.
Monvelle	biconstituent nylon-spandex	Monsanto Textiles Co.
Multisheer	multifilament producer-textured stretch yarn for panty hose	American Enka Co.
Qiana	nylon	E. I. du Pont de Nemours & Co., Inc.
Random-Set	heat-set BCF nylon	Rohm and Haas Co.
Random-Tone	fashion and styling yarns of BCF nylon fiber	Rohm and Haas Co.
Shareen	nylon monofilament textured yarn	Courtaulds North America, Inc.
Stria	bulked nylon carpet yarn, modified twist	American Enka Co.

	Super Bulk	heat-set, high-bulk continuous filament nylon carpet yarn; luxurious thick look of spun nylon	American Enka Co.
	Twix	bulk nylon carpet yarn, modified twist	American Enka Co.
	Ulstron	nylon	Monsanto Textiles Co.
	Ultron	nylon	Monsanto Textiles Co.
	Variline	variable denier continuous filament yarn (patented process)	American Enka Co.
	Vecana	nylon	Chevron Chemical Co.
	X-Static	nylon	Rohm and Haas Co.
	Zefran	nylon	Dow Badische Co.
	Zefstat	nylon	Dow Badische Co.
Olefin	Herculon	continuous multifilament, bulked continuous multifilament, staple and tow	Hercules Inc., Fibers Division
	Marvess	staple, tow and filament yarn	Phillips Fibers Corp.
	Polyloom	olefin	Chevron Chemical Co., Fibers Division
	Vectra	olefin	Vectra Corp., Subsidiary of Chevron Chemical Co.
Polyester	Avlin	filament yarn and staple	Avtex Fibers, Inc.
	Blue "C"	polyester	Monsanto Textiles Co.
	Caprolan		Allied Chemical Corp.
	Dacron	filament yarn, staple, tow and fiberfill	E. I. du Pont de Nemours & Co., Inc.
	Down-to-Earth Tones	polyester	Rohm and Haas Co.

	Encron	continuous fila- ment yarn, staple, fiberfill	American Enka Co.
	Enka	filament and staple	American Enka Co.
	Fortrel	filament yarn, staple, tow and fiberfill	Fiber Industries, Inc., Marketed by Celanese Fibers Marketing Co., Celanese Corp.
	Hystron	polyester	Hoechst Fibers Industries
	Kodel	filament yarn, staple, tow and fiberfill	Eastman Kodak Co., Tennessee Eastman Co. Div.
	Quintess	polyester multifilament yarns	Phillips Fibers Corp.
	Shantura		Rohm and Haas Co.
	Source	biconstituent nylon- polyester	Allied Chemical Corp.
	Spectran	polyester	Monsanto Textiles Co.
	Textura	producer tex- tured polyester yarn	Rohm and Haas Co., Fibers Di- vision
	Trevira	polyester	Hoechst Fibers Inc.
	Twisloc	polyester	Monsanto Textiles Co.
	Vycron	filament, staple, tow and fiberfill	Beaunit Corp.
	Zefran	polyester	Dow Badische Co.
Rayon	Avicolor	solution-dyed filament and staple	Avtex Fibers Inc.
	Avril	high wet modulus staple	Avtex Fibers Inc.
	Beau-Grip	specially treated viscose high- tenacity yarn	Beaunit Corp.
	Briglo	bright-luster continuous filament yarn	American Enka Co.
	Coloray	solution-dyed staple	Courtaulds North America Inc.
	Encel	high wet modulus staple	American Enka Co.

	Englo	dull-luster continuous filament yarn	American Enka Co.
	Enka	rayon	American Enka Co.
	Enkrome	patented acid-dyeable staple and continuous filament yarn	American Enka Co.
	Fiber 700	high wet modulus staple	American Enka Co.
	Fibro	staple	Courtaulds North America Inc.
	I.T.	improved tenacity staple	American Enka Co.
	Jetspun	solution-dyed continuous filament yarn	American Enka Co.
	Kolorbon	solution-dyed staple	American Enka Co.
	Skyloft	bulked continuous filament yarn	American Enka Co.
	Softglo	semi-dull luster continuous filament yarn	American Enka Co.
	Super White	optically brightened rayon	American Enka Co.
	Suprenka	extra-high tenacity continuous filament industrial yarn	American Enka Co.
	Xena	high wet modulus staple	Beaunit Corp.
	Zantrel	high wet modulus staple	American Enka Co.
Spandex	Lycra	spandex	E. I. du Pont de Nemours & Co., Inc.
Triacetate	Arnel	filament yarn and staple	Celanese Fibers Marketing Co., Celanese Corp.

Trademarks of Formed Fabrics

Bidim	polyester, spunbonded	Monsanto Textiles Co.
Cerex	nylon, spunbonded	Monsanto Textiles Co.
Duon	needlebonded olefin	Phillips Fibers Corp.
	needlebonded polyester	
Petromat	needlebonded olefin	Phillips Fibers Corp.
Reemay	spunbonded polyester	E. I. du Pont de Nemours & Co., Inc.
Supac	needlebonded olefin	Phillips Fibers Corp.
Typar	spunbonded polypropylene	E. I. du Pont de Nemours & Co., Inc.
Tyvek	spunbonded olefin	E. I. du Pont de Nemours & Co., Inc.

INDEX